DEMOCRATIZATION
AND
SOCIAL
SETTLEMENTS

DEMOCRATIZATION
AND
SOCIAL
SETTLEMENTS

THE POLITICS OF CHANGE
IN
CONTEMPORARY PORTUGAL

Daniel Nataf

State University of New York Press

To Beth and Colette

Published by
State University of New York Press, Albany

© 1995 State University of New York

For information, address State University of New York
Press, State University Plaza, Albany, N.Y., 12246

Production by E. Moore
Marketing by Theresa Abad Swierzowski

Library of Congress Cataloging-in-Publication Data

Nataf, Daniel.
    Democratization and social settlements : the politics of change in
contemporary Portugal / Daniel Nataf.
    Includes bibliographical references and index.
    ISBN 0-7914-2589-4. — ISBN 0-7914-2590-8 (pkb.)
    1. Democracy—Portugal.   2. Portugal—Politics and
government—1974–   I. Title.
JN85021995
320.9469'09'045—dc20   94–33690
                                                                                  CIP

10 9 8 7 6 5 4 3 2 1

CONTENTS

LIST OF TABLES AND FIGURES

TABLES

FIGURES

ONE

PORTUGUESE DEMOCRACY FROM A COMPARATIVE AND THEORETICAL PERSPECTIVE

Since the 1970s, countries and regions throughout the world have engaged in the difficult transition from dictatorship to more liberal and inclusive regimes. Portugal led that wave of change, ending its dictatorship in 1974, slightly ahead of its southern European neighbors Greece and Spain. At that time Portugal's action was a rare instance of liberalizing change; the Soviet bloc was intact, and authoritarian regimes in Africa, Latin America, and Asia remained firmly in power. Thus, because of its relatively successful democratic transition and consolidation, Portugal was a pioneer in democratization.

The importance of the Portuguese case lies primarily in special characteristics of transition and consolidation that distinguished the country from its neighbors. In Spain the transfer of power from the Franco dictatorship to a more liberal, pluralist regime was based largely upon compromises between the traditional political elite and the opposition, thereby avoiding a sustained period of massive popular mobilization. The military, long a defender of Franco, was an obstacle to change rather than a catalyst. By contrast, Europe's oldest dictatorship ended dramatically through the efforts of the leftist Armed Forces Movement (MFA), which was followed by intensive popular mobilization. Spain's slower, more controlled transition contrasted sharply with Portugal's apparently radical and anarchic process. From the initial coup that overthrew the corporatist dictatorship (April 25, 1974) to the election of a functioning parliament two years later, the country followed an original and complex course that fostered both a narrow alteration in regime and a series of significant socioeconomic changes. The process of political democratization was simultaneously a crisis of participation, economic distribution, and property relations. It involved the extensive nationalization of industrial and bank holdings, the expropriation of land, the blossoming of trade union organizations, worker occupation of factories, and the emergence of more than a dozen political parties.

Portugal adopted a new constitution institutionalizing a competitive electoral system in the aftermath of these sweeping reforms and mass activity. The preamble to the 1976 constitution showed the unique effect of the country's democratization process, providing guarantees about the form of political regime as well as the socialist character of socioeconomic transformations:

> The Constituent Assembly affirms the decisions of the Portuguese people to defend national independence, to guarantee the fundamental rights of the citizens, to establish basic principles of democracy, to assure the primacy of a democratic State of Law and to open the way towards a socialist society, in accordance with the will of the Portuguese people, taking into view the construction of a country which is more free, more just and more fraternal.

While most instances of democratization involve some redefinition of the social contract, exceptional cases such as Portugal question much of the prevailing social settlement involved in the traditional relations among social classes, institutions, public opinion, and political leaders. In that sense, Portugal's experience can be called *expanded democratization.*

Unlike Spain, Portugal has not often been highlighted as a model for democratizers. As long as other transitions to democracy were largely contained within the broad pattern of economic and social organization, Portugal was largely considered an exotic, deviant case with little comparative significance. Despite two decades of democratic consolidation and functioning after the turmoil of transition, the country's experience was not fully appreciated. The study of Portugal's evolution from authoritarian corporatism to revolutionary populism during transition, to political and economic ambiguity during much of consolidation, and finally to membership in the EC within the paradigm of European democratic capitalism has been limited primarily to Portuguese specialists. With the collapse of the Soviet Union and the disintegration of its political bloc, however, conceptualizing a transition to democracy as a process of replacing one set of political institutions with another seems insufficient. As in Portugal, such transitions now entail a fundamental reexamination of the social settlements fostered by previous regimes. In many ways, the collapse of Soviet authoritarianism has produced a pattern of centralized dictatorship, quasirevolutionary transition, and ambiguous consolidation similar to Portugal.

The growing theoretical literature on democratization has not always been sensitive to the interaction between narrow political and broader societal levels of analysis. The political system has been covered in detail, including the causes behind the breakdown of authoritarian regimes as well as the prospects for stabilizing parliamentary democratic arrangements.[1] Schmitter (1986) has pointed to the impact of institutional variables in his discussion of the breakdown of authoritarianism and the transition and consolidation stages of democratization. Specifically, in outlining the prospects for a successful democratic transition, he emphasizes such factors as the importance of a previous parliamentary tradition; the possibilities for institutional adaptation from regional models, which benefited southern European countries surrounded by liberal democracies but created disadvantages for Latin American nations; and the viability of autonomous associational groupings in civil society. He also emphasizes links between international and domestic institutional patterns by noting the role of the European Community in supporting efforts to adopt a Euromodel, regional party links, and the types of treaty obligations that might help or hinder attempts to establish a specific political regime. Moreover, he believes institutional developments have been stimulated by appropriate developments in public opinion and culture and are a product of contacts among citizens in both democratizing and already democratic countries (as was the case in southern Europe).

According to O'Donnell and Schmitter, (1986) the vital actors in the democratization drama were rarely macrosociological in nature, but rather hard- and softliners whose identification was largely determined by their political inclinations and momentary perceptions of strategic gain or risk. As they put it, "the shorter-term political calculations cannot be 'deduced' or 'imputed' to such [socioeconomic] structures—except in an act of misguided faith" (1986, 5). Only rarely or incidentally were the underlying stakes in change presented as a reworking of the basic social settlement among key socioeconomic forces. The main focus of their generalizations about democratization involved a plethora of possible actors and dealt more with the political process (defined as key steps in an uncertain and reversible transition) or institutional outcomes rather than overarching socioeconomic issues.[2] Their comparative assessment of democratization led them to favor a separation of the political and social or economic moments of the democratization process, and the Portuguese experience did not follow this "ideal" course.

While this analysis suggested that countries have a choice to narrow their democratizations to political institutions and pluralist aspects, it is evident that Portugal and the former Soviet bloc have been challenged by both political renewal as well as broader social transformation. Rather than isolate their political moments, give confidence to old elites, and set limits to policy innovation as a condition for elite acquiescence, their democratizations have been more confrontational, open ended, and multifaceted. These commonalities demonstrate our need to study the larger picture of regime and societal change and seek out new frameworks for the analysis of democratization. An empirical examination of the Portuguese case is instructive, showing a country that went through a quasirevolutionary transition to democracy yet managed to become a full, if less developed, partner in mainstream European life, a relatively stable element along the southern rim of Europe.

The literature on Portuguese democratization, while varied and theoretically eclectic, has focused primarily on the political dimension of change, especially after transition ended in 1976. Thomas Bruneau and Alex Macleod (1986) are largely concerned with aspects of institutional structure and process.[3] Walter Opello (1985) provides an interesting assessment of the Portuguese political system within a modernization and political development framework.[4] Nancy Bermeo's (1986) work on the Portuguese revolution and its impact on the land tenure system places more attention on the interaction between institutional events and agrarian social relations. Nicos Poulantzas (1976) makes a concerted if cursory attempt to address the relations between state institutions and the interests or agendas of underlying social agents. He presents an

argument about socioeconomic changes during the 1960s that created crises in the prevailing dictatorships.[5]

Beyond limitations in substantive questions and theoretical
perspectives, comparativists have often failed to underscore sufficiently the unusual dynamics of state-society linkage during the
phases of Portuguese democratization. Rather, in seeking to establish broader generalizations or a regionally derived framework for
analysis, scholars have homogenized southern European experiences. For example, Schmitter (1986) contrasts southern European
democratization as a whole with events in Latin America. He argues
that southern European countries "have entered into, and can be
expected to remain within, the range of institutional variation and
patterns of political conflict characteristic of Western Europe as a
whole" (1986, 3). This tendency to homogenize is not limited to a
single theoretical tradition; even Poulantzas (1976) saw democratization as essentially similar in Greece, Spain, and Portugal because
in all cases the "domestic bourgeoisie" sought a greater share of
political power and stimulated a change in regime.[6] Hybrid scholars
such as Salvador Giner (1986), who combines components of pluralist and class analysis, also tend to generalize about southern European democratizers, considering them instances of modernization
meant to bring the periphery of Europe into the modern mode of the
center, thus resulting in parliamentary-corporatist convergence.[7]

The similarity of Greek, Spanish, and Portuguese transitions
and consolidations should not be taken for granted; only in Porgugal
was there a need to reconcile a quasirevolutionary transition with a
reformist consolidation. The inability of general models to capture
the Portuguese situation can be highlighted by incorporating
Stepan's (1986) discussion of routes to redemocratization, which
focus largely on transition rather than consolidation phases. He
argues that most recent democratizing experiences fall into one of
two basic types. The first involves a "move toward redemocratization [that can] be initiated by the wielders of authoritarian power
themselves" while in the second "oppositional forces play the major
role in terminating the authoritarian regime and in setting or not
setting the framework for redemocratization" (1986, 65).

Within the first type, three variations are possible: the initiating group can be drawn from the civilian political leadership, a military government can provoke a regime change, or the military
within a largely civilian dictatorship can act to preserve its own
institutional interests and depose a hostile government. The second
route also includes several options: the "society led regime termina-

tion" in which "diffuse protests by grassroots organizations" combine with "general strikes and . . . general withdrawal of support for the government" (1986, 78), the "party pact with or without consociational elements" when both the breadth of opposition as well as the consensus on the new regime are demonstrated to the authoritarian leaders, the "organized violent revolt coordinated by democratic reformist parties" in which the authoritarian leaders are defeated and the need for a carefully erected system of consociational obligations is reduced, or the Marxist-led revolutionary war in which revolutionary forces come to power after "defeating the state apparatus and a sector of the social order is displaced without waiting for the results of elections" (1986, 83).

While elements of each route exist in many cases, the degree to which they were blended in Portugal was particularly striking. After his accession to power in the late 1960s, civilian leader Marcello Caetano attempted a short-lived political liberalization seemingly a "move toward redemocratization initiated by the wielders of authoritarian power themselves." By 1974 the military felt obliged to overthrow the Caetano regime. The subsequent period followed routes in which "oppositional forces play[ed] the major role in terminating the authoritarian regime and in setting or not setting the framework for redemocratization." The society-led process did not, as Stepan's model suggests *precede* the fall of Caetano but rather developed and accelerated *after* the Armed Forces Movement had already ousted the old leadership. The construction of a grand oppositional pact occurred simultaneously but was brief and unstable, lasting only a few months during 1974.

What followed was even more complicated. Political parties played an increasingly important role, and the Portuguese Communist party (PCP) was especially strong during parts of 1974 and 1975. In some ways, the country came close to Stephan's model of the "Marxist-led revolutionary war" as the PCP, the revolutionary left, and elements of the MFA sought to establish an MFA-people alliance at the margins of the reformist parties. Reaction to this attempt could be called an organized revolt coordinated by democratic reformist parties (especially the Socialist party), but it was an effort to prevent the consolidation of a Communist regime rather than throw out the corporatist dictatorship. Finally, a kind of party pact was established that by 1976 created a broad, general consensus on the institutional characteristics of the new regime, although the social settlement defining what elements of the leftist transition were to be retained was uncertain.

This complex pattern of developments implies that Portugal was unique among southern European systems. As Gunther et al. (1986) have suggested, Spain primarily followed the route of internal redemocratization coupled with a party pact. Greece also emphasized internal reform without a distinct break with the past. Certainly, Portugal diverged most from the regional paradigm of narrowly political democratization because it *expanded* democratization to social and economic realms rather than simply altered political institutions.

CONCEPTUALIZING CHANGE: THEORETICAL PERSPECTIVES, HEGEMONIC PROJECTS, AND ACCUMULATION STRATEGIES

Political scientists have naturally posed questions about the legitimacy of governments and regimes, especially in the aftermath of a democratic transition. When the turbulence of social change has been limited during transition, this approach captures the essence of events.[8] Nevertheless, Portugal, Nicaragua, and the former Soviet bloc seem deviant when democratization is narrowly conceptualized according to orthodox scholarship. Their common experience of expanded democratization demands a conceptual approach that captures the multidimensional character of change.

Because expanded democratization involves profound questions of power, social relations, and the state, their conceptualization requires a special framework. As Alford and Friedland argue, the three dominant theoretical perspectives—pluralist, managerial, and class—each have specific "home domains of description and explanation" (1985, 3). The pluralist perspective concentrates on the "political behavior of individuals and groups and the influence their interactions have on government decision making" (1985, 4). Empirically, the key elements are citizens, representatives, and officials whose coexistence within a political system is punctuated by a constantly changing set of issues that need to be resolved. When conditions for group organization and demand articulation are present, interest groups will press their demands, which are aggregated and organized by the political parties. The perspective emphasizes the fluidity of the political scene with a wide array of broadly defined groups engaged in the political game. Pluralist analysis seems the most appropriate in situations characterized by the presence of a broad consensus on the political format—normal, non-paradigmatic politics. For the analysis of an expanded instance of democratization in which the basic model of state and society is unsettled, its conceptual relevance diminshes.[9]

The managerial perspective deals with "organizational structures—both inside and outside the state—and the domination of the elites that control their relationships." It focuses on how "organizational structures of power protect themselves both from unorganized participation and from the kinds of issues that they cannot manage or control" (1985, 5). The framework seems especially relevant to the analysis of party-pact or consociational democratizations where the role of organizations and institutions in negotiating the terms of democratic transition is especially important. Despite the fact that all democratization events involve some conflict over the form and function of the state, elite-dominated transitions keep these struggles to a minimum. Expanded democratization fundamentally questions those boundaries and the established patterns of elite domination, making the elite perspective less compelling as a analytical approach.[10]

The class perspective emphasizes the "relationship among capitalism, the state and democracy" (1985, 5). It directs attention to the underlying social tensions intrinsic to class-divided societies given the particular configuration of modes of production. It also posits a key role for class power in shaping the contours of the state and regime. Changes associated with democratization are determined by the ability of the dominant class (or segments) temporarily to overcome or neutralize the contradictions attendant to capitalist development and its hegemony over underlying classes.[11] This, in turn, is related to the intensity of the divisions between competing class segments (intraclass conflict) combined with the strength of antagonisms between dominant and subordinate classes (interclass conflict).[12]

These points are typical of Poulantzas's work. He argues that forms of the state "involve a different balance of forces between the various components and class fractions of this power bloc intelf." For him, the "parliamentary-democratic state" is one in which there is "an organizational framework for the organic circulation of hegemony among different fractions of the power bloc by way of their political representatives" permitting the balance of forces within the power bloc to change without a serious upheaval in the state apparatuses (1976, 91). By contrast, "the exceptional state comes into being in order to remedy a characteristic crisis of hegemony within the power bloc, and in this bloc's relationship with the popular masses" (1976, 92). This perspective has the advantage of linking broad macrosociological phenomena to the political system as a natural part of its home domain. Expanded democratization constitutes a crisis of hegemony that is ultimately a power struggle to establish a basic pattern of social relations. As Alford and Friedland note, "power is observed in the reproduction of hegemonic social relations, that is those that permeate every social institution and are unquestioned by most of the population" (1985, 274). Contests over the terms of hegemonic domination are the cornerstones of expanded democratization, making class analysis especially well suited to examining such cases.

Because the class analysis home domain is relevant to expand democratization, this book employs and elaborates upon several of its core concepts. I evaluate the factors that shaped Portugal's entry to and emergence from hegemonic crisis to an amorphous middle ground (which I have called *dishegemony*) and finally to the more recent reestablishment of capitalist class hegemony. In part, the Portuguese case suggests that expanded democratization stems from long-standing fundamental policy controversies not adequately resolved under the old regime. The collapse of the old political institutions meant that the entire set of institutions, policy limits, value assumptions, and favored interests associated with the policy paradigm came under critical scrutiny. Thus, aspiring parties seeking electoral support must offer generalized critiques of the old system and specify programmatic alternatives establishing support only not for liberal democracy but also a basic social settlement.

Bob Jessop has provided a conceptual framework to help bridge the gap between general concepts found in class analysis; the concepts of expanded democratization and social settlements; and empirical targets of inquiry such as parties, public opinion, trade unions, and economic structures. According to Jessop (1983), a conceptual separation should be made between an accumulation strategy and a hegemonic project. The former is associated with "a specific 'growth model' complete with its various extra-economic preconditions and outlines the general strategy appropriate to its realization" (1983, 91). These growth models span a broad spectrum of alternatives applicable to different capitalist economies. Some are strategies directed largely at marshaling higher growth rates in the Third World, such as import substitution and export promotion. Others are more typical of advanced capitalist countries with some variations on the common theme established after World War II. Jessop has postulated that "Keynsianism is a general accumulation strategy found in various capitalist economies and marking a long wave of accumulation from the 1930s through to the 1970s" (1983, 97). Viewed in this way, specific adjustments to that model become adaptations reflecting the particular balance of forces in each economy and resulting in militarist or welfare-oriented accentuations. For Jessop, the key function of an accumulation strategy is the integration of the circuit of capital, which involves the continued expansion of industrial capital either under its own leadership or when another segment of capital is economically hegemonic.[13]

A hegemonic project is distinguished from an accumulation strategy by its broader purpose. While *strategy* is restricted to the level of economic functions and relations, the *project* encompasses political, moral, and intellectual alternatives. Its point is to "resolve the abstract problem of conflicts between particular interests and the general interest" under the leadership of a hegemonic class or class segment (1983, 100). Moreover it involves "the mobilization of support behind a concrete, national-popular program of action which asserts a general interest in the pursuit of objects that explicitly or implicitly advance the long-term interests of the hegemonic class and which also privileges particular 'economic-corporate' interests compatible with this program" (1983, 100). In part, what legitimacy is to the pluralist emphasis on political institutions, a hegemonic project is to the class perspective: a broad agreement established around a set of institutions and norms guiding the accumulation process. A social settlement is that part of a hegemonic project that creates and sustains a dynamic agreement between and with classes regarding the institutions and policies appropriate to their continued mutual coexistence. Not quite as vast as a hegemonic project but clearly a fundamental component, a social settlement can include the character of industrial relations, the scope of workers' rights, the size of the state sector, and the emphasis on redistributive or welfare policies. Expanded democratization is characterized by the combined democratization of the political regime and the creation of a new social settlement as part of an effort to rework the prevailing hegemonic project.

Guided by these concepts, an analysis of democratization should include an appraisal of the *process* by which a viable hegemonic project is engendered in the aftermath of the collapse of the old order. While the transition from democracy to authoritarianism is typically a crisis involving a regime's legitimacy, it is not always a crisis of social settlements because no reconsideration of fundamental class arrangements necessarily takes place. When intra- or interclass antagonisms become acute, democratization may expand into a crisis of hegemony as the authoritarian regime proves unable to establish an effective accumulation strategy consistent with its old hegemonic project. This may lead to a crisis such as Stepan's "Marxist-led revolutionary war" or, in a less serious case, to an "organized violent revolt coordinated by democratic reformist parties."

To the extent that the crisis in the old order enables political forces to press for broad constitutional and socioeconomic reforms, the emerging hegemonic project becomes increasingly uncertain. Before the collapse of the Soviet Union, the possibility for replacing a capitalist hegemonic project with one inspired by the Soviet model appeared possible in some circumstances—for example, during certain moments of the Portuguese transition. With the collapse of the Soviet Union, however, the likelihood that a completely noncapitalist model will emerge from such a crisis has sharply diminished. More likely, and also applicable for several years to the situation in Portugal, such a crisis might result in *dishegemony*, a condition in which the dominant class cannot assert a broadly acceptable hegemonic project compatible with parliamentary democracy but in which the popular masses are unable to fashion a viable alternative.

Under dishegemony, neither the historically dominant nor the subordinate classes appear able to shape an accumulation strategy that provides efficiency, a politically acceptable degree of equality, and the preservation of democratic institutions. Instead, policies may veer left and right as proponents of contesting hegemonic projects seek to package electorally accaptable solutions to economic crises and institutional ambiguities. Whether a country slips back into authoritarianism or stabilizes as a form of democratic capitalism depends on the strength, success, persuasiveness, and credibility of the proponents.

HEGEMONIC PROJECTS AND DEMOCRATIZATION IN A EUROPEAN CONTEXT

Stepan's routes of democratization and Jessop's concepts imply that a considerable breadth of variation exists in the degree to which hegemonic projects are globally assaulted and replaced during the course of democratization. As I noted earlier, however, some authors have suggested that democratization in southern Europe can be viewed from a regionally homogeneous point of view, an interpretation emphasizing the relative similarity of institutional change and national-popular programs across European political economies. In a post-cold war context there is a greater likelihood that even a dishegemonic situation will evolve in the direction of a hegemonic project consistent with surrounding democratic capitalist states. In Western Europe, therefore, democratizing countries will probably gravitate to what Kesselman et al. (1987) and Bornstein (1984) have called the *postwar settlement*. The term refers to the fact that after World War II, the role of the state was transformed. The "prevailing orthodoxy during the previous history of the capitalist state gave way to Keynesianism in economics and to the 'welfare state' in social policy." Governments broke with anti-interventionist precedents and used "state power for macroeconomic management with the aim of preventing a recurrence of the Depression," thereby supplementing but not supplanting markets (Bornstein 1984, 56). The extension of the state's responsibility for the provision of social services meant that the terms, if not the global nature, of the hegemonic project had been redefined. As Przeworski argues, "this combination of private property, redistribution of income and a strong state seem[ed] like an ideal package for almost everyone," capitalists and workers alike. Not only was Keynesianism a convenient political compromise, but it also positively evaluated the importance of consumption within the accumulation strategies needed to foster successful growth. Thus it made "increases in lower incomes not only [appear to be] just but also technically efficient from the economic point of view" (1986, 62).

Yet as Przeworski and Wallerstein (1985) and Bornstein (1984) have recognized, the postwar settlement was not etched in stone or homogeneously adopted throughout Europe.[14] Bornstein divides the changes in Western Europe into three periods, each pointing to the dynamic character of the postwar settlement.

> (1) 1945 to the mid-1960s, the period during which the new political and social institutions and arrangements (the "postwar settlement") came into being and flourished; (2) the period mid-1960s to 1973, during which economic difficulties and social unrest prompted efforts at rearranging some of the elements of the postwar settlements . . .; and (3) the period of severe economic crisis and political and social instability, 1974 to the present. (1984, 56)

Thus, the democratization of southern Europe (starting around 1974) appeared at a time of growing crisis in postwar arrangements among the countries of Western Europe. To emphasize the convergence of the recent democratizers with *the* European model at a time whan it was facing serious review overplays its static and conclusive nature.

Furthermore, it is evident that the model was never adopted crossnationally in the same manner and to a similar degree. Bornstein, who emphasizes industrial relations, argues that "the power of the state to reorganize industrial relations in ways that might reduce or at least regularize industrial conflict and facilitate smooth economic growth . . . assumed different characters and attained very different degrees of success from country to country" (1984, 56). Despite his narrow concern, his classification of countries implies significant dissimilarities in postwar settlements. He makes a basic division between countries "such as Sweden, Austria and the Netherlands where political elites managed to transform industrial relations by means of institutional arrangements that have been called 'neo-corporatist,' and those such as Britain, France and Italy where no such arrangements emerged and conflictual modes predominated" (1984, 56). Broadly speaking, the basic geographic pattern divided Europe into northern neocorporatist and southern conflict models, with Britain joining the south, Austria the north, and Germany indecisively placed in the middle.[15]

The impact of this geographic pattern upon European democratization efforts further dispels the idea that democratization should necessarily result in the implementation of a *common* postwar settlement. For Portugal, Spain, and Greece, democratization occurred in the European region in which parliamentary neocorporatism was weakest. In Spain and Portugal, dictatorial corporatism had been the prevailing orthodoxy. Hegemonic projects had evolved in a manner that structurally excluded subordinate classes from independent participation, enforcing a policy paradigm from above. Within that paradigm a limited pluralism of interests (Linz, 1973) could contest policies, but consensus or legitimacy was not subject to free and fair electoral ratification. The dictatorships' national-popular programs stressed elitist, paternal, and nationalist themes (as well as an imperial-colonial one in Portugal).

Portugal's participation in NATO notwithstanding, the Salazarist form of corporatism conflicted extensively with both northern and southern versions of the Western European settlement. It clearly jeopardized the evolving accumulation strategy based on closer economic ties to Europe and a greater distancing from the colonies. Because of the flux in European postwar settlements at the time of the dictatorship's demise, conflict between contesting national-popular programs might have been expected.[16] The fall of dictatorships heralded the arrival of the political center-piece of postwar Europe's reconstruction: parliamentary democracy, the most consistently consensual element of postwar settlements. By contrast, given the balance of political forces, the social and economic content of policies within parliamentary democracy depended upon the plausibility of hegemonic projects.

Portugal's geographic location on the southern rim of Western Europe made it a likely candidate for a conflict model of postwar settlement. Bornstein's argument about the conditions stimulating the divergence in northern and southern models allows us to examine Portugal's potential relevance to either model. Bornstein offers a set of reasons explaining why neocorporatist forms emerged in Sweden and Austria. First, the union movements effectively organized a high proportion of the working population and had well-staffed and well-financed bureaucratic bodies. National leaderships could reliably exert centralized control of rank-and-file members. The union movement was composed of a single, principal peak organization or several bodies with a history of cooperation or nonideological competition. The role of communists was limited in such instances. With similar structural features, capitalist organizations were disinclined to make broad ideological attacks upon the rights and legitimacy of organized labor. In addition, the state itself had "a long tradition of welfare activities" as well as "efficient, centralized bureaucratic structures" and "a special sort of linkage with organized labor" (Bornstein 1984, 58). Either a powerful social democratic party (Sweden) or strong consociational mechanisms brought contending interests together.

The national economies of each country were strong and competitive, but due to the relatively small size of their domestic markets they tended to be export oriented. Industry's dependence upon foreign markets gave both workers and capitalists a strong interest in collaborating to improve productivity, keep costs and inflation down and keep the economy growing rapidly enough to create employment that compensated for job losses in markets facing competition from economies with lower labor costs. The closing of the circuit of capital was fostered by the limited alternatives to export-oriented growth, resulting in the effective channeling of resources to the industrial sector. This was fostered either by state policy or the banking system, largely with the acceptance of subordinate classes. The hegemony of the industrial part of the capitalist class over the accumulation policy was essentially uncontested.[17]

The coincidence of these characteristics resulted in a relatively successful hegemonic project that not only developed methods of maintaining the framework of capitalist accumulation, but also devised a relative consensus over the nature of the accumulation strategy, policy paradigm, and redistributive outlays to subordinate classes. This was accomplished by a system that did not necessarily neglect organized labor and labor parties within the policy network. Rather, it encouraged the participation of working-class peak organizations and became an important tool for maintaining the growth model and regime legitimacy.[18] Przeworski's characterization of the democratic class compromise as combining private property, redistribution of income, and a strong state as an ideal package for almost everyone seems particularly appropriate in such cases.

By contrast, the pattern in the conflict-based regimes of southern Europe was characterized largely by the absence of northern features. Membership in trade unions was lower in comparison to the neocorporatist regime, and proportion of the unorganized working class remained significant. Rather than single peak organizations representing labor, the unions were divided along political and religious lines. The politicization of the union movement was also expressed in the important role typically played by each country's Communist party in influencing the predominant trade union confederaton.[19] The relative radicalism of the trade unions was met by a hostile bourgeoisie that did not eagerly accept the legitimacy and claims of unions. The greater radicalism of the left and the unions was further bolstered by the weaker tradition of the welfare state, although this varied according to place and time. Divided between Communist and Socialist or social democratic camps, the left's role in governing was relatively small. In Italy the Socialists occasionally joined the Christian Democrats but always as a parliamentary minority, and in France the left was out of power throughout the 1960s and 1970s until François Mitterand's successful campaign in 1981.

Bornstein also mentions the strength of the national economy as a variable, although one less easily incorporated than some others. Both France and Italy had very strong postwar recoveries, which contributed to the growing power of labor in the 1960s. The models of accumulation varied among the countries, with the state typically playing a strong role but with differences effected by large, medium, and small capital.[20] Both Italy and France were less industrialized and maintained large numbers of small and medium-sized firms, which contributed to the dilution of urban working-class power and a less unified hegemony among capitalist segments than in the neocorporatist cases.

To what degree can the characterization of southern European countries as polarized, fragmented, noncorporatist, and weakly hegemonic be extended to states whose democratization occurred only when the postwar settlements were themselves in crisis? More important, how has Portugal emerged from an expanded democratization, intrinsically predisposing it to a more extreme version of weak hegemony, finally to adopt major elements of a new hegemonic project mixing elements from both north and south? Using the concepts set forth in this chapter, this book investigates the conditions relevant to the collapse of the corporatist dictatorship, the expanded democratization of the transition, and the dishegemony of the consolidation of democracy. By identifying key variables and processes, I portray the Portuguese case as one option among several possible courses of democratization.

My main argument can be briefly summarized. Portugal's democratization was predicated upon deep divisions within the traditional ruling elite and dominant class. These divisions could not be overcome because of institutional reasons as well as contradictory interests within the ruling circles that prevented a clear policy direction from emerging. The fall of the dictatorship was an instance of relative state autonomy during a complete collapse of traditional leadership. This enabled the dictatorship's historic political opposition to play a paramount role in articulating a new hegemonic project.

The quasi-revolutionary transition to democracy featured particularly intense competition among political forces as leftist elements sought to expand democratic change to fundamental social and economic reforms. Unable to implant a counter-hegemonic leftist model the transition resulted in a dishegemonic impasse. As the transition ended and consolidation started, political parties played a key role in expressing hegemonic alternatives, with elections taking the form of referenda on models of society. Both left and right needed appropriate social and electoral support to pursue their policy preferences legitimately.

The consolidation of democracy proceeded through four phases of evolution, culminating in the Social Democratic party's (PSD) electoral victory in 1987.[21] The party's success gave it a relatively strong mandate for pursuing democratic capitalism with several elements of the southern conflict model in place. Nevertheless, residues of the revolutionary transition continued to hound the party's attempts to institutionalize its neoliberal hegemonic project rapidly. Signs of creeping neocorporatism were also evident, blunting the country's evolution toward the southern model. Structural characteristics of the Portuguese economy made the neocorporatist, northern model difficult to implement because the country's comparative advantage lay in low wages for a given level of productivity. The government, trade unions, and industrialists all showed ambiguous commitment to tripartite bargaining. Broadly speaking, the Portuguese case illustrates the difficulty of finding suitable institutional and social arrangements to consolidate a hegemonic project in the aftermath of expanded democratization. It also represents an instance in which parliamentary democracy survived despite the radicalism of the transition and the weakness of the traditional ruling circles. In my concluding chapter I compare Portuguese democratization to the process now underway in the former Soviet bloc, where substantial political and social change makes other models of democratization less relevant.

ORGANIZATION OF THE BOOK

The book focuses on historical and empirical themes set forth in this chapter, although I make no sustained attempt to provide a detailed recounting of historic events. Chapter 2 reviews the outlines of the Salazarist hegemonic project and accumulation strategy, singling out the exceptional character of the Portuguese accumulation model and its contradictions before the 1974 coup. The chapter identifies soft- and hardliners within the old regime and in opposition and examines the revolutionary transition to democracy—from April 1974 when the old regime fell to the installation of the constitutional regime in 1976, a period that represented intense competition for hegemonic ascendency among a wide range of social and political forces.

Chapter 3 focuses on the character of dishegemony during the consolidation of democracy. It offers a distinct characterization of the consolidation and deals empirically with events pertaining largely to the political system. I examine the positions of the parties and parliamentary deputies on political and socioeconomic issues to identify the main lines of cleavage, and I relate the pattern of coalitions to the general theme of dishegemony. My basic argument is that as the revolutionary period deposed the leading segment of the dominant class and radicalized the subordinate classes, the political parties were particularly hard pressed to develop a coherent national-popular program either for channeling a revamped capitalist hegemony or for setting the terms of a substantially different arrangement based on a new counterhegemony of subordinate classes. The northern parliamentary corporatism was not immediately available as an option, in part because it was poorly differentiated from the southern authoritarian variant. The conflict-based model that discounted the left and placed the right in permanent control of the government was defied by electoral results that failed to give left or right a conclusive or sustained majority.

This chapter also argues that a strong deterrent to a transition to democratic socialism lay in political differences on the left: a polarization typical of southern European countries undermined the electoral majority that supported some brand of left politics. My examination of the composition of governments and election returns reinforces the idea that Portugal was dishegemonic: that is, unable to sustain the political conditions for an alternative to semiperipheral democratic capitalism yet incapable of finding another hegemonic project. Such a project would have been reflected in a consistent rightist electoral majority and government typical of France and Italy during the 1950s or 1960s and would have been necessary for revamping Portuguese capitalism. While signs of rightist resurgence emerged as early as 1979, only after the last revision of the constitution (1989) which allowed reprivatization of nationalized industries under the tutelage of a majority rightist government, could Portugal be said to have moved distinctly toward a hybrid version of the postwar settlement that Bornstein characterizes as a conflict-based regime.

Chapter 4 investigates the nature of the evolving hegemonic project in terms of its degree of popular consensus. This degree is largely measured with Eurobarometer surveys, which make it possible to examine relationships between variables such as the changing strength of voters' party attachments, the ideological self-placement of respondents and its tie to party vote, and the link between country goals or attitudes toward change and ideological and political divisions. The chapter is especially concerned with the period leading up to the Social Democrtic party's unprecedented single-party majority in the 1987 elections.

Chapter 5 investigates the social basis of political differences. Essentially, the chapter has two key concerns. The first is the extent to which the conditions for dishegemony—divisions within the left and electoral frailty on the right—correspond to structured social differences. Using an ecological approach, I compare the relative electoral stability of the Portuguese Communist party (in a world in which Stalinist forms of socialism no longer constitute a viable alternative to democratic capitalism) to the sharply varying fortunes of the Socialist party (PS), the ideal agent of a northern settlement. An examination of the social roots of ideology and partisanship follows, using Eurobarometer and ecological data. The chapter assesses the degree to which a broad social coalition was generated behind the PSD's national-popular program, thus overcoming historic urban-rural, north-south cleavages. It also addresses the impact of cleavages such as education, gender, age, and religion upon party support and left-right ideological divisions.

Chapter 6 analyzes the relationship between party competition and trade union strategies in an effort to link the emergence of a settlement to conditions mentioned by Bornstein involving the orientation of unions and employers toward corporatist-style negotiations. The splintering of the labor movement into pro- and anticorporatist confederations corresponded to political and ideological divisions within the left. A detailed analysis of trends over the last decade shows that this division was belatedly subject to an incumbent-opposition dynamic, especially involving competition between the Socialist and Social Democratic parties. The erosion of the Communist-influenced General Confederation of Portuguese Workers–Intersindical's (CGTP) anticorporatist stances during the late 1980s corresponded to the flip-flopped conditions of the late 1970s: the Socialists, now humbled and out of power, resented the institutionalization of neocorporatist arrangements by their primary political opponent and thus moved toward the left, closer to the Communists in union affairs. In the meantime, the CGTP—having largely abandoned its hopes for a noncorporatist and more radical left hegemony reflecting the gains of the revolution—came to perceive the corporatist mechanisms as a means for bringing the class struggle into the heart of the state. This led some CGTP leaders to seek a rapprochement with the Socialists and their reformist union confederation the General Workers' Union (UGT).[22]

The consolidation of a semiperipheral democratic capitalist system under Social Democratic oversight redirected strategic thinking on the left to emphasize a defense of labor's gains in exchange for a degree of union cooperation. The atrophy of the Communist alternative and the difficulties in giving more concrete form to democratic socialism led to a peculiar Portuguese adaptation of the European postwar settlement that combined some of the gains of the revolutionary transitional democracy with incipient elements of northern left parliamentary neocorporatism. In this sense, Portugal has proved to be less than a pure conflict-based regime.

Chapter 7 recounts the broad themes of party policy approaches to the dishegemonic situation during the four phases of the democratic consolidation. Focusing initially upon the failed attempts at developing a socialist "third road" that was neither communist nor capitalist, it devotes special attention to the right's strategy for controlling the economy. It examines the impact that such a strategy would have had on different parts of the Portuguese economy, especially as the ascendency of the PSD's hegemonic project shifted the focus from reconciliation and stabilization to reordered relations within the capitalist class. I draw a distinction between competitive and monopolistic segments of that class, showing the conflicts between the general goals of narrowing the differences between Portugal and the rest of Europe and moving away from the low-wage comparative advantage that has proved to be a key ingredient in renewed investment and growth over the last decade.

Chapter 8 offers an overall assessment of whether or not Portugal has joined the twentieth century. It extrapolates the key variables in the Portuguese experience and uses them to develop a typology of democratization that is applied to several countries and especially to parts of the post-Communist world. It uses the former Soviet bloc's experience to highlight the importance of factors that characterized expanded democratization in Portugal. The former Communist world has faced a crisis of hegemony even more severe than Portugal's because they have very weak or nonexistent capitalist classes to lead the democratization process. Political agents have been confronted with the need to assert national-popular programs that negate the authoritarian and irrational aspects of real socialism yet reconcile the emergent class contradictions implied by the installation of capitalism. Like Portugal, they are at the edge of modern Europe, often with conditions more like those of conflict-based regimes than of northern neocorporatism.

My analysis of Portugal suggests that the dishegemonic experience will be even more acute in Eastern Europe, although this depends on how well political parties propose acceptable combinations of new institutions and policy approaches given the extant social and electoral topography. The Portuguese experience underlines the fact that during expanded democratizations, weakened historically dominant classes and elites cannot rely on structural power alone to assure a transition to capitalism under conditions of political democracy. The situational aspect of power—who is in policy-making positions and under what conditions—will play an especially critical role in both creating and legitimating accumulation strategies and social settlements.

Chapter 8 concludes by restating the need to combine the social and political dimensions of analysis to understand the specific trajectory followed by a democratizing country. Undoubtedly, the range of variability among hegemonic projects and internal social settlements is limited by structural and contextual factors. Yet a complex combination of specific historical events, preexisting policy divisions, types of newly available party coalitions given the pattern of ideological and electoral cleavages, and even the timing of political business cycles may determine many elements of the democratization process. Scholarship should be directed not simply to the explanation of relatively homogeneous outcomes but also to the exploration of factors influencing divergences in process or outcome. In this book I combine specific historical analysis with structural and situational factors to describe Portuguese democratization and offer a framework for the study of democratization elsewhere.

TWO

THE END OF THE DICTATORSHIP
AND ITS HEGEMONIC PROJECT

Portugal's dictatorship under long-term ruler Salazar has been called dependent capitalism, sui generis capitalism, or a middle ground between liberalism and socialism.[1] Given the duration of the regime, it is unlikely that any single characterization applied consistently for the entire period. Rather, the government's economic orientation showed some flexibility over the decades, shifting from the antimodern orthodoxy of Salazar to a more robust industrialization effort with growing infusions of foreign capital during the 1960s and early 1970s. Particularly during the 1970s, the inability of Portuguese industrial capital to establish a clear model of accumulation that corresponded to the growing ties to European markets and capital meant that the dictatorship lacked direction: the colonies-based strategy lingered as a historical alternative to the modern European choice, placing the regime in the impossible position of seeking to maintain both options under increasingly taxing political, military, and economic conditions.

The collapse of the government in 1974 represented the beginning of the end for the colonial option and the corporatist-imperialist hegemonic project that Salazar assiduously fostered for decades. Caetano was no more successful in reconciling the European-colonial schism within the dominant class than he was in substituting an *Estado Social* for the *Estado Novo* as the national-popular program meant to rally the nation. The fall of Caetano was in this sense reflective of the ambiguity of Portuguese ruling circles, which were unable to choose between accumulation strategies and could not effectively discard the institutional-philosophical complex represented by the authoritarian colonial corporatist regime. This chapter examines the historical antecedents to Caetano's ouster and develops an argument concerning the key policy conflicts that immobilized the dictatorship. It explains the entry of the military in terms of the old regime's inability to provide an effective resolution to those conflicts and argues that as a consequence the traditional elite and dominant class lost control of the transition. This opened up a much larger role for the extraregime opposition, which was able to impose a much more leftist agenda upon events. By the start of the consolidation period in 1976, reformist softliners had gained control of the process but now faced the difficult task of reconciling gains of the revolution with the often divergent goals of electorally based parties as they form governments.

SHIFTING ACCUMULATION STRATEGIES UNDER THE DICTATORSHIP

The installation of António de Oliveira Salazar, first as minister of economics in 1928 and then as prime minister, occurred during economically uncertain times. Salazar dealt with rising government debt and trade imbalances in the aftermath of the 1926 military coup by using traditional economic orthodoxy: fiscal restraint in an effort to reduce demand and sound government budget policies to decrease the blossoming deficit.[2] The management of macroeconomic policies, however, soon yielded to a broader conception of an accumulation model based on a kind of autarkic, colonially based corporatism. Inspired by Catholic integralism, this model was meant to serve as an alternate to purely liberal-market as well as centrally planned economies, and also deal with the deterioration of world trade during the Great Depression.[3] More important for Salazar, it solved several political problems related to establishing the relative positions of the various segments of Portuguese capital, thereby creating a social basis of support for the new order.

The importance of Salazar's model lay especially in orchestrating a relative balance among rival elements of the dominant class, a point often insufficiently emphasized in other works dealing with this period. Boaventura Sousa Santos (1990) and Nicos Poulantzas (1976) essentially agree that agrarian capital was the hegemonic fraction through World War II and possibly to the 1960s. Nevertheless, this argument fails to underscore the balancing act that the regime was forced to play that affected rural and urban capital. This balance was reflected in the main economic policies: the Wheat Campaign, the Colonial Act, and the *condicionamento industrial.* Passed in August 1929, the Wheat Campaign was targeted at farmers, especially the large estate owners (*latifundistas*) concentrated in the southern half of the country where most of wheat was grown. The Wheat Campaign provided fertilizer and machinery subsidies and placed limits on the importation of wheat. According to the legislation, it was meant to "dignify agriculture as a most noble and most important of all the industries and as the first factor of economic prosperity for the nation."[4] The language as well as the substance of the legislation indicated the importance the government placed on the interests of landed capital and its key role in the national-popular program, given the development of productive forces at that time.[5] We cannot infer, however, whether this single, albeit significant, policy clearly established the economic hegemony of that class segment. As Sammis (1988, 104–7) has noted, the Wheat Campaign tied landowners with industrialists such as Alfredo da Silva (head of Companhia da Uniã o Fabril (CUF), which made fertilizers) and firms that made implements for the mechanization of agriculture. In this sense, the Wheat Campaign was an effort to spur agricultural output by reinforcing the market for nationally produced industrial goods.[6]

The Colonial Act (1930) favored those segments of the domestic dominant class whose production could be absorbed by colonial markets. This was accomplished by structuring economic ties with the colonies to limit the development of competing industries and open markets. Despite considerable dissension between industrialists seeking greater protectionism and wine and wheat growers seeking freer trade, policies directed at the colonies managed to appease elements among both: wine growers found protected markets for their table wines; textile manufacturers obtained cheap cotton from the colonies and earmarked their internationally uncompetitive goods for the colonial market.[7] Even commercial capital benefited from the preferential tariff rates given to Portuguese exports shipped on domestically chartered carriers. Like agriculture, the colonies were seen as a key component of the new national-popular program, reinforcing the country's imperial mission while bringing together contending elements of the dominant class. From the regime's perspective, the colonial policies made good use of "the very idea of Empire which . . . brought to our spirits an idea of unity and an optimistic sense of grandeur, indispensable for stimulating energies and eliminating the indifference and narrow-mindedness which threatened to wear away our thoughts, plans and efforts."[8] In short, these policies sought to bind both the masses and the dominant class to a single hegemonic project.

In a further measure meant to distinguish Salazar's corporatism from liberalism, the *condicionamento industrial* obligated entrepreneurs to obtain government approval before establishing a company (so the government could assess whether there was a need for additional firms in a given market), introducing new technology, or markedly increasing production (to ensure that excess production would not occur). As Correia de Oliveira, minister of the economy in 1945, explained, "we created systems of 'condicionamento' or the reserve of the internal market with the theoretical objective of avoiding overproduction and with the practical result of impeding competition, which was thought to be excessive, among domestic producers."[9]

The policies associated with the *condicionamento* helped establish the basis for the balance between large and small or medium capital. For large firms, the policies helped assure markets after expensive industrial investment, which might otherwise not have occurred, by restricting new product lines to larger, more capitalized enterprises.[10] For small and medium firms, it made it possible for "almost all of them to survive to this day as industrialists."[11] This was done by restricting entrance into old product lines, which were often dominated by small and medium producers. While the future of small and medium capital may not have been as rosy as Correia de Oliveira supposed (as I discuss later in the chapter), the accumulation strategy under Salazar was meant to support capital of various sizes rather than foster free-market competition likely to undermine weaker producers and sectors.[12]

Engendered during more autarkic times, these policies were not uniquely representative of the economic hegemony of landed capital or the domination of the economy by a classic *comprador* bourgeoisie, a mere conduit of foreign capital. By restricting foreign investment, particularly in sectors such as insurance and shipping, and limiting the sale of Portuguese enterprises to outsiders, the government stifled foreign investment in Portugal until the 1960s. As Sammis (1988) and Nataf and Sammis (1990) have pointed out, the

Portuguese dominant class was heterogeneous: while some major segments resembled a classic *comprador* bourgeoisie with strong ties to foreign capital and colonial markets and primarily engaged in trade, other significant elements favored domestic production and industry. This was part of the compromise that constituted the Salazarist model. It sought to preserve a role for both industry and agriculture through mildly import-substituting policies directed at the domestic and colonial markets in isolation from extensive direct intervention by foreign capital (especially within Portugal as opposed to the colonies). Small and medium capital was to be represented within the policy paradigm by elements of the *condiciona-mento*. The dominant class was further unified by antilabor policies prohibiting strikes, independent trade unions, and democratic political parties.[13]

Many authors commenting on the postwar period have emphasized the relative decline of both landed capital and small and medium firms. Sousa Santos (1990) has argued that landed capital increasingly lost its structural dominance during the 1950s, although its relative ideological and instrumental impact within the regime did not erode until later.[14] Others have remarked that the postwar period saw a growth in the power of large monopolistic groups, although the relationship between them and the regime has been the subject of controversy. Communist leader Álvaro Cunhal has argued that the regime was effectively dominated by an alliance between the state and the monopolies, constituting "a few hundred large capitalists and landowners and their agents" coming into rapidly growing opposition with "the great masses of the population—all the non-monopolist classes and strata" (1975, 31).[15] Similarly, Rafael (1976) emphasizes the decline of small and medium capital under Salazarism and suggests that Portugal reached a context-specific version of monopoly capitalism during the last decade of the old regime's existence. Poulantzas underlines the role of the monopolies within the Portuguese *comprador* bourgeoisie, a pro-regime element unlikely to break with the old system, and contrasts it with the domestic bourgeoisie, which he claims was the major force for democratization. Maxwell (1986) and Makler (1979) mention that the Portuguese dominant class was led by a set of key families whose assets dominated the economy. The following section evaluates the notion of the large monopolistic groups and assesses to what extent they might have been considered hegemonic in the postwar period as part of a shift in accumulation strategies.

Monopolistic Groups and Postwar Hegemony

The Portuguese economy during the dictatorship was characterized by the increasing centralization and concentration of capital.
In 1930 there were actually more owners than workers (a 1.3 to 1
ratio). By 1970 the number of owners had declined from 644,000 to
76,700 while the number of workers increased from 494,000 to
1,019,300 (a .08 to 1 ratio).[16]

While a large number of firms persisted into the early 1970s,
they were typically small and poorly capitalized: fewer than 6 percent of all firms held 73 percent of all the capital. In several sectors,
a high level of monopolization existed, with capital-intensive industries such as cement or steel represented by a very few or a single
firm. Typically, such industries were tied to one or more of the large
groups, which were often associated with a major bank and family.
The groups were usually concentrated in certain markets and products.[17] Thus, despite the fact that the groups were partly composed
of firms implanted in the key industrial sectors of the economy,
they were not identical in terms of the types of investment held.
Rather, their variable placement opened the possibility of policy
conflicts among differently situated groups.

Sammis (1988) argues that some of the groups were historically
tied to the anti-industrial commercial or colonial segments. Espírito
Santo (Banco Espírito Santo e Comercial de Lisboa) was based on
trade with the colonies, while the Miranda group (Banco Português
do Atlântico) stemmed from wine commerce. Based on her examination of stock portfolios, Sammis concludes that at least until the
1960s, Espírito Santo along with Banco Burnay and Banco Nacional
Ultramarino were the most significant nonindustrial groups. They
were heavily involved in colonial extractive industries or agricul-
tural-export commodity production. Moreover, they often had associations with foreign capital and thereby had characteristics similar
to a *comprador* bourgeoisie.

Other groups had assets concentrated largely in the industrial
sector and tended to have fewer ties with foreign capital. Mello's
large conglomerate, CUF, was tied to the Totta bank and had
invested heavily in industrial manufacturing; the Champalimaud
family with its associated bank Pinto e Sotto Mayor was also a
major industrial actor. These firms (especially CUF) tended to be
vertically integrated and had some ties to the colonies insofar as
they were sources of raw materials used in industrial production
within Portugal (for example, cotton and oilseeds).

During the period after World War II but before the start of the colonial wars in the early 1960s, divisions among these groups were relatively sharp. The regime was faced with the choice of continuing protectionism or adopting a more open policy. Given the changing international context, the perpetuation of a protectionist balance between industry and agriculture was increasingly stressful. Domestically, pressures mounted for economic policies that would continue the industrial expansion experienced during the war. Industrial firms had long displaced commercial ones, and the need for new markets for their goods become critical after the war as export markets were more fully satisfied by other recovering industrial economies.[18] Any effort by the regime to accede to the industrialists' interests with policies designed to stimulate development through further industrial concentration would have meant turning to a different model of accumulation. Accelerated industrial growth and concentration of capital would have undermined the regime's ties to small and medium capital as well as landowners and perhaps obliged it politically to incorporate the growing strata of workers that industrialization would engender.

The regime continued its policy of compromise among the segments of capital. To placate industrialists' desire for development aid, the government was able to secure a substantial investment program from the Economic Cooperation Administration (ECA), a U.S.-tied agency meant to assist Europe's postwar recovery. The $388 million investment was nearly two-thirds financed by the ECA and included a considerable segment for domestic industry (28 percent) and much less for agriculture (3 percent). While this percentage was clearly advantageous for industrialists, landowners were partly appeased by funds directed to colonial development (which would reduce pressure for internal north-south colonization and land redistribution) and electrification (which would be based on hydroelectric power, enabling irrigation systems to be installed).[19]

This program gave a small nod to domestic industrialists but was not a turn toward European postwar settlement because it required no democratization and was specifically directed to the further development of the colonies during a period of decolonization elsewhere. The tendency to find avenues of compromise when choosing accumulation strategies was retained in the First Development Plan (1953). Although it maintained some emphasis on agricultural development, the plan was primarily directed at industrial projects that reduced foreign imports, fostered the building of physical infrastructure, and continued colonial development. It did not specifically call for significant industrial reorganization.[20]

Rather than the fundamental reorientation of the 1930s, the late 1940s and 1950s represented a deepening of the classic strategy of accumulation. The era continued to focus on the import-substituting industrial growth of national capitalists in a protected market. It accepted the growing importance of the monopolistic groups but sought to minimize the impact on agriculture and small and medium firms. Domestic development remained linked with the colonies, which provided cheap raw materials, markets for uncompetitive surplus industrial production, and profits for *comprador* elements involved in the extraction of resources and their reexportation to other Western European markets, often in concert with foreign capital.[21] Rather than transforming the parameters of Portuguese economic development, this period was largely confined to economic policies consistent with the regime's historic social support. Such continuity managed to undercut the ability or desire of potential intraregime softliners to appeal to extraregime elements and challenge the basic framework of Salazar's hegemonic project.[22]

Portugal's entry into the European Free Trade Association (EFTA) in 1958 and the infusion of foreign capital from the mid-1960s through the early 1970s helped to redirect the accumulation strategy from the classic model of import substitution to export promoting. In particular, foreign direct investment in industry went to labor-intensive manufacturing, where low wages and a repressed work force could provide a competitive advantage (for example, in electronics, clothing, and automobile assembly). Finished goods were meant for both domestic consumption and export, while semifinished products were destined for export only, a part of the production globalization associated with multinational corporations (MNCs). From 1959 to 1972, imports from the colonies decreased from 14.2 to 11.6 percent of all imports; exports to the colonies declined from 29.8 to 14.7 percent.[23] Traditional exports (with the exception of textiles and clothing) declined, while modern industries such as chemicals and machinery increased. By 1970, industrial production contributed 46 percent of GNP, up from 37 percent in 1960. In many key export industries, the percentage going to Europe increased while colonial exports languished or declined.[24]

However limited, the economic liberalization of the 1960s threatened to undermine the delicate balance historically sought by the regime. Small and medium enterprises were directly threatened by liberalization and foreign investment because they were the least capable of competing due to limited resources and antiquated technology. They depended on the special advantages provided by the *condicionamento*, colonial markets, and cheap raw materials associated with the classic accumulation strategy. *Comprador* elements wanted the colonies to pursue their exploitation of African resources and reexportation activities. By contrast, industrial monopolistic groups could benefit from collaboration with foreign capital through technology transfers, investment, and other assistance. Tied to foreign capital, Portuguese capital would be better able to tap European and American export markets, thereby reducing the country's (already declining) dependence on the colonies.

Poulantzas (1976) argues that the main shift in the Portuguese economy involved the emergence of a domestic bourgeoisie, a segment of nationally owned capital spawned by foreign investment. He claims that this segment was neglected by the regime and thus was favorable to the opposition. Poulantzas's understanding of the Portuguese economy, however, suffers from his desire to generalize from Spanish and Greek cases, which were subject to much greater foreign investment than Portugal was. In Portugal, the key divisions were *not* between a neglected domestic bourgeoisie pressing for democratization against a retrograde *comprador* segment composed of the monopolistic groups. Rather, three key points apply. First, the monopolistic groups were not homogeneous. Some were more industrial than others and had different links with the colonies and *comprador* activities. Some were clearly *comprador* and depended upon privileges that only continued Portuguese dominion could guarantee, while others were engaged in industrial activities that might have prospered under neocolonial arrangements.

Second, the industrially oriented monopolistic groups were not mere conduits for foreign capital but rather a national bourgeoisie, albeit one weakened by the agrarian-colonial-protectionist accumulation strategy necessitated by the class alliance. Their associations with foreign capital were not meant to subvert Portuguese industrialization but were instead meant to redirect it in a period when the old strategy could no longer be sustained.

Third, industrial groups' alliance with the truly retrograde elements of the dominant class (the landowners, colony-linked *compradors*, and inefficient small and medium firms) was indicative of their relative lack of hegemony. The programs and state aid that industrially oriented monopolies received were conditioned by the need to appease segments whose industrializing inclination was limited.[25] Thus, if one segment of Portuguese capital seemed unduly excluded from its proper place within the policy paradigm, it was the industrially oriented monopolistic groups.

The evolving alternative to the classic model was based on a partial and slow adoption of a development option more oriented to Europe. Expanded trade among countries along the European rim was signaled by Portugal's entrance into the EFTA.[26] Changes in the foreign investment code after a spurt of foreign loans also marked a greater internationalization of the economy. Finally, once Portugal's major trading partner, Great Britain, made overtures to the European Economic Community (EEC) (which were initially rebuked by France in 1963, although Britain was eventually admitted in 1973), the gradual shift toward Europe became an option that the regime could hardly resist. In 1972 the government signed an agreement with the EEC that promised to open the Portuguese market to significant competition from the outside. Full membership in the EEC, however, still required Portuguese political changes such as democratization and decolonization. Rather than take that political leap, the regime worked in relatively small steps to appease softliners, who were inclined to favor a limited version of the European postwar settlement, while not alienating hardliners.

Despite the relative decline of the colonies in the Portuguese economy, certain industries still had reason to cling to the hardliners' imperial hegemonic project and economic strategy. For example, textile manufacturers faced tariffs when European exports reached a certain ceiling and had to tolerate higher levels of competition with foreign firms in the domestic market. Although textile exports to Europe increased in the years before the fall of the corporatist regime, this was attributable to "new investments by foreign firms who took advantage of low tariffs and a cheap labor force."[27] By comparison, the colonial market was overwhelmingly supplied by Portuguese textiles. Thus, a major industry centered in small and medium enterprises had reason to resist further Europeanization of the economy.

In contrast to the dispersed textile industry, the firms most likely to benefit from European integration were larger, more concentrated, and tied strongly to foreign capital: chemicals, glass, naval repair yards, and machine construction. The economic softliners were the modern, advanced industries already experiencing various levels of integration with the global and regional economy. The *comprador* bourgeoisie, along with smaller, less capitalized, and unproductive firms, were the economic hardliners less able and willing to embrace the political and social approaches to democratic capitalism found throughout Western Europe.

While the juxtaposition between large, modern, capitalized, and Europeanized firms with small, traditional, protectionist-colonial firms split the Portuguese bourgeoisie, it did split it well, or at least not well enough. During the 1960s, the distinction between *comprador* and industrially oriented groups diminished. Groups centered around the banks Totta Açores (CUF), Borges e Irmão, and Português do Atlântico each had holdings in extractive or agricultural industries based in the colonies, although most of their holdings were in industrial firms likely to benefit from European integration. Banco Pinto e Sotto Major (Champalimaud) held virtually its entire colonial portfolio in industrial investment, which predisposed it well for a postimperialist future. Although the industrial-monopolistic groups remained distinct from the purely comprador ones, they exhibited some structural ambivalence. Politically, this weakened the strength with which fundamental choices among alternative accumulation strategies could be posed as clear alternatives between the softliner Europeanist course or the hardliner classic model emphasizing retention of the colonies.

Salazar's presence in the government ensured the prevalence of continuity over change. His departure in 1968 and replacement by Marcello Caetano seemed to open the door for greater political debate about the regime's accumulation strategy and overall hegemonic project. The new incumbent promised some kind of economic and political liberalization. The regime's National Union party was opened to allow factions, specifically in the form of an *ala liberal* (liberal tendency) that advanced a more Eurocentered program in the National Assembly. Pinto Leite, Francisco Sá Carneiro, and Pinto Balsemão articulated preferences that put them at odds with admirers of the classic model such as Franco Noqueira and Almeida Garrett. The latter continued to hold the hardline position favoring the retention of the *condicionamento* and colonies, arguing that Portugal would otherwise constitute only an insignificant rectangle on the edge of Europe in contrast to its imperial reign over the colonies.

Among elements of the Portuguese bourgeoisie, structural differences seemed reflected in public stances. *Comprador* groups such as Banco Espírito Santo e Commercial de Lisboa and Banco Nacional Últramarino concentrated their attention on Portugal's colonies and the need to defeat the liberation movements. They were joined by textile producers who lamented the possible loss of colonial raw materials and sought to preserve traditional markets in the colonies. Associations representing industries dominated by small and medium firms drew attention to the difficulties such firms would have without the *condicionamento* and protective tariffs. Landowners faced with very low agricultural growth rates, rising costs, and decreasing land values also resisted Europeanization, which would cause wage rates to increase, facilitate labor migration, bring about greater competition in agricultural markets, and diminish the importance of colonial markets for wine.

Industrially oriented groups such as those centered around Banco Totta Açores, Banco Pinto e Sotto Mayor, and Banco Português do Atlántico concentrated on the need to bolster domestic industrial development, increase market competition, and engage in more effective cooperation between public and private sectors. They and other large firms advocated colonial industrial investment rather the traditional *comprador* trading activities (Sammis 1988, 234–36). These groups were the most closely drawn to the Europeanist line.

Caetano's Failed Democratization: Weakness of the Softliners

Failed democratization in the years 1968 to 1974 symbolized the weakness of intraregime softliners. The framework developed by O'Donnell and Schmitter (1986) conceptualizes both failed and subsequently successful democratization. They argue that democratization is a process involving the short-term calculations of several groups, starting with the breakdown of the old regime and ending with the consolidation of the new one. These groups can be divided into those within the regime and those outside—the intra- and extraregime elements. Both groups can be further subdivided in accordance with their political positions: softliners show a willingness to support a democratization process, while hardliners resist. Intraregime hardliners favor retention of traditional authoritarianism; extraregime hardliners favor replacing the old dictatorship with a new revolutionary regime that has similar methods if different targets of repression.

In addition, democratization involves both a change of political institutions and a choice among accumulation strategies with hegemonic domestic consequences. Therefore, the terms *soft-* and *hardliners* take on additional meaning. Because the Europeanist accumulation strategy required political democratization, softliners were those who sided with both new institutions and a change in economic direction. Conceivably, this might have included elements within and outside the regime, with such a coalition providing the basis for a reformist transition to democracy. In contrast, intraregime hardliners were clearly those favoring both authoritarian corporatism and the protectionist-colonial accumulation strategy. Extraregime hardliners, however, escaped easy classification. Their revolutionary goals overshadowed the ambitions of softliners and instead aimed at the establishment of a broad counterhegemonic project meant to overturn the class system altogether.

O'Donnell and Schmitter have made several points regarding successful democratization. Softliners must be able to take control of the process in which "authoritarian incumbents begin to modify their own rules in the direction of providing more secure guarantees for the rights of individuals and groups" (1986, 6). A prolonged process, democratization often starts with partial liberation, which, if "not too immediately and obviously threatening to the [prevailing] regime[, will] tend to accumulate." (1986, 7). The process is still reversible: the intraregime softliners have to coax the hardliners into going along, while the reformist extraregime opposition must be convinced that the softliners will ultimately prove successful.

The staying power of the regime's hardliners is partly determined by the dictatorship's past policy successes. When they are numerous, vulnerability to change is diminished, and the rules guiding a democratic transition (and the intraregime hardliners' ability to limit social and economic changes, if not forestall any change in regime) are determined by the regime itself. When the regime has faltered significantly in foreign or domestic policy, the process is more open and uncertain. Occasionally (and for Schmitter and O'Donnell, ideally) the transition is structured around a set of pacts among elites, which may include a range of actors, civilian and military. It is possible for the intraregime softliners who initially provided the stimulus for reform to lose control in a second phase to a more militant opposition as rising mobilization puts greater pressure for faster and more general reforms. In pact-structured transitions, however, the regime's acceptance of new political parties and other independent interest groups is exchanged for constraints upon policy choice and distribution of benefits. This separates the political moment (changes in the governing institutions) from the economic moment (which is linked to property relations and accumulation strategy) and thereby reduces incumbents' risks when accepting the process. If such policy constraints are adequate, political hardliners are increasingly excluded as the substantive uncertainty associated with democracy diminishes. Eventually, as the costs of repression increase with the institutionalization of democracy, the process becomes much harder to reverse.

How do these arguments and concepts apply to the six years of Caetano's rule dubbed Marcelismo? In order for liberalization and democratization to have started, a basic divergence between hard- and softliners must occur. As my analysis has emphasized, democracy and economic liberalization were at best part of Europeanist accumulation strategy. With varying intensity, it was favored by certain elements within the dominant class—including, to some degree, the industrial monopolistic groups and foreign capital. These groups constituted the dominant-class basis of support for the civilian softliners as represented by the *ala liberal* within the National Assembly. A significant part of the extraregime opposition also generally supported political democracy. Why, then, didn't Caetano forge an effective alliance with the softliners in and out of the regime and successfully pursue the transition to democracy and a Europeanist accumulation strategy? Why was a military coup needed to overcome the hesitations of the incumbent political elite?

For a brief period, Caetano appeared to be pursuing a softliner alliance. The years between 1969 and 1971, the *primavera* (spring-time) of his government, seemed a classic liberalizing prelude to fuller democratization The *ala liberal* was allowed into the legislature. Caetano pledged to construct a social state mirroring, at least in intention, the welfare states of Western Europe; and allowed open elections within the trade unions. Independent policy centers such as SEDES (Society for Economic and Social Development) were formed, and dissidents such as Mário Soares returned from exile. The colonies became overseas provinces with an added measure of autonomy from metropolitan Portugal. Technocrats associated with the Europeanist view expressed their opinions forcefully: Rogério Martins, the minister of the economy, proposed a Law of Industrial Development meant to restructure the Portuguese economy along the lines of export promotion and further European integration by reducing protectionism and limiting the scope of the *condicionamento*'s application. In general, these policies suggested a shift away from the balancing of dominant-class interests favored by Salazar in favor of a modernizing alliance of large, industrially oriented groups and foreign capital.

This alliance proved to be fragile. By 1972 much of the *ala liberal* had departed from the National Assembly, and the modernizing technocrats in government had left their posts. The predisposition of the government for balancing had frustrated the modernizers because it maintained closer links with the colonies and retained more of the *condicionamento* than modernizers preferred. Union elections came back under closer government control. Prospects for Europeanization dimmed; the soft-liner coalition proved ephemeral.

What accounts for the failure of Caetano's liberalization to be carried out? Why wasn't the theoretically leading segment of the dominant class able to assert its hegemony and thereby redefine the national-popular program? Several reasons account for the short-comings of the *primavera*.

One key reason for the reversals of the later Caetano years rests with the character of the dominant class itself. Although industrially oriented groups and foreign capital had become quite important in the Portuguese economy, nonindustrial groups could not be taken lightly. For example, the *comprador* Espírito Santo group was a large, well-financed element with a strong presence in Lisbon among policymakers. Moreover, as I have mentioned, certain industrial groups had *comprador* ties—for example, CUF and its link to colonial agriculture. Overlaps between industrial and land ownership also diluted modernizing efforts. Although foreign capital had grown considerably during the 1960s, it still was not the weightiest part of the economy. Small and medium enterprises, while diminished overall, still predominated in many industries, especially traditional ones such as textiles.

The dictatorship's repressive labor policies also brought some degree of unity to the dominant class. Trade unions could be more easily controlled, recalcitrant labor leaders harassed, and strikes broken by force. Low wage rates engendered partly by these conditions attracted both foreign capital (which had entered Portugal particularly for that reason and typically invested in labor-intensive export industries) and relatively inefficient small and medium enterprises. From an employer's perspective, the potential negative effects of political liberalization upon labor markets and enterprise control weakened zeal for democratization. Because a middle way between protectionist-colonial corporatism and market-European liberalism was elusive, the determination of dominant-class softliners to press for a complete break with the classic model was not as resolute as hardliners' desire for continuity rather than renovation.

In addition to considering the internal contradictions afflicting the dominant class, we must also examine the extraregime opposition in terms of its attractiveness as a potential alliance partner for intraregime softliners. As I discuss later, the domestic and colonial policy objectives of the opposition, both soft- and hardliners, were sufficiently radical to make regime change seem risky to the political elite and the dominant class.

Within European Portugal the extraregime opposition had long been divided into antagonistic parts.[28] Since the early years of the cold war, the regime's opponents had been drawn into the ideological conflicts between Communists and more moderate leftists, despite some short-lived unity around the presidential candidacy of Humberto Delgado in 1959.[29] During the 1960s, the colonial war stimulated the growth of a student movement in the universities and antiwar activism in general. This helped rekindle the energies of the opposition, although it further fragmented it into a set of revolutionary Maoist and Trotskyist subgroups. The 1969 elections were contested by two opposition organizations: the Democratic Electoral Commissions (Commissões Democráticas Eleitorais—CDE), inclined toward the Portuguese Communist party, and the Electoral Commission for Democratic Unity (Commissão Eleitoral de Unidade Democrática—CEUD), closer to Socialist positions.[30] At that time the opposition was less radical in its demands than it came to be a few years later; it mostly sought political liberalization and a recognition of the legitimacy of the African liberation movements.

After the government's inevitable victory in the 1969 elections, the opposition strove to maintain a more enduring political and social presence. The CDE attempted to keep its operation going after the legally sanctioned electoral period, while some opposition members (especially Communists) sought to use the liberalization of the trade union laws to organize workers better, both in opposition to the regime as well as for more limited economic gains. It is important to note that the turmoil within the classic accumulation strategy was not simply a top-down affair involving conflicts among firms and sectors of the economy, although this was a critical component. As Logan (1985) and Arrighi (1985a) have argued, pressures from below played a role in reducing the appeal of involuntary corporatism, although Logan's (1985, 151) point seems essentially correct: "the existence of a working class made a difference in the evolution of Spain and Portugal . . . [but on the whole it] was a secondary actor."

Nevertheless, after 1969, labor peace was not effectively provided by the regime as strikes and mass demonstrations, took place, although legally prohibited. They involved sizable numbers of workers and occurred in various key industries throughout the economy. In 1969 they affected (among others) major automobile plants, cement, tobacco, tires, textiles, chemicals, and shipbuilding; in 1970, hospitals and fishing; in 1971, batteries, doctors, textiles, and bank workers (mass demonstrations); in 1972, electronic assembly, fishing, transports, and agricultural workers; in 1973, bank workers (mass demonstrations and work stoppages), fishing, and airline workers; and in 1974 before the coup, chemicals, textiles, and insurance workers (mass demonstrations and work stoppages). In addition, student demonstrations and strikes were endemic at universities.[31]

The public sector was relatively quiescent during Caetano's rule, giving credence to Logan's (1985, 150) argument that a "bureaucratic class entrenched in the state apparatus opposed demands for liberalization." With certain elements of the dominant class it shared an interest in the protectionist aspect of the classic accumulation strategy. In a sense, this aspect was similar to the Italian postwar settlement, which also featured a bloated state apparatus staffed by political patronage that was meant to assure a degree of loyalty to the reigning parties. In Italy and France, however, worker rebellions still occurred; and both countries had the advantage of drawing upon democratic institutions to overcome these crises.[32] Portugal's social settlement lacked the legitimacy provided by democratic political arrangements. Despite the transformation of the social structure during the quarter century since the end of World War II, the regime had left itself with few legitimating principles that could quell working-class activism.

Labor and student turmoil, coupled with the fact that the vilified Communists were taking advantage of Caetano's political opening, complicated efforts of intraregime softliners to convince vacillating elements within the regime to support further democratization. Sensing that democratization could not be substantively circumscribed to negotiated agreements among moderate partners softliners could not assure recalcitrant elements that a democratic future would be better than the present. Hardliners continued to insist that political liberalization exclude any possibility of timely decolonization. In a pactlike reform process, this demand would have been non-negotiable, a position that the opposition could not accept.

Caetano's inability to sustain the *primavera* radicalized the opposition even more. By 1973, at the Third Congress of the Democratic Opposition in Aveiro, the CDE and CEUD attempted to coordinate their activities better. Furthermore, a broad leftist agenda, which included a critique of capitalism and an insistence on socialism, was advocated during the 1973 electoral campaign. The regime's hardliners could now take comfort in the theory that further liberalization would bring radical leftists into power who favored immediate decolonization and nationalization of industries. This argument not only convinced truly *comprador* elements and neocolonially inclined industrial groups, but also lessened the softliner convictions of those interests that stood to gain most from Europeanization. In retrospect, had the intraregime softliners been able to solidify an alliance with the opposition in 1969—initiating a gradual withdrawal from the colonies, political liberalization, and new social policies—the prospects for renovation rather than continuity would have been vastly improved. Instead, the failure to consummate that alliance strengthened hardliners within both the ruling circles and the opposition.

The opposition to the regime was not confined to continental Portugal; it was clearly leftist in the colonies of Mozambique and Guinea-Bissau and had a large leftist component (MPLA) in Angola. The prospect of dealing with a radical African independence movement was not encouraging from the point of view of protecting *comprador* interests. Had the dictatorship started a process of negotiation with the liberation movements, some accommodation of industrially inclined interests might have been possible. Eventually, even Gulf Oil Corporation was able to continue its operations in postcolonial Angola (Cabinda), protected from sabotage by Cuban troops. Nevertheless, the unwillingness of the regime to consider African political movements as anything other than terrorist contributed to a self-fulfilling theory that the opposition was composed of radicals who could not be trusted.

By the end of the Caetano regime, Portuguese politics had reached a historic impasse: neither the regime's ruling circles (with numerous internal divisions and political ambiguities) nor the civilian opposition (divided between hard- and softliners with a long tradition of cold war enmity) could marshal the resources to force a decision between the Europeanist and classic strategies of accumulation, to say nothing of a more radical leftist alternative. Symptoms of regime disaggregation abounded as military efforts faltered, domestic dissent increased, and international pressure mounted. That disaggregation was evident in the regime's political isolation as the remaining European colonial power but was also due to the economic consequences of the 1973 oil crisis. Until the military's intervention in 1974, civilian leadership within and outside the regime was unable to overcome internal divisions and provide effective hegemonic direction. Unlike General Charles de Gaulle, who overcame the Algerian crisis and established the Fifth Republic in France, Caetano simply presided over the collapse of the Portuguese empire and corporatist dictatorship.

THE OLD REGIME FALLS: THE RELATIVE AUTONOMY OF THE STATE, THE MILITARY, AND THE THREE PHASES OF THE REVOLUTIONARY INTERLUDE

On 25 April 1974, MFA officers overthrew the Caetano regime.[33] The military wanted to resolve the impasse involving dominant-class interests and start negotiations with civilian sectors to form a workable alliance and hegemonic project. Why did the military assume the role of key policymaker and institution builder, a relatively autonomous state? One answer is the failure of civilian leadership to create a context for policy adaptation. Nevertheless, this situation only set the stage for the military, which needed its own specific motivations to justify intervention.

The military felt the brunt of the regime's policies. Its years of combat had not brought it closer to success; instead, long tours of duty under harsh conditions had fostered resentment and a desire for change. Because the rigors of the three-front war had depleted the number of candidates able to fill officers' positions, the government promoted officers from civilian military recruits, even over officers of the professional army who were on the promotion list.[34] This move deeply frustrated professional officers and ultimately led to the formation of the MFA.

The MFA united officers with specific professional grievances, and many officers concluded that those grievances could only be satisfied by solving the colonial question (Graham 1979). Whether a solution involved immediate decolonization (favored by the extraregime opposition) or a more protracted, negotiated process (associated with intraregime softliners), it clearly meant the end of a key component of the classic accumulation strategy and the time-tested method for dealing with disharmony among segments of the dominant class. Most important, because any rapid changes in colonial policy required dramatic action such as the April coup, the entire edifice of the dictatorship, with its insistence on balancing classic and Europeanist accumulation strategies, might be open to general contestation. The MFA thrust itself into the role of policymaker and institution builder as a way of dealing with both professional grievances and perceived threats to the military as an institution. In keeping with Stepan's argument, this was a variant of "redemocratization initiated from within the authoritarian regime." "The military-as-institution, though at one time a component part of the authoritarian regime, [sought] to overthrow either the civilian political leadership or the military-as-government because it [came] to believe that the continuation of the authoritarian regime [was] detrimental to its long-term core institutional interests" (1986, 73).

The institutional motivations of the MFA explain only the specific, limited objectives of the movement. What remains to be explored is whether the MFA constituted a true case of relative state autonomy in which the interests of some parts of the dominant class were sacrificed in order to protect larger political interests (Poulantzas 1978). Or was it something more radical and different whose behavior stretched beyond the relative autonomy concept?

Events after the April coup show the MFA's ambiguity on this point. The military established a Junta da Salvação Nacional (National Salvation Council) that reflected both intraregime softliners and the extraregime opposition.[35] The provisional government's president was General António Spínola who, along with other officers such as Galvão de Melo and Pinheiro de Azevedo, identified with the military softliners. Adelino da Palma Carlos became the government's first prime minister and, with Francisco Sá Carneiro, represented civilian intraregime softliners.[36] In this sense, the MFA did seem to resolve dominant-class discord in favor of the Europeanist tendency. But the new government also included other figures—Mário Soares, head of the Socialist party, and Álvaro Cunhal, long-time chief of the PCP—who reflected the extraregime opposition. Within the military, Rosa Coutinho, Costa Gomes, and Vasco Gonçalves were strongly connected with the leftist, hardline opposition.[37] The MFA and the new government were more than a simple case of relative autonomy. They united not just the old regime's softliners with the opposition's reformist elements (Socialist, Social Democratic, Republican, and so on), but also included revolutionary extraregime hardliners who had little sympathy for the Europeanists and their accumulation model.

The heterogeneity of the forces within the new government made it inevitable that no clear policy direction could be established or maintained. Three phases exist between the initial coup and the start of the constitutional regime: from 25 April 1974 to 10 March

1975, from 11 March 1975 to 25 November 1975, and from 26 November 1975 to 25 April 1976. These phases correspond to the shifting alignment of political and social forces within the government and society.

The first phase was largely devoted to working out conflicts within the dominant class, which no longer had an intrinsically supportive regime. Other classes and social forces pressed for economic and political gains but generally within the framework of the softliner alternatives. The second period featured a radicalization of government following Spínola's abortive coup on 11 March. It substantially broadened the debate over accumulation strategy by bringing extraregime opposition (especially hardline elements) into policy-making posts. The hot summer of 1975 ended with the termination of the Vasco Gonçalves government on 12 September 1975. This was an important turning point in the realignment of forces because softliners greatly enhanced their positions within the government, to the detriment of opposition hardliners. From that point until 25 November 1975, when the revolutionary hardliners were removed from power (particularly in the armed forces), the tide turned against a broad alternative to a capitalist model of accumulation and moved toward combining rapid decolonization with closer ties to Europe and political democratization.

The role of private versus public accumulation was only partly resolved by the time the Socialist minority government was installed in 1976. Following the crises that generated the initial coup against Caetano, the subsequent two years reflected a profound disorientation among the Portuguese bourgeoisie. The hegemony of financial-industrial Portuguese capital (stripped of its *comprador*-colonial parts) and foreign capital could not be firmly established until after the second constitutional revision of 1988–89. Postrevolutionary governments were pressured from above to move in the Europeanist direction, yet pressures from below perpetuated ambiguities in the accumulation model for a decade and a half.

Phase 1: 25 April 1974 to 11 March 1975

In first phase, government bodies were dissolved, including the president, the National Assembly, and the Council of State, and the ideological apparatus of the corporatist state was dismantled—for example, the Portuguese Youth (Mocidade Portuguesa) and the Portuguese League (Ligue Portuguesa). Caetano formally handed power to Spínola, and the MFA established the National Salvation Council. The Armed Forces Movement declared itself in favor of decolonization, democracy, and development. The opposition parties issued their first statements, with the Communists emphasizing an end to the colonial wars, the protection of democratic liberties, and the role of elections; the Socialists highlighted the need to negotiate immediately with the independence movements about the right of African people to self-determination and independence. Within a few days, the leaders of the extraregime opposition, Álvaro Cunhal and Mário Soares, arrived and, along with other political groups, entered into talks with the MFA.

The mid-May appointment of Spínola as president and Palma Carlos as prime minister demonstrated the Europeanist inclinations of the new leaders. During May, Spínola met with several prominent industrialists, bankers, and employers' associations. The Association for Portuguese Industry (AIP) soon declared its support for the junta and underlined its desire for the defense of free enterprise and closer ties with the European Community.

The first provisional government included both soft- and hardliners among the extraregime opposition, with Soares as minister of foreign affairs and Cunhal as minister without portfolio. Sá Carneiro, who had quit the old National Assembly in frustration was made an adjunct to the prime minister, a sign of the softline liberal tendency. The Communists were put in charge of the newly formed Ministry of Labor and issued statements deploring, in their opinion, the generalized strike wave that only served the cause of fascism.

The incompatibility of the extralegal opposition and the Europeanists became more apparent over time. The Europeanists, an expression of the interests of large industrial and foreign capital, found that several obstacles impeded their hegemony. First, despite the presence of the PCP in the Ministry of Labor, an unprecedented strike wave continued, hitting the larger foreign and national firms in particular. Spínola went to Porto to say that "democratic ideals and liberty [were] being criminally undermined by forces aiming at destruction and anarchy" (Morais and Violante 1986, 268). The strikes, however, were often opposed by the PCP, which was the best organized political force on the left. They seemed instead to express years of pent-up working-class frustration. Spínola's democracy and the Europeanists' accumulation strategy depended upon the retention of the country's main advantages: low wages, industrial peace, and good proximity to European markets. A distinct separation of the political and economic moments, Spanish style, was needed to ensure Europeanists' adherence to the transitional process.

Second, the Europeanists faced a left-wing tendency within the MFA. In June, Spínola and Sá Carneiro attempted to expand the president's power to conduct foreign and domestic affairs, but their request was refused at a plenary session of the MFA. On 8 July Palma Carlos went to the MFA-dominated Council of State, again requesting a change in the provisional constitution, only to be refused as Spínola had been. The next day he announced his resignation as prime minister.

The appointment of Vasco Gonçalves as prime minister of the second provisional government on 17 July signaled the further erosion of the Europeanists' position.[38] During the next year, he became associated with the ascendency of the hardline opposition, even though the next government had representatives of the PPD/PSD (Sá Carneiro's party) as well as the PS and PCP. In late July, Spínola tried again to bolster his institutional authority, especially concerning decolonization—and exacerbated the tension between the intraregime softliners and the opposition. Despite his efforts, the decolonization process continued apace; an agreement with Guinea-Bissau was reached by the end of August, and a transitional agreement finalized with Frelimo in Mozambique in early September.

The initial showdown with the Europeanists came at the end of September when Spínola attempted to mobilize a silent majority for a massive demonstration in Lisbon. The left was able to unite against Spínola, with the PS and PCP mobilizing against the president's maneuvers while other parties (for example, the Christian Democrats—PDC) and military officers (such as Galvão de Melo) supported his plans. The coordinating council of the MFA's program, the Council of State, and the National Salvation Council all held meetings in which Spínola failed to carry the day. Because he could not gain public support to change the prevailing alignment within the MFA and among the parties, Spínola resigned on 30 September. Costa Gomes was appointed president, and Vasco Gonçalves continued as prime minister of the third provisional government. The elimination of Spínola was an essential step in distancing the Europeanist tendency; in Spain, the creation of a government-in-exile was announced, bringing together frustrated intraregime softliners and hardliners.

During the first few months after the overthrow of Caetano, two themes dominated—at times pitting intraregime and extraregime elements against each other; at other times forging common ground between intra- and extraregime softliners against hardliners. The first theme was anti-fascism, an almost instinctive civilian and military response based on a visceral repudiation of the principles and institutions of the old regime. Anything thought to have benefited from the dictatorship was tainted and intrinsically suspect. The Europeanists, represented during the dictatorship in the *ala liberal* and after the coup by the Spínola-Palma Carlos-PPD/PSD-Sá Carneiro troika, suffered considerably because they did not pursue their opposition to authoritarian corporatism more actively and sooner. This poisoned their relations with military officers predisposed to take decisive action rather than pursue the prior regime's balancing act among dominant-class segments. The civilian extraregime opposition was quite radical by the time of the coup and able to play up its long history of opposition to fascism to a receptive MFA and the general public. Anti-fascism united the extraregime opposition and lent it militancy in the face of intraregime softliners.

The second theme was building democracy, essentially an institution-creating endeavor that played a subdued role during the first phase. Other than creating or legalizing multiple political parties, legalizing trade unions, and eliminating remnants of the corporatist regime, the process had little impact. Many issues, however, continued to fester throughout the transition to democracy. One was the question of the unity of the trade-union movement (which the PS opposed and the PCP and Intersindical union movement preferred). In addition, there were many troubles with the Catholic Church concerning its control over Rádio Renascença and the need to revise the Concordata with the Vatican to allow for divorce, issues dealing with individual rights and pluralism under a democratic political framework.

Unlike the anti-fascism theme, this one was likely to split the extraregime opposition into soft and hard lines and forge a more conciliatory attitude among intraregime and extraregime softliners. Because softliners were partly defined by their political positions (favoring tolerance for opposition and liberal democratic political institutions), both Socialists and liberals could theoretically find common ground, despite conflicts about the exact distribution of the president's and prime minister's power.

Both anti-fascism and building democracy were more explicitly linked to the strictly political dimension of the new regime's national-popular program than to the design of a new accumulation strategy. During the first phase, these two themes only had economic implications: they allowed trade unions to press for higher wages and better working conditions (freedom of association), thereby eroding the low-wage accumulation strategy. Decolonization meant at least a partial repudiation of the state's corporatist function of balancing mutually contradictory accumulation strategies. Otherwise, the MFA's program was vague about the character of its preferred accumulation strategy.[39] The parties were undergoing much internal reformation as they held their first legal congresses and, as in the case of the Socialists, were still dealing with the opposition's radicalism inspired during the last years of the dictatorship.[40] They could not be expected to direct themselves immediately to the long-term question of accumulation strategy. Although the anti-fascist sentiment included an antimonopolist component, no direct actions against the monopolistic groups were taken during the first phase.

Phase 2: 11 March to 25 November 1975

The first phase ended with the growing alienation of the Europeanist softliners from the democratization process. The eleventh of March 1975 witnessed the culmination of this alienation in an abortive coup attempt by Spínola and his supporters. The failure of the coup transformed the political situation, further reducing the influence of the intraregime softliners and allowing radicals to press forward with a concerted antimonopoly strategy. Soon afterward, the MFA and the governing bodies were transformed, with the Council of the Revolution and the MFA Assembly now guarding against additional destabilizing attempts. Melo Antunes, an important intellectual among the MFA officers, declared that the *via socialista* was now proper for Portugal. By the end of March, the government was reconstituted. While it retained the three core parties (PS, PCP, PPD/PSD), it now included more elements from the left (MDP, ex-MES). The spirit of antifascism engendered by the failed Spínola coup intercepted the process of building democracy, fostering a lasting institutionalized role for the MFA and lending it a more radical ideological and programmatic orientation.

Spínola's failed coup made it possible to transform the regime's class coalition even further. Although the Europeanist segments of the domestic dominant class had seen their access to power diminish in the first phase, it nearly disappeared altogether in the second. The monopolistic groups, both industrial and *comprador*, were subject to nationalization in a series of decrees from the Council of Ministers soon after the coup attempt. On 14 March banks and insurance companies became the first targets, given their importance as holding companies and credit sources for the monopolistic groups. Almost immediately afterward, the industrial bourgeoisie was subject to similar treatment: Siderurgia Nacional (Champalimaud's steel plant) was nationalized, followed by cement, cellulose, tobacco, transportation, petroleum, electricity, and so on. By September, a wide range of firms had been taken over, including the large shipyards outside Lisbon as well as CUF.

Over the next few months, agrarian capital was also subject to expropriation. The government set up an agrarian reform program that identified properties legally subject to state takeover, often belatedly endorsing the actions of rural workers already occupying the southern latifundias.[41] The PCP chronology of events mentions that on 28 March "the creation of the cooperative 'Estrela Vermelha' (Red Star) was a decisive step starting the transformation of southern Portuguese farms, applying the principle of the land for those who work it" (PCP 1982, n.p). Clearly the process of change had moved far beyond dominant class bickering so typical of the Salazar/Caetano years; now, several leading segments of the Portuguese bourgeoisie and the economic system itself had come under full scale attack. The material basis for the new state-centered collectivist political economy was rapidly being created.

The assault on the old order was most intense from March through early September, the hot summer of 1975. In July the PS and PPD/PSD left the fourth provisional government. The fifth provisional government, again headed by Gonçalves, was constituted on 8 August but lasted only twenty-two days: the prime minister was dismissed on 30 August. By that time, the Gonçalves government had completely undermined its ties to the extraregime softliners, both civilian and military. Officers within the MFA produced the Document of the Nine, outlining the main points of criticism against Gonçalves's rule, which had carried with it escalating violence and confrontations throughout the country. After some deliberation within the MFA—particularly among the nine officers who had produced the document; Otelo Saraiva de Carvalho, head of COPCON; and Gonçalves and Costa Gomes, part of the ruling triumvirate—a decision was made to create a sixth provisional government headed by Pinheiro de Azevedo in early September.

Nevertheless, the process had not yet run its course. The Portuguese transition to democracy had resulted in something less than dual power in the classic Leninist sense but certainly more than a modest change in political system. The transition brought into question the choices now facing the new country: any proposed hegemonic project faced the difficulty of reconciling parliamentary democracy (the Constituent Assembly had been elected in April) with the mass mobilization and direct democracy of the hot summer.

Between the beginning of the sixth provisional government and 25 November, power flowed tenuously between formal institutions and the street. By mid-September, some soldiers had formed Soldiers United Will Win (SUV), a radical organization questioning the political credentials of the traditional military hierarchy.[42] Arms flowed outside of controlled circles to revolutionaries frustrated with the change of direction implied by Gonçalves's removal. The charismatic leader Otelo and his COPCON forces were now officially in opposition to the sixth provisional government and supported the devolution of power to the streets. In October, conflict between the Communists, who were influential in organizing mass protests and demonstrations, and the Socialists increased. The PCP accused the PS of a right turn and the PS declared that Cunhal's party exercised excessive control over the mass media and acted one way in government (more or less responsibly) and another in the streets (provocatively).

By November, these conflicts had grown more acute. The PS and PPD/PSD held mass meetings calling for stability, while the small PRP-BR (the Portuguese Revolutionary Party-Revolutionary Brigades) called for armed rebellion. On 12 November, the day after Angolan independence, construction workers surrounded the Parliament, trapping the prime minister and deputies inside. Over the next few days, street politics escalated. Those who favored *poder popular* (popular power) held mass meetings while the softliner parties (PS and PPD/PSD) held their own assemblies. President Costa Gomes warned of impending civil war. On 20 November the MFA's Revolutionary Council replaced General Otelo with a more moderate officer, Vasco Lourenço, as commander of the Lisbon military region. On 24 November the Communist-influenced Intersindical trade unions staged a two-hour general strike in Lisbon's industrial belt, protesting the political and economic situation. Otelo and COPCON criticized proposed changes in military personnel meant to remove elements too strongly linked to the revolutionary left or the PCP.

The events of 25 November clarified the political situation. The integrity of the provisional government was restored after military elements associated with the revolutionary left were defeated by Jaime Neves and his Amadora Commandos. Leftist officers such as Otelo and Carlos Fabião were removed, and COPCON was eliminated as an independent force. Changes in the composition of the Revolutionary Council reinforced the general purge of leftist officers. *Poder popular*, as well as PCP plans to use its MFA-people strategy to circumvent other parties, lost its influence in the government and MFA.[43]

The crackdown on the revolutionary left reflected the continuing conflict within the old extraregime opposition over the course to follow. The limited consensus around anti-fascist goals and measures, which to some extent included PS and PCP acceptance of the nationalization of *comprador* and industrial groups, broke down during the summer. Unity within the left around the theme of building democracy was shattered as the Communists (and other elements of the revolutionary left) relied upon the MFA-people strategy, which promoted direct ties to the military and reduced the importance of Parliament or the multiparty provisional governments. That strategy especially favored the PCP; April elections for the Constituent Assembly had shown that the PCP's influence as an electoral party was slim, especially by comparison to the PS. Naturally, the Socialists and other major parties to the right perceived the approach as a direct challenge to the democratization process conceived in parliamentary-institutional terms. The softliners' fears about the viability of national democratic institutions could not be overcome by PCP denunciations about the undemocratic character of fascist attacks on agrarian reform, Communist headquarters, and so on. For these parties and their many sympathizers, anti-fascism could not work as a substitute for a weak commitment to building democracy.

There were differences about the ideal political model. Despite the nationalization of some major industries, there was little real agreement on the accumulation model or the strategy to be implemented. The Communists favored an antimonopolist vision that seemed akin to a Portuguese new economic program: commanding heights of the economy under state control, increased state planning of the economy, and the retention of small and medium capital operating in a controlled market setting. To some extent, the Socialists may have also accepted these general parameters, at least during 1975–76.[44] Nevertheless, little else drew the left together.

Except for the Communists, parties on the revolutionary left backed *poder popular*, which focused on the workers' and residents' commissions that were oriented to direct democracy. In addition to limited political support, a vast range of critical obstacles impeded the successful realization of this option. Despite the state's corporatist pretensions under Salazar, it was still relatively weak and lacked the requisite talent or internal organization to compensate for private accumulation functions, even in conjunction with workers' commissions. The cold shoulder from Europe and the U.S. meant that any implementation of popular power in a revolutionary Portugal would impose very severe sacrifices and require the concerted use of repression. This alone would have undermined support among all those concerned with building democracy, making the exercise an impossible revolution (Mailer 1977). The Communists' accumulation strategy had similar political and economic problems. The key issue was whether there really was a third way capable of changing the fundamental dynamic of the classic model of accumulation, even in its Europeanized version: low wages, chronic balance-of-payments deficits, and growing dependency on European and American markets and capital.

Inevitably, the accumulation strategy based upon the MFA-people alliance would have faced insuperable contradictions. Limited capitalist support would have eroded quickly as wage increases were granted to maintain workers' loyalty—a presumed requisite for regime survival. At least in the short term, falling investment would have further diminished productivity, redoubling wage-induced inflation. In order to maintain external demand in the face of rising wages and decreasing productivity, sharp devaluations would have been needed, contributing to the inflationary spiral. In the absence of viable foreign markets, unemployment would have risen perhaps disguised as underemployment through state subsidies—further depriving the economy of productive investment and compounding other problems.

The viability of an import-substituting accumulation strategy, generally favored by the Communists, dubiously assumed that investment, markets, and raw materials could be effectively derived from Portugal's population of ten million and its small territory in combination with newly developed second- and third-world markets. PCP economists reasoned that worker enthusiasm for the new accumulation model would limit wage demands and encourage sacrifices for the long term. But deep strains in the economy due to foreign pressure and substantial internal opposition might well have resulted against fascists of all kinds, enforced by the military and PCP-controlled trade unions.[45] The implementation of such an accumulation strategy would have eliminated any possibility of building democracy in cooperation with Socialists.

The PS provided the only viable opposition accumulation strategy, although without pressure on the left, the Socialist party might have adopted the deradicalized Europeanist solution favored by the PPD/PSD sooner. For Soares's party, the European route was painless in several respects. Politically, it tapped the Socialists' numerous ties to other Western European parties, particularly the German Social Democrats and to a lesser extent the French and Italian Socialists, who together could fashion a Social Democratic Europe through the EC Domestically, it encouraged the consolidation of parliamentary democracy and ensured a regime in which the Socialists would play a very important role.

Economically, a greater continuity would reign under the Europeanist option as attention shifted further to the Old World and away from the former colonies. The PS favored Portugal's entry into the European Community because substantial aid would follow. Foreign capital could supplement state and domestic private capital within a mixed economic model acceptable abroad and at home. Under ideal circumstances, the European economic option would feature growing productivity, noninflationary wage increases, the growing competitiveness of Portuguese goods, and the concomitant lessening of balance-of-payments problems.

The key to the Socialists' accumulation strategy was finding a workable compromise between the interests of workers and capital. The appeal to workers would be largely through economism: rising wages, fuller employment, and a gradually expanding welfare state. It would be granted some anti-fascist legitimacy if it kept former monopolies either in the state sector or under government oversight. With European markets opening and additional aid from the EC, even small and medium firms might learn to live without the colonies, despite heightened competitive pressures. The scenario might yield a model of accumulation closer to Mitterand's France than Kohl's Germany, perhaps combining state ownership of key firms with an essentially market-driven system. This could form the basis for Portugal's postwar settlement and move it toward the neocorporatist social democracy prevalent in northern Europe. Still, it required a workable domestic coalition, either within the extra-regime opposition or between intra- and extraregime softliners.

Unable to create that coalition on the left, the Socialists in the last phase of the Portuguese transition focused on building democracy in conjunction with their major softliner ally, the PPD/PSD, and sealed the victory of the Europeanist accumulation strategy, albeit with leftist residues. Could a hybrid accumulation strategy, less radical than that favored by the PCP and the revolutionary left but more leftist than that represented by the PPD/PSD-PS alliance, be implemented as a kind of unique democratic socialism. Had the Communists discarded the MFA-people strategy, strongly endorsed the European outlines of a new political system, and shed the illusion of Eastern European socialism, this might have been attempted. Instead, although the Socialists remained the vital political agent shaping the future political economy, their options were limited by political dependencies.

Phase 3: 25 November to 25 April 1976

After the November victory of the softliners, the emphasis returned to building democracy in the European mold: radicals were purged from the military; the Constituent Assembly continued its job of drafting a new constitution in a climate of relative stability, continuing until elections in April 1976. To a surprising degree, the constitution proved true to the political action plan that the Revolution Council passed after Spínola's failed coup. That document stated that "socialist pluralism comprehends the coexistence in theory and practice of various forms and conceptions of the construction of socialist society [and] rejects the implantation of socialism by violent and dictatorial methods." It acknowledged political pluralism by defending "the existence of various political parties and currents of opinion, even if they do not necessarily defend socialist options." The constitution was passed by the Assembly on 2 April 1976 with its pluralist and socialist components largely intact.

Chapter 3 examines the democratic consolidation, which still featured substantial transitional residues despite a movement in favor of a softliner alliance backing a Europeanist, democratic capitalist course. I have characterized the first years of the consolidation as dishegemonic, or lacking a distinct hegemonic project representing a broad social consensus. Dishegemony was expressed in the Socialist elements of the constitution, the continuing presence of a important nationalized sector of the economy, the agrarian reform, and the sustained ideological divisions among the parties and trade unions.

To a degree perhaps only exceeded by recent transitions in Eastern Europe, Portugal experienced an expanded democratization in which the traditional elites and classes lost control over major elements of political and social change. In turn, the state and the parties and forces controlling the government acquired substantial relative autonomy to determine the nature of the evolving hegemonic project.

THREE

DEMOCRATIC CONSOLIDATION
UNDER DISHEGEMONY

Portugal's democratic consolidation followed a turbulent period. During the two-year transition, the country experienced six provisional governments, intensive divisions about the structure of the new regime, and questions about fundamental social relations. The transition ended during a phase in which a key struggle resolved the terms of a workable political settlement: the events of November eliminated prospects for a revolutionary, leftist dictatorship and made it clear that only a European-style parliamentary democracy was broadly acceptable. There was much less agreement on the social settlement, which the new regime was to help establish. The constitution had codified many of the gains of the revolution, including the nationalization of industry, agrarian reform, and many workers' rights, but also left an important role for private enterprise. As democratization expanded to included a vast array of issues, the task of the consolidators in government was to overcome dishegemonic uncertainties, establish a policy paradigm, and implement relevant policies.

Although Schmitter and his collaborators seemed assured that liberal democracy would survive, the consolidation still faced both the radicalism unleashed by the extraordinary transition and a prior history of failure as a democracy. Wiarda (1988, 75) has emphasized that the "litany of the Portuguese republic is the oft-repeated history of a futile effort to erect an inorganic, liberal parliamentary system in a county where organicism, centralism, and unity had always been the dominant characteristics." Portugal *had* changed during the years before democratization: it was more modern and cosmopolitan, inclining to a great degree of liberalism than in the past. In addition in the course of the transition, the corporatism-protectionism-colonialism framework had been shorn from the evolving hegemonic project. The radicalism of the transition had partially resurrected a leftist "organicism, centralism, and unity" but without successfully imposing it as a hegemonic alternative.

During the democratic consolidation, both the popular masses and the remaining elements of the dominant class sought new political formulas and social settlements that took into account the unwillingness of all important political forces to engage in civil war, a question essentially settled by the events of 25 November 1975. Brute force and frontal confrontation yielded to a war of maneuver in the contest for hegemony. Democratic institutions offered an attractive terrain within which the Europeanist softliners could reorganize themselves both politically and economically and the subordinate classes could hope to defend gains of the revolution, possibly with the added legitimacy of electoral endorsement.

The consolidation period was only partially dishegemonic. The transition process settled one aspect of indecision regarding accumulation strategy. Except for the PCP and some third worldists, the elimination of the colonial-protectionist strategy meant that although the Second Portuguese Republic would have to deal with the perils of European integration and the eventual elimination of protectionism, issues could now be resolved in a much narrower framework of policy choice. The lingering issue of political identity as a colonial power or a mere rectangle on Europe's periphery had also been overcome: Portugal as rectangle would frame the new debate. The statist, authoritarian, elitist, rural, and conservative traditions that Wiarda ascribed to Portugal were associated politically with colonial empire and the antiquated sense of community identity and regime legitimacy. Portugal was in this sense unlike Latin American countries, which developed their authoritarianism domestically without the colonial power identity and colonies-Europe alternative. For Portugal, dishegemony was relative rather than absolute: the scope of debate over property relations was much less a discussion about the fundamental direction of economic policy, which had been settled for most important actors. Dishegemony was a residue of the revolutionary aspects of the transition. While inspiring much emotional debate, it managed to limit itself to terms that could be handled under democratic institutions and conditions.

FROM DISHEGEMONY TO DEMOCRATIC CAPITALISM: FOUR PHASES

The postrevolutionary period can be divided into four phases, each characterized by specific political and economic conditions but generally featuring the progressive establishment of a more liberal, bourgeois hegemony. Throughout each phase, frustrated attempts to install a new left-inspired political economy demonstrated the severe obstacles to sustaining a creative and nonauthoritarian alternative to democratic capitalism. With the collapse of Marxist-Leninist regimes in Eastern Europe and the Soviet Union, the traditional Leninist strategy of smashing the capitalist state lost much of its attraction; yet parliamentary socialism proved no less evasive in Portugal.

I argue that apart from structural obstacles to any counterhegemonic project, the ultimate decline of a leftist alternative was facilitated by the inability of the popular masses and their political representatives to offer a clear alternative backed by party cooperation rather than competition. Instead of engaging in productive ideological compromise and strategic alignment, relations were flawed by principled differences and short-time horizons emphasizing momentary sectarian advantages. The war of maneuver was more successfully pursued by the old intraregime softliners. The overall reorientation of society along leftist lines would have implied a series of parallel ideological breakthroughs in various institutional spheres and along major principled lines. Instead, divisions over political economy within the left remained as deep as those between the left and the right, reducing the attraction of left ideas.

Each phase of the consolidation period involved continuity as well as new elements that aided the resurgence of the right and the implementation of a renewed model of capitalist accumulation. The major distinction among the time periods concerns the political situation: the relative weakness of the traditional power holders coupled with the diminished importance of street politics, meant that control over government afforded extraordinary discretion over policy choices.

Rather than changing the underlying pattern of party politics, each phase only confirmed the strategic advances of the right and the political impasse on the left. The first phase began in 1976 with the election of the minority Socialist government and ended in 1979 as the Democratic Alliance (the AD, composed of the PSD/CDS/PPM—the center and right parties) came to power. The second phase covered the AD government from 1979 to 1983. The third phase encompassed the period from 1983 to 1987 when eclectic governing arrangements prevailed. The fourth phase started with the 19 July 1987 victory of the PSD, which formed the first single-party majority government, and continues to the present (after the 6 October 1991 elections further confirmed the success of the Social Democrats). These phases are charted in table 3.1, which shows the political composition of governments and the parties that voted for them in Parliament.

TABLE 3.1. Political Composition of Governments in Portugal, 1976–94

Dates	Parties Represented in the Government	Parties Voting in Favor of the Government
23 July 1976– 8 December 1977	PS, Indep. (Soares)	PS, PCP, PSD
30 January– 27 July 1978	PS, CDS (Soares)	PS, CDS
28 August– 14 September 1978	Indep. Presidential (Nobre da Costa)	PSD, CDS
25 October 1978– 7 June 1979	Indep. Presidential (Mota Pinto)	PS, PSD, CDS
1 August 1979– 3 January 1980	Indep. Presidential (Pintasilgo)	PS, PCP
	End of First Phase	
3 January– 8 December 1980	PSD, CDS (AD) (Sá Carneiro)	PSD, CDS
9 January– 11 August 1981	PSD, CDS (AD) (Balsemão)	PSD, CDS
2 September 1981– 19 December 1982	PSD, CDS (AD) (Balsemão	PSD, CDS
	End of Second Phase	
9 June 1983– June 1985	PS, PSD (Soares)	PS, PSD
June 1985– 21 July 1987	PSD (Silva)	PSD, CDS
	End of Third Phase	
	Start of Fourth Phase	
July 1987–	PSD (Silva)	PSD

Phase 1: 1976–79

The election that brought about the first constitutional government of the Second Republic was rather inconclusive. As indicated on table 3.2, no party obtained a majority, although the Socialists received a plurality of the votes. Together, the Socialists and Communists held over 58 percent of the seats in the new Parliament. The old extraregime opposition was once again faced with the strategic dilemma inherited from the transition: coalesce efforts to avert a return to fascism and defend gains of the revolution, or continue with the divisions resulting from the ambiguity of the PCP's position on building democracy.[1] Despite the deep fissures that remained from the conflicting strategies of *poder popular*, MFA-people, and building democracy, some conditions favored the left, which emerged with a supportive constitution and the leading segment of the inherited capitalist class in state hands. At least in theory, these conditions could have been used to fortify the Socialist elements of the constitution with more specific policies during the democratic consolidation.

TABLE 3.2. National Election Results: 1975–91 (in percent)

	Party				
Election	PCP	PS	PSD	CDS	Other
1975	16.4	37.89	26.3	7.6	11.9
1976	14.3	34.8	24.3	16	10.6
1979	18.8	28.0	45.1	(AD)	8.1
1980	16.9	28.1	47.1	(AD)	1.9
1983	18.2	36.3	27.0	12.4	6.1
1985	15.5	20.8	29.8	9.7	27.4
1987	12.2	22.3	50.1	4.3	8.8
1991	8.8	29.6	50.4	4.4	5.0

Note: The reported figures include all coalitions by the PCP and PS as well as the scores for the MDP in 1976 within the PCP total. The PRD obtained 18.8 percent of the vote in 1985, accounting for the large increase in the "other" category for that year, which also includes blank or spoiled votes. All figures are from STAPE, the government electoral commission.

Nevertheless, the establishment of a left majority required conditions that were not met in this phase or in any future one. The votes on each article of the newly ratified constitution demonstrated that the extraregime opposition had undergone an enduring split during the revolutionary period, effectively destroying much of whatever solidarity the anti-fascist struggle had forged. Table 3.3 shows the overlap among the parties voting for each cluster of articles. The patterns reveal that the constitution was essentially the product of agreements among the softliner parties, the Socialists, the social Democrats, and to a lesser extent the PCP or CDS, the only party that voted against the constitution as a whole.

Clearly, the constitution was a compromise among the various parties. It represented several models of accumulation but captured especially the leftist-favored gains of the revolution by legally sanctioning a set of structural changes to the economy and greatly enhancing the position of workers and trade unions. Notably, it excluded the private sector from certain parts of the economy, made land reform and nationalization irreversible, emphasized cooperatives, promoted workers' participation in management, prohibited employer lockouts, and so on.[2] It seemed to combine the popular-power conception of workers' control with the Communist emphasis on nationalization and land reform and the Socialist concern for associational freedoms and individual rights.

TABLE 3.3. Overlap in Party Votes for 1976 Constitution

	Party Combinations			
	PCP/PS	*PS/PSD*	*PS/CDS*	*PSD/CDS*
Political Articles				
Agreed	16	27	25	24
Disagreed	20	9	11	12
Economic Articles				
Agreed	9	26	17	16
Disagreed	18	1	10	10
Social Articles				
Agreed	1	1	2	1
Disagreed	1	1	0	2
Overall Percent				
Agreed	40	84	68	63

Instead of immediately choosing a policy emphasizing bitter confrontation, the PSD as the main party of the right avoided a radical oppositional stance while the PS, the electorally prevalent left party, sought to establish a common ground with both the right and left. The war of maneuver did not pit a secular, Socialist, revolutionary left against a clerical, capitalist, fascist right. The revolutionary period fashioned a milder alliance of forces whose common commitment to process moderated the sting of the conflicting traditional cleavages. Although the CDS did oppose the constitution, this phase was somewhat comparable to Spain's consensus period lasting roughly from 1977–79. The key difference was the more active and explicit role of the military in Portugal. Overall, a demure tripolarization of the political spectrum—Communist, Socialist-Social Democrat, and a poorly defined right—came to characterize this phase.

The differing coalition strategies of the PS and PCP during this phase presaged the general pattern of interparty relations through most of the consolidation period. Having failed to secure their position through the MFA-people alliance, the Communists pursued the majority of the left. The party realized that without assistance from the MFA or a supportive elected government, it could not maintain key policies such as nationalization and land reform. Therefore, the PCP pressed the PS to make it a formal or informal partner in government. Nevertheless, the PCP's radicalism was largely directed at the PS—and particularly its leader Mário Soares, who many Communists felt had betrayed the revolution.

Although the opportunity existed for a Mitterand-style government, Soares had neither the personal inclination nor the ideological predisposition necessary to engage the PCP constructively. The Socialist leader portrayed himself as having saved the country from *Gonçalvismo*, as a person unwilling to sacrifice liberty for socialism and mindful of the sociological givens of the country. He was more conservative than the Communists and arguably intolerant of any rapport between the two parties. For Soares, the point was to overcome the crisis to save the revolution, a process that meant primarily the consolidation of parliamentary democracy. During the transition the Socialist leader had deplored "deficits of the nationalized enterprises as well as those in the private sector . . . the progressive anarchy of production, the generalized indiscipline in the world of labor, the abuses practiced in the name of Agrarian Reform." He criticized the "strategic unrealism" of the far left and mentioned that the PCP's flirtations with that faction put the Communists in a very difficult position for "negotiating seriously with the PS a durable leftist politics which would consolidate revolutionary gains and definitively push back the counter-revolution" (Soares 1979b, 29–30).

Soares's thinking did not change much after the hot summer of 1975. Faced with the choice of aligning with the totalitarian left or a politically uncertain right, the Socialists opted in 1976 to do neither and instead formed a minority government. This suited many within the party who anticipated the emergence of a pattern of Portuguese political alignment that was, in fact, realized in Spain after its 1982 elections: a Socialist party with a majority to form its own government, the Communists in disarray and in seemingly irreversible decline, and the right divided by factionalism and unable to present a coherent governing alternative. The perception of the Socialists as the most significant actor in the Portuguese party system was a key assumption of the party as well as of others. Bruneau and Macleod (1986, 7), for example, call the PS "the pivotal party of the political system" and cite Jean-Claude Colliard (1980, 80) who adds that it was "the essential axis of political life [as] governments are made around it." This was particularly true in the first and third phases, although the majoritarian pretensions of the party were never realized.

The Socialists' pragmatism meant they were an interclass party trying to maintain the broad electoral appeal intrinsic to a catchall approach. This pushed the PS into the difficult position of trying to establish a social settlement based on the northern European model, including a vaguely articulated sense of an expanded welfare state while restructuring the accumulation process to give a meaningful role to both domestic and foreign capital as well as the state productive sector. The party resisted further bipolarization along capitalist-Socialist lines, groping for a European yet originally Portuguese third way. During this time, the political disorganization of capitalist interests produced added stress. It was both the key to deepening an iconoclastic leftist constitution and integrating a resurrected capitalism further into Europe.

The nature of the Socialists' predicament can be illustrated by a comparison with Spain. Felipe Gonzalez's PSOE played the role of left-reformist catchall party in the aftermath of the breakup of Súarez's UCD, gaining a parliamentary majority from 1982 to 1993. But the terms of the Spanish transition were altogether different: negotiations between the various parties from 1976 to 1979 had already narrowed the scope of left ambitions to a realm that ruling circles found tolerable (Gunther 1986, 1993; Maravall 1982; Maravall and Santamaria, 1986). Like the Portuguese PS, the PSOE had to represent bourgeois interests while demonstrating an ostensible commitment to social welfare and the popular masses. Nevertheless, because the issue of capitalism versus socialism was never on the policy agenda, the party did not have to deal with the dishegemonic context faced by the PS. Despite earlier radicalism during an initial part of the transition, the PSOE under Gonzalez was never expected to do anything other than engage in a modernized, somewhat progressive management of capitalism during the democratic consolidation. The PS had to do more than manage: the constitutional order urged it to create a classless society, not just a more humane or efficient capitalism.

In practice, the PS pursued indecisive policies that were greatly constrained by balance-of-payments difficulties and the need to deal with the International Monetary Fund.[3] Austerity policies combined with a general strategy that stimulated domestic private investment inevitably led to antagonism with the hardliners on the left; the CGTP and PCP had staked their futures on the retention of the revolutionary structural reforms of the economy. The Revolution Council was the constitutional tribunal making sure that government legislation suited the "spirit of April." Such praetorian democratization worked differently in Spain, where the military was conservative. In Portugal, on the other hand, the MFA had been strongly affected by the left. Therefore, to some degree, the Socialists were obliged to play the role of the moderate liberal opposition to the more radical left, which caused it to lose credibility with some of its left wing (as with the exit of Lopes Cardoso and the formation of the UEDS) without gaining much from right-wing softliners. These softliners used the PS only for the convenience of its building democracy stance, giving time for parties of the right to regroup and ultimately turn against the PS.

The PS's precarious role as an uncommitted middleman of Portuguese politics was demonstrated in the fall of the PS government in February 1978. Because the right still had not developed a clear strategy for dealing with the aftermath of the revolutionary process (its leading class segment, the old monopolistic groups, having been pushed out of play) the events that followed revealed the indecisiveness of the counteroffensive. At first the CDS proved willing to form a new government with the Socialists, intent on keeping the PS from drifting to the left. After only six months, however, the CDS balked at further collaboration with its more leftist partner, leading to the first in a series of three presidentially appointed governments.

The Nobre de Costa and Mota Pinto governments essentially represented President Ramalho Eanes's own conception of the ideal governing model: the *bloco central*, a government of centrist parties, would provide the ideal balance between building democracy and class compromise. Eanes had played the key role of arbitrator within dishegemony since his election in July 1976. Supported then by the PS and parties to its right, he was also a product of the contradictions emergent from the transition. He not only symbolized the military's role in bringing about the end of the previous regime, but was essential to the forces that countered the radical left in November 1975. After the failure of the PS-CDs government, he was confronted by the lack of a right or left working majority. This forced him to devise means for keeping several institutions afloat: the government, which could not depend on a party majority; the Parliament, whose approval for legislation was unavoidable; the Revolutionary Council, which continued to give voice to the more leftist claims of the revolution; and the military as a whole, whose control by civilian authority was still not definitive.[4] Faced with a parliamentary context in which the right-wing parties were unable to provide an alternative of their own with the PS or by themselves, Eanes devised these governments as an interim device, which, intentionally or not, ultimately gave the right sufficient time to regroup politically.

The first phase gave the Portuguese population a negative impression of the left. On the one hand, it could not provide a stable governing model because of the differences separating the PS and PCP; on the other, the Socialists suffered from the inevitable problems associated with instituting a contradictory hegemonic project in which the constitution was strongly left while the party's alliances were largely to the right. As the "party of hard times" it was obligated to administer austerity policies during a blance-of-payments crisis and poor international economic conditions after the first oil shock. In contrast, the right waited for the worst to fall on the Socialists, hoping that the hard times would change at a moment when the right could reassert itself. By avoiding much governing responsibility in the immediate aftermath of the revolution, the intraregime softliners under Marcelismo could present themselves as carriers of a revitalized Europeanist hegemonic project rather than the austere third way of the Socialists.

Phase 2: 1979–83

In early legislative elections held 2 December 1979, the right campaigned as the Democratic Alliance and gained a slim two-seat majority in the Assembly, allowing it to form its first government. While possessing only a thin mandate (the popular vote for the left still reached over 50 percent), the right achieved an important milestone in its effort to define its place within the evolving political economy.

The search for a modern but conservative posture had not been easy for the Portuguese right which was accustomed to a tradition of corporatist and authoritarian unity. Its conception of the permanent values and ideas of the nation were shattered by the end of the colonial empire, and its economic ideas were assaulted by the revolutionary nationalizations during *Gonçalvismo*. Most important, after nearly a half century of political domination, an unstable, novel, and possibly unfriendly set of institutions and actors emerged to replace the right in power. Instead of retaining the certainties of the old regime, the first five years after the coup had marginalized the right within a rapidly changing situation involving new national identities that were increasingly Eurocentric rather than Luso— Socialist or liberal but not corporatist. Thus, after the period of presidential governments and continued political equivocation, the right's successful pursuit of a bipolarizing strategy was as much an effort at self-clarification as anything else.

That strategy emphasized the contrast between the Marxist left, including the PS and PCP, and non-Marxist parties such as the PSD and CDS. To a considerable extent, the strategy was geared to self-definition by negation of others—the right became what others were not. As the party of liberal intraregime softliners, the PSD's part in a new democratic order was particularly hard to pin down. In 1975, PSD leader Francisco Sá Carneiro had insisted that his party had nothing to do with the center-right, being instead a party of center-left orientation, predominantly Social Democratic. At that time the party's program conveyed principles in keeping with the general label: guarantees to private property, support for workers' participation in management through a scheme of *cogestão* or coparticipation. More social welfare, more progressive taxation, and mild agrarian reform were coupled with a call for effective right of self-determination for the colonies.

By espousing these principles, the PSD distanced itself from the corporatist, Integralist right. In the context of Portugal's revolution transition, however, a mildly Social Democratic program was not likely to be seen as progressive by important, typical Social Democratic constituencies such as the labor movement. This party represented European-colonialist struggle within the ruling circles rather than the realization of a long working-class struggle for political incorporation within a reformist political setting (like that of the Swedish Social Democrats). The extraregime opposition had a more credible claim to representing working-class aspirations.[5]

Some of the right's agenda had been partly accomplished by its election to power: it had convinced a substantial part of the electorate to place the blame for hard times on the Socialists, Communists, MFA, and constitution. But much of its success was due to anti-incumbent feelings rather than positive attraction to a well-articulated program of the modern democratic right. As I explore in more detail in chapter 7, the right was self-conscious about its need to show concrete economic policy successes despite governing as an anti-system government.

The AD's success in renewing its parliamentary majority in the 1980 legislative elections reinforced the basic direction of politics that was typical of this phase. The coalition continued to govern as an antisystem government, forced to accept a constitution and a revolutionary legacy upon which it blamed all problems. As Bruneau and Macleod (1986) have discussed, the constitutional revision of 1982 did less to alter the class character of the document than to reorder institutional relations between Parliament and the president. Lacking a qualified majority, the AD could not transform the legal order in dramatic ways as long as the PS remained an unwilling partner. By 1983, tensions within the coalition resulting from unsuccessful economic policies and personality disputes inside and among the parties led to new elections, signaling the end of the right's first encounter with governmental leadership in the postauthoritarian period.

In 1981–82 I conducted a survey of deputies hoping to pin down more precisely the major lines of ideological cleavage among the members of Parliament and their parties. The survey focused largely on ideological identity and agreement as well as party proximities. The questionnaires were handed to the administrative assistants of the Socialist and Social Democratic parties; the Communist, Popular Democratic Union (UDP), and Center Democratic Social (CDS) parties either refused outright to participate or agreed in principle without producing any completed forms. Fortunately, the sample size was increased somewhat through the addition of smaller parties such as the Popular Monarchical party (PPM), the Association of Independent Social Democrats (ASDI), and the Democratic Socialist Union of the Left (UEDS). The inclusion of the smaller parties allowed a broader representation of the political spectrum. In any case, the limited number of respondents (N=20) limited the statistical importance of these results. They are included here only to suggest confirmation or denial of my general analysis.

The questionnaires included more than one-hundred questions with a range of concerns. Of particular interest here are two types of questions: those asking for self-placement of the individual vis-à-vis the four major parties and their major political and ideological principles, and those asking for general ideological locations of both the respondent and the party to which the respondent belongs. Because the number of respondents from any given party was too low to make meaningful statements about direct party-ideology relationships, the results of the survey were reorganized to enhance the relationships between general perceived party proximities and ideological placement.

Table 3.4 depicts the relative placement of deputies and parties on a left-right scale between 1 and 10. A high score indicates an inclination to the right; a low score favors the left. The respondents were grouped by party into two categories: right, which included those from the PPM and the PSD; and left, including the ASDI, Socialists, and UEDS. This led to a slightly greater representation of the left than the right (12 to 8).

TABLE 3.4. Deputies' Political Tendencies and Perceptions of a Party's Ideological Placement

	Party				
	PCP	*PS*	*PSD*	*CDS*	*SELF*
Respondents' Political Tendency					
Right	3.1	3	4.9	8.1	4.7
Left	1.7	3.5	6.8	9	3.3
Average	2.3	3.2	5.9	8.6	4
Distance from					
Center	2.7	1.8	0.9	3.6	1

Note: 1=Left; 10=Right

Table 3.4 shows that the CDS was perceived as extremely ideologically isolated despite its alliance with the PSD. It was clearly on the right extreme of the spectrum, but the deputies generally placed themselves on the center-left (not surprising given the distribution of the respondents by political tendency). Nevertheless, the CDS's relative extremism anticipated its steady decline in subsequent phases. In addition, these results imply a repudiation of the traditional Portuguese right to the extent that it was most expressly represented in the CDS.

Perhaps of greater long-term significance for the emerging party system was the relative placement of the PSD and PS. The right deputies placed the PSD as virtually identical to themselves: only slightly right of center, presumably where much of the electorate also resided. This perception was in line with the PSD's long-term strategic orientation to be the single dominant party of the right. Conversely, the other major party, the PS, was seen as farther from the center by the rightist deputies.[6]

The leftist deputies reversed the placement of the PSD and PS. The PSD was more extreme, the PS closer to the center. The PSD was placed nearly one-third more right than themselves and twice as distant from the self-placement mean of 3.3 for the leftist deputies. These deputies placed the Socialists at nearly an identical ideological location as themselves. While the composition of the sample may have naturally predisposed leftist deputies to claim a proximity close to the PS, the general trend in the party system—making the PS and the PSD the major parties of the left and right respectively—coincided with these results.

The scores for the Communist party were particularly curious. While the bulk of the respondents predictably placed the PCP on the far left of the spectrum, two deputies of the right gave the party a score of 10. Written comments on the questionnaires expressed the view that the Communists constituted an authoritarian, centralizing party, making it more similar to rightist dictatorships than to the Social Democratic left. This resulted in a higher average score for the Communists (that is, less left than the PS) among the deputies of the right. Ironically, its mean score then appears less extreme to the right than to the left, while the intent of the rightist respondents was surely the opposite. Nevertheless, also relevant was the Communists' distance from the center, 2.7 points, which made the party only slightly less extreme than the CDS, even given the benefit of high scores. These results partially obscure an underlying reality for the PCP: its relegation to a political space of its own.

The meaning of these ideological placements can further be understood by using deputy responses to a proximity scale. They were asked to indicate the degree to which they felt close to the party positions of the CDS, PS, PCP, and PSD on basic principles and policies. The deputies were presented with eight issues: property principles (private versus public), preferred macroeconomic organization (marked versus plan); trade union policy, industrial policy, agricultural policy, foreign policy, and their general conception of democracy. To the extent that they agreed with the stand of a given party on these issues, they gave the party a high score on a 1-

to-10 scale. Thus, a high score indicated a kind of consensus position with regard to the stand taken by a given party.

TABLE 3.5. Deputy Ideological Proximity to Parties by Issue

	PCP	PS	PSD	CDS	PCP	PS	PSD	CDS
	Party				*Party*			
		Property Form				*Macroeconomic Policy*		
Deputy's Tendency								
Left	3.7	8.7	4.7	2.2	3.5	8	4.2	2
Right	1.2	4.6	8.8	6.6	1	4.6	8.8	5.4
Average	2.5	6.8	6.5	4.2	2.4	6.5	6.3	3.8
		Trade-union Policy				*Industrial Policy*		
Deputy's Tendency								
Left	5.5	7.8	3.8	1.7	4	7.5	4.3	3
Right	1.2	5.2	9	5	1	4	6.4	3.8
Average	3.5	6.6	6.2	3.2	2.6	5.9	5.3	3.4
		Agricultural Policy				*Foreign Policy*		
Deputy's Tendency								
Left	4.8	7.2	3.5	1.7	3	8	5	3.7
Right	1.4	3.8	7.4	4.8	1	6.4	8.8	6.2
Average	3.3	5.6	5.3	3.1	2.1	7.3	6.7	4.8
		Democracy				*Overall*		
Deputy's Tendency								
Left	2	8.8	5.5	3.8	3.8	8	4.4	2.7
Right	1	8	9	8	1.1	5.2	8.3	5.7
Average	1.5	8.5	7.1	5.7	2.8	6.9	6.6	4

Several patterns were present in table 3.5. Not all areas produced the same degree of agreement. The greatest disagreement appears in two areas: trade-union policy and agricultural policy, which produced the sharpest opposition between left and right as well as within each. For example, with regard to agricultural policy, the PS obtained its lowest proximity rating from the left, 7.2, as well as its lowest from the right, 3.8. There was a similar pattern for the PSD, with only a predictable reversal of scores by tendency. The division within the left was also shown by the relatively high score received by the Communists, 4.8, from those on the left. Trade-union policy was similarly divisive within the left; the PCP's score was not much lower than that for the Socialists, 5.5 versus 7.8. The PSD recorded its second lowest left score on that issue (3.8), while receiving a very high score from the right (9). Despite the formation of the Socialist/Social Democratic—sponsored UGT trade-union confederation, the underlying issues regarding the politicization of the trade-union movement and its radical or reformist character had not been resolved (see chapter 6).

Issues such as property relations, macroeconomic organization, and foreign policy showed some antagonisms between left and right but without the sharpness associated with the other items and without as much divisiveness within the left. The survey revealed that the PS and PSD offered a distinct set of preferences that were equally liked and disliked by the respective tendencies. Thus, the left favored the PS on property relations to the same degree that the right favored the PSD. This implies that the parties, despite a somewhat diluted ideological fervor through much of the democratic consolidation, still represented alternative directions for socioeconomic development for the deputies in 1982. The parties' average scores underscore the degree to which they represented a convergence point around the center.

With regard to the smaller parties of the left and right, two patterns stand out. First, both were ideologically marginalized in comparison to either of the other larger parties, even by those most likely to hold common points of view. Second, the Communists appeared more marginal to the political system than the CDS, somewhat in contrast to the conclusions of table 3.4.

It is apparent that the CDS was closer to the mainstream on some issues than others. It received its highest averages for property form, foreign policy, and democracy. It should be noted, however, that this did not imply much gain in left support; rather, these were relatively consensual issues for the right. Indeed, other than for democracy, rightist deputies consistently gave the party much lower scores than those received by the PSD. The CDS was clearly within the same camp as the right deputies but perhaps not precisely at the same site. For the leftist deputies, the CDS was not especially admired for any of its stands but was most attractive on foreign policy and democracy.

The PCP was far from the mainstream on nearly all issues. Its average scores never exceeded 3.5, while its overall average was only 2.7. If we look simply at the left, we see that the PCP attained its highest scores on the trade union and agricultural issues. These, as I have mentioned, were internally divisive for the left—in the case of agriculture, leading to the resignation from the Socialist party of Lopes Cardoso and António Barreto, both former ministers of agriculture. But the generally low sympathy for the Communists underlines the importance of the communist–anti-Communist cleavage within the Portuguese system which anti-fascist unity could not overcome even within the left. The survey confirms the softliner-hard liner distinction within the extralegal opposition.

The building-democracy element of the transition and consolidation periods was understandably of great importance to the deputies, whose positions in government depended upon a particular political settlement. Three-quarters of the respondents listed democracy as the most important issue of all those listed. Their perceptions of each of the parties necessarily played a vital role in shaping their conceptions of which could be relied upon to foster a parliamentary and democratic political format when considering coalition options.

Deputies were asked to assess their proximity to each party's conception of democracy. An impressive general consensus formed around the Socialist party. Apart from the high score from those on the left (8.8), the Socialists received nearly as high a score from the right (8.0) as the PSD received (9.0) and obtained as high a score from rightists as did the CDS.

In comparison to the right, leftist deputies were particularly reluctant to identify democracy with the CDS, which hardly surpassed the score received by the Communists (3.8, 2). During democratic consolidation, the definition of what constituted an antisystemic party was critical. The complete isolation of the PCP from the mainstream on this critical issue, as evidenced by its mean score of only 1.5, meant that its political marginality was based less on socioeconomic policy differences than on its failure to shake its Leninist trappings, which as Budge and Herman (1979) have argued generally for politically antisystemic parties, undermined its trustworthiness as a strategic ally.

Phase 3: 1983–87

The collapse of the AD government in December 1982 and the decision by President Eanes to dissolve the Parliament underscored the continuing dishegemony engulfing Portuguese politics. Turmoil developed despite the continued existence of an AD majority as well as the Council of State's vote in favor of continuing with the present Parliament. The right's majority had lost its cohesiveness; party competition within and across the alliance suggested that the right had not yet found the ideal blend of ideology, program, and electoral representation. The end of the AD government was dramatic, with the resignations of CDS leaders Freitas de Amaral and Basílio Horta from their party positions and deposed Prime Minister Pinto Balsemão claiming that he would apply himself full time to "putting an end to the treason of which I was a victim."[8] The destruction of the AD was in many ways self-inflicted. The alliance remained divided between the PSD, which as a party of *barões* was forever in a state of internal competition among personalities and factions for leadership positions, and the CDS, which sought to capture part of the PSD electorate to the right but also realized that its prospects of getting into power without the PSD were remote. In part, the end of that alliance reflected the impact of internal party conflicts and interparty competition operating within a leftist constitutional order that the AD could erode but not overturn. These conditions meant that the right reproduced some of the problems that had troubled the left: a short-time horizon based on sectarian or momentary gains. Partisanship and personalities helped undermine the common interest in establishing the ideological and structural basis for prolonged class hegemony through control of government.

The AD collapsed under circumstances similar to those in many capitalist democracies: a downturn in the business cycle. The alliance originally reached power during the burst of prosperity produced by the growth policies of Minister of the Economy Cavaco Silva, who served in the first AD government headed by PSD leader Francisco Sá Carneiro. After Sá Carneiro's death in a plane accident, subsequent Balsemão administrations were confronted with deteriorating domestic and international economic conditions. Mounting balance-of-payments difficulties combined with economic contraction to diminish popular support for the AD government. For once, the right was saddled with the political inconvenience of incumbency during austerity. Despite the stability that the AD coalition had promised, it could not overcome the dour times that emerged during its governance. (See chapter 7 for additional details.)

The 1983 elections were decisive in reordering the right's political organization. Unlike the left, the right was less divided over fundamental principles of political economy, which meant that there were fewer reasons for maintaining two competitive organizations, especially because it undermined the prospects for gaining and retaining power. As figure 3.1 shows, the CDS started its long-term decline that year and fell to its lowest point yet. While the CDS faded, the PSD obtained its highest total ever as an independent party (29 percent). Overall, the right lost nearly 8 percent of the total vote and over one-quarter of its 1980 vote. These elections signaled the start of the long-term ascendance of the PSD as the single major party of the right, eclipsing the CDS, which slipped further in the 1985 and 1987 elections. This change was critical to the long-term termination of dishegemony and the firm establishment of the

Europeanist strategy. During this phase of consolidation, the right could more effectively concentrate its resources behind one organization and better hone its message.

For the Socialists, the 1983 elections helped renew visions of a PSOE-like destiny as the majority party. Although it substantially improved its electoral performance, gaining the 8 percent of the electorate that the AD had lost, it did not reach a single-party majority. In 1983 it benefited from the anti-incumbent swing to the opposition coincident with poor economic times. In this particular cycle, the AD suffered. In 1985, after two years of a grand coalition between the PS and PSD with Socialist leader Mário Soares as prime minister, the Socialist party not only lost the 8 percent it had gained but another 8 percent as well, reaching an unprecedented low with only a fifth of the electorate.

Rather than signaling a major change in policy, the 1983 elections actually represented a period of continuity within dishegemony. The AD offered an antistatist vision meant to provide the ideological underpinnings of a modernized right, yet its disintegration left the Socialists as the party of dishegemony, neither clearly confirming the AD's policy directions nor directly repudiating the confused political economy emerging from the turbulent transition. By 1985, the Socialists' failure to capitalize on a parliamentary plurality was affected by the party's lack of consistency and coherence. Naturally, it paid the price for austerity policies, which were either provoked earlier by the AD (whose first government stimulated excess demand) or by circumstances outside of party control (for example, a downturn in European and U.S. markets).

The 1985 elections started the decisive reshaping of the Portuguese political system, especially on the left. The PCP initiated a period of continuing decline. The Socialists were deserted by an electorate frustrated with the party's bad-times connotation and tantalized by a new party with a vaguely center-left placement: the Democratic Renewal party (PRD). A fluid and sizable part of the electorate filled the political space between the Socialists and the left wing of the PSD. In 1985, that electorate went to the PRD, the party associated with President Eanes, and dealt the PS a huge defeat.

The volatility in the electorates of the major parties is illustrated in table 3.6, which shows the standard deviations in the votes across the four phases and for the entire period of elections (1975–91). From 1975 to 1983, the Socialists experienced about twice as much electoral volatility as the PSD. By contrast, the Communists experienced little change. The third phase, which for statistical purposes redundantly includes the 1983 elections as a starting point and concludes with the 1987 elections, featured unprecedented fluidity in what had been a stable four-party configuration. The last phase included only the 1987 and 1991 elections and indicated a return to stability—but with a smaller PCP and CDS, a collapsed PRD, a dominant PSD, and a slowly growing PS. The last phase highlighted the right's consolidation behind the PSD as the party of the useful vote (*voto util*): a strategic merger of votes behind the single party most likely to succeed. The PSD increased its previous vote by two-thirds, rising from nearly 30 percent to over 50 percent.

TABLE 3.6. Standard Deviations for Major Parties, 1975–91 Elections[9]

	Party						
Phase	PCP	PS	Left	PSD	CDS	Right	Other
1975–79	1.8	4.1	3.1	2.1	3.9	4.6	1.6
1980–83	0.7	4.1	4.8	1.8	2.0	3.9	2.1
1983–87	2.5	7.0	9.0	10.3	3.4	7.0	9.5
1987–91	1.7	3.7	2.0	0.2	0.1	0.2	1.9
1975–91	3.1	5.9	7.3	11.1	4.2	7.0	7.2
Overall Deviation As percent of Mean Vote	21.0	20.0	16.0	29.0	44.0	6.0	2.0

The entry of the PRD did little to provide a new opening for the Portuguese left: the PS would not form a coalition government with the PRD after the 1985 elections. This made it possible for the PSD to form a minority government and take credit for the economic upswing that previous years of PS-led austerity had done so much to produce. By 1987, the PRD had vanished as an important political actor, leaving only the PS and PCP to continue dividing the spoils of the leftist vote. The legendary impasse on the left was not broken during legislative elections. Only presidential elections seemed to shift the center of gravity into the left's terrain; in both 1980 and 1986, the candidate endorsed by the left won against a rightist alternative. This particularly frustrated the right in 1980, when it sought but failed to consolidate its control over both elected branches of government. The left could marshal its energies much more effectively when the PCP and revolutionary left perceived the need to unite with the reformist softliners in the anti-fascist struggle. The importance of that dimension of Portuguese politics continued to make its presence felt but could not provide a basis for a positive program bridging other differences.

Phase 4: 1987 (Continuing)

The main vectors of the fourth phase have already been established: an unprecedented single-party majority obtained by the PSD, continuing fragmentation and reorganization on the left, and an apparent susceptibility of centrist voters to anti-incumbent and business-cycle influences. In this period, the right finally found both message and messenger. It was equipped with a modernized liberal, antistatist, and confidently Europeanist appeal that avoided the obscurantism and authoritarianism of clerical corporatism without assaulting the sensibilities of Catholic voters. In Cavaco Silva, the right discovered an economist whose competency and attractive vision could help it overcome historic internal antagonisms over accumulation strategy. This phase has represented the ascendancy of the intraregime softliners to a hegemonic position in Portugal's political economy. Like the PSOE in Spain, the renewal of the PSD's majority in 1991 has meant that voters in Portugal have placed their faith in the party that can most credibly provide stable management of democratic capitalism.

Chapter 4 will examine more closely the extent to which the rise of the PSD was associated with a changing ideological climate in public opinion. Was the PSD's support linked to a more generalized right-wing swing indicative of an unambiguous hegemonic mandate? Before we proceed to that issue, I will draw on historical patterns found in the first four phases of democratic consolidation to speculate about future phases or changes in the Portuguese political system.

Scenario 1

The first scenario is based on the continuation of economic good times for the remainder of the PSD's term (1994–95) assuming that no other issues gain sufficient importance to displace those associated with the economy. This would lead to the further repudiation of revolutionary aspects of the political economy and more firmly entrench the Europeanist softliners in power under the PSD. The CDS, representing only a corrosive influence on the right's global hegemony, would continue as an insignificant party or perhaps even disband altogether. As of 1993–94, this scenario seems unlikely to be realized given the current downturn in the economy and the 1994 municipal elections that showed a sharp drop in PSD support.

Whether this attrition in PSD support will be sufficient to change the overall dynamic of the phase 4 party system and policy paradigm is unclear. Depending on the impact of a weaker economy on popular perceptions, the PSD might continue to hold on to its governing role because the left is not in a position to offer a real alternative. Under such conditions, the Socialists would remain the main opposition party, clearly competing in the conventional Social Democratic terrain of managing democratic capitalism. The party whose program claimed to have as an objective "the construction, in Portugal, of a classless society" will have come full circle: it now proposes a more efficient, if humane, management of capitalism.[10]

Should the PSD find the economy on an upswing by the time of the next elections, the Communists would drop further from the political scene, unable to overcome the collapse of real socialism in the disbanded Soviet Union and abandonment by intellectuals, union leaders, and even key long-time party stalwarts. These disaffected Communists might experiment with a variety of ideological and party orientations, with some perhaps running as independents on a PS list (like former CGTP leader José Judas, who has been elected mayor of Cascais). The concept of hegemony for the left would become less based on class control over the state and move increasingly to cultural and redistributive struggles typical of contemporary Western European politics.[11] In this scenario, the left is transformed within bourgeois hegemony into the matrix of pluralist politics and generally abandons any conception of socialism as a class-based alternative to capitalism.

Scenario 2

The second and third scenarios assume that the economic situation between 1991 and 1995 deteriorates either somewhat or sharply. In both cases, depending on the exact set of conditions, the PSD would come under increasing pressure to apply monetary policy to avoid balance-of-payments deficits. Manipulating exchange rates in ways allowed to national officials of EC countries, the government would attempt to devalue the escudo to compensate for relatively high domestic inflation and make Portuguese goods

cheaper abroad. Such action might well produce inflationary pressures, requiring the government to curb domestic demand and thus
produce the classic downturn in the political business cycle that has
been so important in bringing down other governments.

Elements of the second scenario have appeared in Portugal, but
the adverse conditions may not yet be sufficiently severe to undercut the PSD's support dramatically. Nevertheless, it is important to
remember that the PSD's majority in Parliament has depended on
gaining roughly 45 percent of the popular vote. Given its 1991 election total of slightly over 50 percent, anything over a 5-percent
transfer of votes to other parties (or abstentions of those voting for
the party in the last elections) would cost the PSD a parliamentary
majority and the possibility of forming a single-party majority government.

If the PSD experiences more than a 5-percent drop but remains
the largest party, it may attempt to form a new government either
by itself or in coalition. Assuming that the CDS remains a possible
partner, the PSD would be attracted to it as the basis for a minimum
winning coalition. In this way, the AD would be resurrected, bringing with it a degree of uncertainty for the right given the strong cen-
trifugal tendencies evinced in the Balsemão governments of the
early 1980s. Because the two parties are not very distinctive, this
renewed coalition would not affect policy outcomes significantly.
Instead, it would only redistribute the responsibility for pursuing
policies to two parties rather than one.

If the PSD could not form a government with the CDS, it
would be faced with the choice of attempting to govern as a minority government or forming a grand coalition with the Socialists. In
the former case, a return to the situation after the 1985 elections—
with a PSD plurality and Cavaco Silva as the probable prime minister (assuming he does not run for president or otherwise abandon
the leadership of the PSD)—would imply a government of short
duration. The PSD would attempt to ride out the downturn, timing
the call for new elections with an anticipated upswing. Naturally,
this would have to be negotiated with the other parties and would
place great pressure on the CDS (assuming it held the difference
between the PSD's plurality and a parliamentary majority) to go
along with the PSD's plans.

Given the Socialists' experience between 1983–85, the party
would probably prefer a minority PSD government because it would
not in all likelihood be inclined to act as the junior partner in a PSD-
led government. The minority government would be more vulnera-

ble to PS pressures and less able to spread the blame for failed policies. The electoral circumstances of the Socialist party would continue to improve with the decline of the PCP and the erosion of the
PSD, whose voters would be split between the PS and CDS. Depending upon the further evolution of the economic situation and other
issues at election time, the PS might only be able to consolidate
itself further as the major opposition party, a catchall for leftist,
Republican, secularist, and progressive moderate voters. It would
not attain a majority and possibly not even a plurality in the 1995
elections. Table 3.7 shows the possible voting and government outcomes for each scenario.

TABLE 3.7. Alternative Scenarios for the 1990s:
Election Outcomes and Governments

	Party			
	PCP	*PS*	*PSD*	*CDS*
		Scenario One		
Election Results	5	32	52	3
Government			PSD only with Parliamentary Majority	
		Scenario Two		
Election Results	6	39	41	6
Government		Grand Coalition with PS-PSD	PSD Minority	PSD-CDS Coalition
		Scenario Three		
Election Results	13	38	35	5
Government	PS-PCP Coalition	PS Minority	Grand Coalition	

Scenario 3

If the economy experiences a very sharp drop or a significant
weakening in combination with another set of circumstances (such
as an extraordinary PSD scandal, departmental incompetence, corruption, or a badly bungled campaign— (for example, featuring
intraparty leadership competition and lack of solidarity to avoid
blame for the current circumstances), a third scenario might sur-
face. The PSD's electoral results would decline to a point where it
lost both its majority and its plurality. Aversion to the PSD would
not help the CDS, which would remain a party on the outer margins

of the political system, unable to become a partner in a minimum winning coalition. Thus, the right would be removed from government, the softliner-led dominant-class coalition frayed.

Unlike either of the other two scenarios, in which bourgeois hegemony is essentially maintained intact, scenario 3 envisions a resurgence of the left without a fundamental reorganization of its party forms: in short, a renewed if far more anemic dishegemony typical of phases 1 and 3. The Socialists would be the plurality but not the majority party. The PCP (or another party or coalition left of the Socialists) would be boosted back to earlier electoral results in the low to mid-teens. Governing options would include those typical of phase 1 (PS minority government), phase 3 (grand coalition of PS and PSD with a PS prime minister), or an altogether new experience: a PS-PCP coalition like the one that helped PS leader Jorge Sampaio with the Lisbon local elections in 1990. The 1994 local elections might be a signal that the electorate is ready to consider a return to mild dishegemony given the PS plurality, faint PCP resurgence, and the success of the PS-PCP coalition in Lisbon.

Without a PS single-party majority, the Socialists would be faced with conditions similar to 1983, when the party was forced to continue austerity policies without reliable parliamentary support to carry it through the economic cycle. A renewed coalition with the PSD would be plagued by recollections of that party's defection in 1985. The Socialist leadership might prefer a minority government with more ability to move left or right for support rather than accept a formal governing alliance with the PSD. Formal or informal dependency on the PCP could open up the long-avoided majority of the left question, with all its electoral and policy uncertainties. The Communists might have a different view of the political system than they did in 1978 when the party helped bring down the first Socialist government only to face a consistent loss of influence to the right afterward. At this point, the PCP might be willing to accept any share of power it is offered, but its lack of significant internal reform and its polarizing effect on the electorate would probably lead PS leaders to avoid a formal arrangement and instead rely on brokered support as a minority one-party government.

It seems likely that this scenario would sustain the dishegemonic character of the Portuguese political system more than either of the other two because it rekindles a period of left majorities without left governments but after a prolonged reconstruction of a capitalist political economy. Should these conditions reappear, the impasse of the past would continue into the future: a left, which can only govern as an unstable and unpredictable surrogate for the right's own governance, encouraging a renewal of rightist rule.

These three scenarios do not necessarily exhaust the realm of possibilities for the evolution of Portuguese politics. One key alternative involves the Socialists' long-held dream of becoming the Portuguese PSOE. This might be possible if the left effectively consolidated nearly all its votes behind the PS, much as the right did with the PSD in phase 4. What remains to be determined is whether the Portuguese electorate and social structure is inclined to consolidate its vote in such a manner. The next two chapters investigate the attitudinal and partisan composition of the Portuguese electorate as well as the social bases of party support. The goal of these chapters is to determine the nature of cleavages that have helped the PSD gain its current majority and could shape the development of future governing coalitions.

FOUR

THE RISE OF THE PSD AND EMERGENCE OF A NATIONAL HEGEMONIC PROJECT AMONG THE MASS PUBLIC

The previous chapter identified the four phases of the democratic consolidation and the conversion of an uncertain dishegemony into an emergent intraregime softliner domination symbolized by the PSD majorities in phase 4. The rehegemonization process by which liberal capitalist institutions were constructed after the corporatist period and the revolutionary interlude involved a transformation of the party system. As Bruneau and Macleod (1986) remark, party politics were all-absorbing during the consolidation. Moreover, in the absence of a capable historic dominant class, party leadership and the political institutions generally were decisive for redefining the nature of the new national arrangements.

The rise of the PSD as a dominant party in Portugal during phase 4 is undeniable. Less clear, however, is whether its electoral success corresponded to a meaningful shift in ideological inclination and partisan attachment among the mass public, making its governance indicative of genuine hegemony. This chapter will address that general issue by examining the following specific questions:

1. How strong was the PSD's support? Where did it come from? How enduring was it likely to be?

2. Was the success of the PSD associated with an ideological change signaling the emergence of a new ideological hegemony or largely a momentary electoral phenomenon?

3. To what degree can the change in the Portuguese party system from phase 3 to 4 be explained by a political business cycle or other short-term cues rather than deeper ideological or partisan conversion? The key issue here is whether the PSD's success was strongly associated with improving economic circumstances or at least the *perception* of improving economic conditions.

4. Did the change in the party system correspond to a shift in the class coalition supporting alternative party options? The presence of a shift in the class coalition supporting alternative party options? The presence of a shift that moved working and new middle-class segments further to the right in general and the PSD in particular could also indicate the emergence of a basic consensus around liberal capitalist institutions by those key social strata whose support for a leftist alternative would be vital. This issue concerns the social bases of the parties' support and will be examined in detail in chapter 5.

The investigation of these questions will depend largely upon survey data available in Eurobarometers conducted from 1985 to 1988. Certain strengths and weaknesses are associated with reliance on this research instrument. Notable limitations include the fact that the surveys polled one thousand Portuguese citizens, a sizable number for judging overall traits but less useful for breaking down the sample into representative subgroups classified by party affiliation, class, gender, religiosity, and so on. Many of the questions in the surveys were not relevant to my themes of interest; other questions should have been posed but were not. Nevertheless, the Eurobarometers did provide data that I could use to make comparisons over time.[7]

I justify the use of survey data by the importance that electoral success assumed for asserting classlike party power and decisively shaping the basic political economic institutions and social relations. The party system symbolized the frustrated attempts of the left to recast its appeal as a viable governing option and, conversely, the success of the right to jettison its corporatist and authoritarian legacy and offer a modernized softliner image of Europeanized competent moderation. Therefore, the investigation of the nature of public opinion and the social basis of electoral support is a necessary step in discussing the changing character of hegemony. Chapter 7 will focus upon the shifting pattern of policy to address the related but distinct issues concerning the structure of the economy and nature of the accumulation strategies that correspond to the demise of dishegemony.

PARTISANSHIP IN FLUX: PHASE 3 AS A PRELUDE TO CHANGE; PHASE 4 CONSOLIDATION

Eurobarometer 24 was conducted after the 1985 elections, which ended the PS-PSD government and replaced with a minority PSD government squarely in the midst of phase 3. The results from those elections indicated the growing dissatisfaction with the political impasse that the PS-PSD government represented: the PS lost nearly 45 percent of its 1983 vote, while the recently created Democratic Renewal party received a shocking 19 percent of the vote. By comparison, the other parties only experienced minor shifts (see table 3.2 for actual percentages). The right experienced virtually no change from its 1983 totals, while the PCP only dropped slightly. The key partisan shift involved apparent defections from the Socialist party, with the PRD as the beneficiary.

The striking number of likely PS defections implied that the party's 1983 support had been broad but weak. Although Eurobarometer 24 was the first survey conducted after that election, it did not have a question about party attachment to gauge the depth of voter commitment to a party. Eurobarometer 25 was conducted in April 1986 and included the party-attachment variable. By comparing the degree of party attachment with the respondent's last party vote and current voting intentions, it is possible to assess the strength of ties between a party and its voter. By repeating this process using subsequent Eurobarometers, researchers can monitor changes in party attachment and offer some determination about the solidity of the PSD's rise.

Table 4.1 shows the percentages of respondents either declaring to have voted in the last elections or expressing a current vote preference by their degree of party attachment.[2] The values for the two voting variables essentially parallel each other, a pattern repeated in most Eurobarometers.[3] For this reason as well as for the sake of brevity, only "party last vote" will be used as an indicator of partisan preference. Rather than discuss table 4.1 in isolation from the other surveys, we will examine the surveys longitudinally to analyze relevant patterns.

TABLE 4.1. Party Attachment by Last Vote and Vote Intention,
Eurobarometer 25

	PCP	PS	PSD	CDS	Other
		Party Last Vote			
		Attachment			
Great	20	0	5	3	5
Some	21	7	13	19	15
Merely					
sympathizer	49	62	65	67	68
None	11	31	17	11	13
		Vote Intention			
Great	19	0	5	3	8
Some	20	8	14	18	15
Merely					
sympathizer	56	62	64	68	68
None	6	30	17	11	10

Table 4.2 presents the crosstabulation between "party last vote" and "party attachment" variables over time. The strength of party attachment was highest among Communist voters, almost twice that obtained by the PS and PSD when comparing the combined totals for the first two highest levels of attachment. At its peak in 1985, the PCP claimed almost 7 percent of the entire electorate as either "very" or "fairly close." When we look at the electoral trend over the three-year period, the PCP's fortunes skidded; the average vote for the first four surveys was 12.1 percent but for the last three it dipped to 7.5 percent. Still, a fairly consistent 30 to 40 percent of its voters claimed to have a significant degree of attachment.

The PRD, whose total vote fell dramatically both in the polls and in elections, had very low levels of party attachment, only slightly more than half as much as the two major parties. In fact, the surveys make it clear that the PRD was a classic flash party whose voters were probably drawn largely from those dissatisfied with the Soares-led government but who had not yet decided to vote for the PSD. The remarkable bounce found in the PS total for Eurobarometer 25—when its vote jumped from 26.8 to 41 percent—corresponds to an equally astonishing downswing for the PRD, from 17.7 to 4.3

percent. In all likelihood, the 1985 elections were largely a vote *against* the PS rather than a vote *for* the PRD. The inability of the latter to change the political equation substantially resulted in a resumption of the previous general pattern with two large and two small parties.

TABLE 4.2. Party Attachment by Party Voters, 1986–88

			Eurobarometer					
	25	26	27	28	29	30	Mean	Std. Dev.
PCP Attachment								
Very close	14	25	10	4	11	9	12	6
Fairly close	6	16	16	25	11	27	17	7
Merely sympathizer	59	50	56	57	60	56	56	3
Not close to party	20	9	19	4	19	9	13	6
Total Vote	8	14	10	5	10	7	9	3
PRD Attachment								
Very close	0	0	3	5	—	0	2	2
Fairly close	4	13	17	3	—	0	7	6
Merely sympathizer	44	63	43	71	—	71	58	13
Not close to party	52	25	37	21	—	29	33	11
Total Vote	4	5	5	3	7	0.8	3	2
PS Attachment								
Very close	5	6	2	5	2.4	3	4	2
Fairly close	13	18	11	7	12	16	13	4
Merely sympathizer	61	50	59	69	62	65	61	6
Not close to party	20	25	28	20	24	16	22	4
Total Vote	41	35	31	31	36	40	36	4
PSD Attachment								
Very close	5	5	2	7	3	2	4	2
Fairly close	13	30	14	11	7	12	14	7
Merely sympathizer	67	51	65	69	59	66	63	6
Not close to party	14	15	20	14	31	20	19	6
Total Vote	38	40	39	53	48	43	43	5
CDS Attachment								
Very close	4	13	4	0	1	2	4	4
Fairly close	11	17	11	0	6	32	13	10
Merely sympathizer	64	57	79	92	65	61	69	12
Not close to party	20	13	7	8	18	5	12	6
Total Vote	8	5	4	5	4	8	6	2

The PS, the PSD, and the CDS all had relatively similar levels of attached voters (between 15 and 25 percent). The PS was slightly distinct in that its range was narrower, never exceeding 24 percent compared to the PSD's 35 percent. As mass parties, the PS and PSD did not engender deep commitment; even in 1987, the PSD only had 18 percent of its voters expressing a significant level of party attachment, completely consistent with other scores. This suggests that the PSD was not embraced by a massive flood of new followers, although the fact that its percentage did not go down noticeably despite a major increase in its vote total indicates that it was at least able to hold its own.

The CDS never had much of a committed following and lost all of them in the 1987 elections, although a few returned later when it no longer matter (as indicated in Eurobarometers 29 and 30). For all parties, the largest category was "merely sympathizers," indicating that they all had less than unequivocal support. On average, the PS, the PSD, and the CDS had 82 percent of their voters claiming to be either "sympathizers" or "not close to any part."

When looking at the survey-based vote estimates (table 4.3), we can see that the 1985 results were especially noteworthy. The left (PCP plus PRD plus PS) actually obtained a very high overall percentage of the vote, suggesting that many centrist voters remained or became attracted to the PS or PRD. The sum of the actual left vote in 1983 was almost identical to its 1985 electoral total (54.5 versus 55.1 percent), as moderate voters in 1985 generally sought options to the left of the PSD but rejected the PS. The apparent shift from the PS to the PRD may have predisposed them to greater subsequent openness to the right, although the movement away from the PS was not unprecedented, having occurred already to a degree during phase 2 and the AD government. The electoral totals as derived from the Eurobarometers show a drastic movement away from the left from 1985 until the July 1987 elections, with the PSD as the main beneficiary.

After 1985, the Socialists regained some of the electorate lost to the PRD but not enough to thwart either the generalized movement of voters to the right nor the PSD's ability to form a single-party majority in Parliament. In fact, the 1987 elections were not effectively recorded by the Eurobarometers; the polls never show the PS total as falling below 30 percent after 1985, despite the party's crushing loss in those elections when it received only 22.3 percent. The gradual rise of the Socialists' actual vote to nearly 30 percent by 1991 did not reveal a broad movement to the left. The global left vote showed no change due to the decreases posted by the PCP and PRD. Phase 4 has featured a sustained and significant electoral gap between left and right in the latter's favor.[4]

TABLE 4.3. Left-Right Electoral Support 1985–88, 1991

	Eurobarometer								
	24	*25*	*26*	*27*	*28*	*29*	*30*	*Mean*	*Std. Dev.*
Tendency									
Left	61	54	54	45	39	47	48	48	8
Right	36	46	45	43	57	52	51	49	7

	Election		
	1985	*1987*	*1991*
Left	55.1	41.2	40.7
Right	39.5	54.4	54.8

As indicated by the relatively small standard deviations, both the PS and the PSD maintained a narrower band of overall support variation after 1985 than did the smaller parties. While the high scores of the CDS and the PCP were nearly two and a half times larger than their low scores, the PS and PSD had similar ranges, with high scores varying slightly more than half as much. These results suggest that the larger parties had attained a stable configuration during this period. Furthermore, the survey figures show that phase 4 actually began very soon after the 1985 elections, which only represented a brief instance of instability in the Portuguese political system.

The rise of the PSD was well under way by 1986 when the polls showed it had already attained historically high levels of voter support. The key period, however, was not reached until the interlude between April and October 1987, when the PSD level of support blossomed from slightly under 40 percent to over 52 percent. Because elections were held in July, it is also likely that the boost in support came in the two months immediately preceding the elections. Subsequent polls show PSD support dipping nearly 10 percent within the next year. Therefore, the PSD must have benefited from some combination of short-term cues and highly favorable campaign effects to have succeeded in luring as many voters as it did in such a limited time period. Although the electoral trend was clearly toward the right, it was still likely that the PSD's victory was a product of good timing, an effective campaign, and possibly some combination of electorally inspired changes in policy to remind voters of the government's (and incumbent party's) generosity. This did not necessarily mean that the PSD would fail to repeat 1987's winning formula (as the 1991 elections made abundantly clear); instead, it simply suggests that the PSD may have mastered certain skills, including timely management of economic outcomes and effective campaigning for strategic votes among those least committed to the CDS. Future success would depend on a credible leadership's convincing, effectively delivered appeals to the highly fluid elements that flocked to the PRD in 1985 seeking an alternative to the PS and the divided or minority governments of phase 3.

IDEOLOGY AND THE PARTY SYSTEM: HEGEMONY OR BOA FORTUNA

I have argued that the PSD's success corresponded to a general rise in the right's electoral fortunes, although short-term factors seemed especially vital in boosting Social Democratic popularity around election time. The Eurobarometers allow us to investigate ideological factors as one element in the right's electoral ascendency. The simplest measure of ideology is respondent self-placement on a left-right ten-point scale. Table 4.4 displays the results for each of the Eurobarometers, and table 4.5 couples them with the "party last vote" variable to link ideology with party support.

TABLE 4.4. Ideological Self-placement, 1985–88

| | | | Eurobarometer | | | | | |
Ideology	24	25	26	27	28	29	30	Mean
Left	17	14	20	14	14	22	14	16
Center	64	70	63	65	58	58	64	63
Right	19	17	18	21	27	19	19	20

Table 4.4 shows the recoded left-right variable in seven Eurobarometers.[5] The peak level of support for the right coincided with the PSD's high point in 1987. Peak support for the left did not exist during election years, rising instead during interim periods. Overall, rightists were slightly more numerous than leftists, although the vast majority of respondents were centrists. The relative stability of the three categories suggests that fundamental and enduring shifts did not occur in the distribution of ideological predispositions. Rather, a momentary attraction to the party of preference seems to be associated with a greater propensity for respondents to shift their declared stand in the direction of that party's ideology. For example,

despite a relatively low number of self-declared leftists just before the 1987 elections (as measured by Eurobarometer 28), the number goes up substantially after the election with no clear long-term change indicated.

TABLE 4.5. Ideology by Party Voters, 1986–88

				Eurobarometer			
	25	26	26	27	28	29	30
Mean							
			Ideology and PCP Voters				
Ideology							
Left	92	70	76	71	82	75	78
Center	6	30	24	28	18	13	20
Right	2	0	0	1	0	13	3
Total Vote	9	9	14	10	12	7	10
			Ideology and PRD Voters				
Left	40	16	25	11	0	46	23
Center	48	72	78	82	100	57	73
Right	12	12	0	7	0	0	5
Total Vote	5	4	5	5	0.7	2	4
			Ideology and PS Voters				
Left	40	13	19	15	33	19	23
Center	55	83	78	79	62	74	72
Right	6	4	3	6	5	7	5
Total Vote	40	40	35	31	37	38	37
			Ideology and PSD Voters				
Left	4	2	2	1	1	3	2
Center	45	74	66	62	66	64	63
Right	50	25	32	37	33	34	35
Total Vote	38	38	40	41	47	44	41
			Ideology and CDS Voters				
Left	7	7	0	0	0	0	2
Center	71	61	69	47	56	62	61
Right	23	32	31	53	44	38	37
Total Vote	8	8	5	5	4	9	7

When examining the parties individually (table 4.5), the relation between ideology and vote becomes somewhat clearer. Not surprisingly, the Communists' voters were overwhelmingly from the left, with nearly all the rest coming from the center despite the fact that the party was the least centrist of any. The PRD obtained its support mainly from centrists and to a much lesser extent the left. That party's voters had an ideological mix almost exactly identical to the Socialists', bolstering the assumption that the two parties traded votes among the center-left electorate. Like the PS, the Social Democrats obtained between two-thirds and three-quarters of their votes from the center, although for the PSD that balance was made up almost entirely of rightists as compared to the leftist balance for the PS. The CDS nearly reversed the proportions between center and right, obtaining most of its support from the latter. Thus, only the PRD and PS overlapped to a significant degree, showing the PRD's redundancy within the PS's political space and accounting for its mercurial character.

Another means of assessing whether ideological drift to the right accompanied the PSD electoral victories is to follow a set of attitudes associated with the right and left over time, noting whether sympathy for issues favorable to either side fluctuated with election results. The Eurobarometers generally did not provide an ideal means for this task, although to some extent the "country goals" variable (which asks respondents to choose one factor among four choices as the most important goal) incorporates the idea.

The goal most likely to be associated with the right stresses "protecting law and order." This choice was listed as the top country goal by about 40 percent of the respondents. The values in table 4.6 suggest that this attitude corresponded to shifts in electoral outcomes in two ways. As measured by Eurobarometer 24, when the PRD reached its zenith in 1985, "order" was least frequently cited compared to any other time; "rising prices" peaked instead. Eurobarometers 27 and 28, however, show that "order" rose in saliency precisely during the interlude (1987) when the PSD captured its electoral majority.[6] In the first instance, the shift toward "rising prices" coincides with the end of the two-year austerity under the PS-PSD government and confirms my general interpretation of the PRD's success. In the second instance, "order" in Portugal might well be interpreted in terms of governmental stability, which would account for the right electorate's strategic voting as well as the rest of the electorate's general drift to the incumbent PSD. The decline in attention to prices would bolster the view that previous economic problems had lessened under PSD rule, also contributing to its electoral success.

The items included in the Eurobarometer do not facilitate a thorough examination of the attitudinal correlates of party vote and ideological self-placement. The inability to follow left-right differences over time makes it hard to trace interactions between such attitudes and party vote. In Eurobarometer 28, only "order" had a distinct right bias, while other items—especially "protecting free speech"— were disproportionately tied to left parties. This slight trend can be best observed by combining the three other items and merging the parties into left and right groupings (see table 4.7). Because the relationship was not strong, it seems unlikely that ideology measured even in this manner could effectively explain the sudden rise in the PSD vote.

A final Eurobarometer variable that can be used to estimate ideology is attitudes toward society. This item asks respondents whether they would be most satisfied with revolutionary change, gradual reform, or valiant defense of existing society. Under normal circumstances, it might be expected that change-oriented respondents would tend to be on the left, with valiant defenders of the status quo on the right. In the specific circumstances of postrevolutionary Portuguese society, with change showing a rightward drift, leftists might have interpreted the question as, Should *revolutionary* society be defended? Table 4.8 presents the percentages in the three answer categories for the seven Eurobarometers.

TABLE 4.6. Country Goals, 1985–88

	Eurobarometer							
	24	25	26	27	28	29	30	Mean
Goal								
Order	37	42	39	37	43	39	44	40
Give people more say	11	11	11	14	9	11	11	11
Rising prices	45	38	42	41	39	43	37	41
Free speech	7	10	8	8	9	7	8	8
Prices+say+ speech	63	59	61	63	57	61	56	60

TABLE 4.7. Left-Right and Country Goals

	Party Tendency		
	Left	*Right*	*Percent of Total*
Goal			
Order	35	65	45.1
Prices+say+speech	43	57	54.9
Percent of total	39	61	N=583

Chi-Square: 0.07

TABLE 4.8. Attitudes toward Change, 1985–88

			Eurobarometer					
	24	25	26	27	28	29	30	Mean
Goal								
Revolutionary change	14	6	6	5	4	5	5	7
Gradual reform	74	79	81	80	80	79	83	79
Defend society	12	14	13	15	16	16	12	14

Between the October 1985 (Eurobarometer 24) and April 1986 polls (Eurobarometer 25), there was a dramatic drop in the percentage of respondents seeking revolutionary change. After April, the value hovered consistently around 5 percent. The 1985 elections once again seem to be exceptional, with very strong sentiments favoring change and apparently rebelling against the PS. By contrast, the 1987 poll shows the lowest number of voters seeking revolutionary change. That election was not one favoring change but rather continuity, thus helping the incumbent PSD.

By tracing the percentage of people in each of the goal categories who were voting for a left party (table 4.9), we can note the possible ideological bias carried by the change variable. In 1985, there was hardly any difference between the left's total vote and the percent of support it provided to all three answer categories.[7] This result reinforces the idea that dishegemony persisted through phase 3, because as many wanted to defend the existing society as pursue revolutionary change. Phase 4 appears to begin shortly afterward as the PSD government consolidated itself and increasingly established the Estado Laranja. The left became sharply associated with the "revolutionary change" option. By October 1988, three-quarters of the support for "defending existing society" came from the right; only three years before, nearly two-thirds had come from the left. This also suggests that as the PRD and PS declined electorally, the left was increasingly inhabited by frustrated advocates of the revolutionary gains of the twenty-fifth of April who were unable to find a political vehicle for forestalling the more liberal order favored by the PSD.

Although the inconsistency of Eurobarometer questions makes it difficult to use a cluster of attitudes to measure ideology and party vote over time, Eurobarometer 28 (conducted only a few months after the important July 1987 election) offers the possibly for a cross-sectional examination. That poll had a series of opinion questions that might provide some understanding of the meaning of left-right contrasts.

TABLE 4.9. Attitudes toward Change and the Left, 1985–88

	Eurobarometer							
	24	*25*	*26*	*27*	*28*	*29*	*30*	*Mean*
Goal								
Revolutionary change	63	76	89	77	68	58	62	70
Gradual reform	60	52	52	43	40	49	52	50
Defend society	61	58	49	38	38	43	26	45
Total left vote	61	55	54	44	41	48	49	50

Note. Cell entries indicate the percentage of respondents in each goal category who voted for the left

The variables that proved statistically significant against a recoded ideology variable included poverty, religion, human rights and freedom, protection of nature, and several issues involving cooperation with the country's problems with or separately with other EC countries. The ideology variable was recoded from its 1 to 10 continuum to five discrete steps, resulting in the following left-right percentage distribution: 5.5, 18.6, 37.7, 26.9, and 10.4.[8] This differentiated left-right cleavages to a point where internal distinctions within the variables could be preserved while still reducing the overall number of categories.

On most issues, the far left and the moderate left lined up identically. Neither viewed sacrifices for peace as especially important; both were similar regarding the importance of the struggle against poverty, the respect for freedom and human rights, and (to a lesser extent) the importance of revolution. They conflicted, however, on the importance of defending national interests against the superpowers (the far left agreed and the moderate left did not) and on the importance of protecting nature and fighting pollution (the far left disagreed and the moderate left agreed).

The middle position, which represented the modal value, was generally quite specific and distinct from either the left or right. While it tended to agree with the left regarding the importance of poverty and freedom and human rights, it was more inclined to support pan-European approaches to most national problems than was the left or the right. Like the moderate left, it also gravitated to protecting nature. Overall, the distinctiveness of its position suggests that it was more left than right but also more Europeanist than nationalist.

The rightist categories were mainly distinguished by clear differences on the desirability of pan-European approaches to problems. The moderate right, unlike the middle position, was consistently against pan-Europeanist approaches to problem solving, while the far right occasionally favored such collective approaches as helping to "develop regions of the country" or "ensuring energy supplies." There was more agreement between these categories regarding freedom, revolution, and poverty (the latter two had low importance); the relatively high importance of defending one's religious faith; and the need for sacrifices for peace. The far right was particularly distinctive in its antipathy toward human rights, which the moderate right neither excessively supported nor opposed.

In terms of political parties, most of the relationships with opinion items were not statistically significant, although certain residuals were especially large for some items and parties. For instance, there were differences between the Communists and Socialists concerning issues related to poverty and the elimination of the gap between rich and poor, which the Communists were more inclined to support than the Socialists were. The left—the Socialists, in particular—was more reluctant to agree that sacrifices were important to ensure national defense than the right was, which also tended to support sacrifices to defend one's religious faith. The relatively high consensus on the importance of fighting poverty and eliminating the gap between rich and poor underlined the comparative absence of sharp left-right contrasts on these equality issues. This suggests that issues strongly differentiating the old right from the left were mostly related to noneconomic variables, an interesting point that deserves further probing with a more comprehensive questionnaire.[9]

In addition, other divisions between the PS and the PCP were apparent, particularly with respect to "sacrifice for human rights" and "sacrifice for freedom." Contrary to what we might expect, the Communists were more likely to be pro-sacrifice than the Socialists were. Among the parties on the right, some differences were found among issues related to protecting nature, sacrifices for the environment, and human rights and freedom. In all cases, the PSD was more left than the CDS; in the case of environmental issues, the PSD was more left than the left parties themselves (with the exception of the PRD).[10] The Social Democrats displayed more postmaterial and liberal traits than the left as a whole or the CDS, although PCP voters did show great sympathy toward human rights and freedom, both of which are connoted with postmaterialist political values. To complicate matters further, when combining the postmaterialist country goals "giving people more say" and "protecting freedom of speech," the PCP (and to some degree the PRD) was the only party overrepresented, while the PSD was underrepresented.

Summarizing the relationship between issues and the parties, I see a cleavage roughly along modern-traditional lines, with the values of the old right (such as strong nationalism and defense, the importance of religion, and the low priority of political liberty) contrasting with a less nationalist, more secular, and politically libertarian stance. The CDS was best linked to the traditionalist side, while Communist voters expressed sympathy for the politically liberal items.[11] Thus, despite the Communists' public image as a totalitarian party favoring repressive political forms, its voters were actually more accurately described as libertarian left. The Socialist party, which tended to have a public persona emphasizing its commitment to libertarian values, attracted voters less liberal than those favoring the PCP. The Socialists' voters were also secular but less nationalist than the PCP's. The Social Democrats were more nationalist and religious but remained generally more liberal and modern than the CDS. These results, with my previous caveats about PCP voters, generally confirm my expected overall assessment of party-ideology links.

A second line of cleavage relates to the materialism-postmaterialism split. The cleavage was most evident when postmaterialism was limited to environmentalism and divorced from political liberty. This pit the left and the CDS, which both tended to be more materialist, against the PSD, whose voters placed a greater emphasis on protecting nature and the environment. Among the materialists, the left was internally differentiated, with the PCP more favorable to attempts to deal with poverty and the gap between rich and poor than the Socialists were. Regarding the PSD, results tended to reinforce the public's mainstream and center-right impression of the party, although the party's symbolic orange was blended with a touch of green. The CDS was more classically old right, conforming with its public image and my previous characterization.

Despite the links between voters and attitudes, the weakness of those ties suggests that although a mild ideological hegemony might have been associated with the PSD's electoral success, such an explanation is inadequate by itself. Rather, as I suggested earlier, short-term cues and incumbent-opposition dynamics rewarding parties for good times might have been important in explaining the 1987 outcome. To examine these hypotheses further, I will study two sets of relationships. First, I relate respondents' perceptions of the performance of the economy and their personal finances over the last twelve months to party vote. A strong statistical relationship between PSD voters and respondents who felt that the economic news was positive means that economic performance rather than ideological conversion was the key factor shaping the outcome. Second, the respondents might have been rewarding the incumbent party for good times in more diffuse ways, as measured by "satisfaction with life" and "satisfaction with democracy" variables.

The crosstabulation of "party" with "general perceptions of the economy over the last twelve months" proved statistically significant and confirmed the expected pattern: PSD voters were more likely to have a positive view of the economy. By contrast PRD, PCP, and PS voters all were disproportionately likely to say that the economy had gotten worse or stayed the same. An even stronger tendency was displayed when individual household finances over the last twelve months were considered: again the PSD was the beneficiary of such perceptions, as was the CDS. When I considered ideology and these variables, I noted a similar relationship, with the right being favored among voters with positive perceptions of the general economy and especially personal finances. Generally, voters who perceived economic good times were likely to reward the incumbent party disproportionately, although incumbency effects cannot be easily separated from ideological ones. In addition, the data does not immediately establish whether voters moved to the right in parallel with a political transition toward the PSD, thus signaling the emergence of a rightist ideological hegemony, or whether their electoral support was an opportunistic reward to the incumbent party that happened to be in the right place at the right time.

The long-term significance of the links among ideology, perception of general economic improvement, and PSD vote for reshaping Portugal's political economy depends on their durability. By examining the relationship among these variables as they apply to the other incumbent party situation in 1985, we can assess the tendency for incumbent parties to be generally attractive to those holding positive perceptions of the economy.

In 1985, the government was led by Socialist leader Mário Soares, although the PS was part of the PS-PSD coalition. If sympathy toward the incumbent party, rather than simply the right, was more likely from voters with positive evaluations of the economy, a disproportionate number of Socialist voters should have held such views. True to expectations, the PS picked up the support of 40 percent of those who said that the economy had improved, compared to

28 percent of the total vote. Had there been a larger number of voters sensing an improved economy, the 1985 elections would have been dramatically altered: the Communist vote greatly diminished and the PS vote substantially enhanced. As the plurality party, the PS would have enjoyed the fruits of the economic upswing between 1985 and 1987. Conceivably, phase 4 would have been marked by Socialist rather than Social Democratic party hegemony. Unfortunately for the Socialists, nearly 45 percent of respondents said that the economy had gotten worse, compared to only 20 percent who saw improvement, undermining its aspiration to be the dominant party.

By 1987, the PSD had good reason to think, "What a difference two years can make!" The percentage of respondents claiming that the economy had improved tripled to nearly 60 percent. Fully 61 percent of those perceiving an improving economy voted for the PSD, more than twice as many as those who voted for the Socialists. In fact, the PS obtained a share of this category roughly comparable to that of the PSD in 1985 (29 versus 31 percent). What changed was that the other parties obtained almost none of this category's vote. Incredibly, the PSD had nearly managed to monopolize credit for an economic upturn. Even more impressive, those voters who said the economy had gotten worse gave the PSD a plurality. For the left, the 1987 elections were a disaster; the incumbent party was richly rewarded for good times, and continued a trend since 1985 for the right to be more attractive to those perceiving an improving economy. The left saw the number of voters admitting to a worsening economy decline, and the percentage of those in that group supporting the left eroded as well.[12]

These results suggest that the PSD's success can only partially be explained by specifically economic perceptions and imply that the period of PSD governance must have been associated with a generalized sense of improving conditions. The Eurobarometer provides two variables that tap this factor: "life satisfaction" and "satisfaction with democracy." Both show the expected increases. The percentage of respondents saying they were satisfied with life increased from 55 percent in 1985 to 78 percent in 1987. But the most notable change concerned "satisfaction with democracy" which doubled its 1985 percentage, rising from 40 to 80 percent. Not only were the specific economic aspects of good times associated with those miraculous two years, but diffuse contentment with life in general and the political system increased as well.

CONCLUSION

Several patterns have confirmed the emergence of a coherent modern right able to establish a credible national-popular program. The association between the right and perceptions of an improving economy seem to go beyond a narrow reward to incumbency, a trend apparent as early as 1985. By 1987, incumbency further reinforced the predisposition to link good times with the right, making the PSD's electoral rise that much more impressive.

The Communists were relegated to being a minor protest party depending on electoral faithfulness from strongly attached voters on the ideological left or those dissatisfied with current economic conditions. While Communist voters expressed libertarian and egalitarian attitudes, party leaders could not convert these into an inspiration for reformulating the party to make it a viable actor within the democratic system. The PCP might have received a boost if economic conditions had turned sour because its electorate was deeply implanted among economic pessimists: in 1985, 70 percent of them voted for the Communists.

The Socialists found themselves in the unenviable position of being in the wrong place at the wrong time. The incumbent party was certain to be rewarded by those perceiving an improving economy, but the percentages of those with such perceptions blossomed only in 1987, not 1985. The PS did not decline as much as the PCP and remained the major alternative to the PSD. As befitting its heritage, it attracted a moderate left electorate willing to follow its reformist softliner inclinations.

The PSD proved able to capitalize on improving economic perceptions, evidently by convincing the electorate of its key role in producing the economic turnaround. But it showed some vulnerability to changing economic conditions; an economic reversal could turn the tide and reward the PS. The PSD could never rely on a large core of strongly attached supporters who might carry the party through hard times. In the past, when the Socialists were in power, poor economic conditions enlarged the percentage of those with negative views of the economy and helped sustain the Communists on the left and the PSD on the right. Nevertheless, only future events can confirm this untested hypothesis: if the PSD is in power during a period in which negative views of the economy multiply, the Socialist party rather than the Communists would be the disproportionate greatest beneficiary. Whether the PS can expect effectively to attract the Communist protest vote to gain a single-party majority will be a key variable affecting the future of the political system.

The success of the PSD should not be reduced to an epiphenomenon of the economy. The fact that satisfaction with democracy doubled during the two-year period of PSD rule may signal a deeper sense in which hegemony has been reestablished. Having won the 1987 election by gaining an absolute majority of the electorate, the PSD presented itself as an alternative to unstable coalition governments of the past. Coupled with passable performance in the economy, the Social Democrats became the regime alternative to dishegemony. The *estado laranja* was more than a party in power; it became a solution to the dishegemonic impasse produced by the revolutionary transition. Chapter 5 reveals the durability of the PSD as a hegemonic alternative insofar as it established a broad social coalition united around the party's neoliberal social democracy and promise of political stability.

FIVE

PARTY STRATEGIES AND THE SOCIAL BASES OF CONTESTING HEGEMONIC PROJECTS

The emergence of an expanded and apparently durable political force in the PSD was the political hallmark of the fourth and latest phase of Portugal's democratic consolidation, the phase that has gone furthest in crystallizing a democratic capitalist hegemonic project. This chapter investigates the nature of the social coalition through which the PSD established single-party dominance and reviews the strategic choices faced by all parties seeking to forge a broad electoral coalition. Both the left and the right had several strategic alternatives for coalescing constituencies with their programmatic orientations. The viability of these strategies depended upon party assumptions about different parts of the electorate, such as political and economic interests, commitment to ideological symbols and values, propensity to vote, and size in proportion to the overall electorate as well the availability of certain coalitions given the dynamics of party competition.

PARTY ELECTORAL STRATEGIES

The left faced serious strategic problems because of the positions taken by the Communists and Socialists during the transitional period. Conflicts over the type of transition taking place (parliamentary, Socialist, or both) led to internecine struggles that reflected the lack of a consensus about the basic dimensions of a counterhegemonic strategy. Although the 1976 constitution was a common rallying point, it could not overcome the interparty tensions, those that had especially surfaced in 1975.

Each party sought to emphasize one of two strategies. Radical and counterhegemonic, the first strategy revolved around defining a core set of constituencies that agreed on key aspects of the transformed, leftist political economy as it emerged from the revolutionary period.[1] Programmatically, this meant finding constituencies likely to favor the retention of a sizable state productive sector, land reform, an enhanced welfare or redistributive role for the state, and a considerable number of workers' rights.

The second strategy of democratic dishegemony was more inclusive and vague. It focused on establishing a consensus about the institutional and legal parameters of the new regime—liberal, parliamentary, and participative—rather than its socioeconomic principles. While espousing a Europeanist vocation, it remained ambiguous regarding the terms of reconciliation between revolutionary gains and a more capitalist accumulation strategy. Essentially a holding pattern, this strategic orientation sought to bring together sociologically equivocal elements such as anti-fascists and prodemocrats along with more distinct social categories such as moderate and semirevolutionary workers and farmers (that is, those favoring revolutionary gains but not wedded to a more generalized anticapitalist or antiparliamentary revolution) and progressive parts of the service sector. Also included were some elements of the bourgeoisie such as small and medium employers who feared excessive market competition or were directly or indirectly subsidized by the state and nationalized firms. Progressive employers of any size who were willing partners in neocorporatist arrangements were also sought. This coalition would pursue voluntary corporatism in the private sector, the retention of a relatively strong state productive sector, and a modified free market providing some protection for small and medium firms and farmers during the process of European integration. It was distinct from appeals made by the right because it was never explicitly anticonstitutional; it did not repudiate the structural changes of the revolution but did add that any future changes would be based on legal processes and popular mandates.

Both the Communists and the Socialists showed signs of deep ambiguity about the two strategies. PCP strategy had long assumed that the old regime was based on the support of a "few hundred large capitalists and landowners and their agents" who would come into conflict with "the great masses of the population—all the non-monopolist classes and strata" (PCP 1976, 31).[2] Before the radicalism of the hot summer of 1975, this view predisposed the party to support a broad anti-fascist revolution that was to be national and democratic rather than specifically Socialist. This meant that although the PCP prioritized political agreement within the working class "with its particularity being the unity of the industrial and rural proletarians," it also sought an alliance with the peasantry and urban petty bourgeoisie. By focusing upon common negatives, anti-fascism, and antimonopolies, the Communists sought to reach beyond its working-class core constituency into other social categories such as "youth, progressive intellectuals, the working masses and the democratic and anti-monopolistic forces" to form the basis for the "unity of democratic and patriotic forces" (PCP 1974, 18–19). Antimonopolist elements also included parts of the capitalist class such as small and medium capital. Thus, the anti-fascist revolution was not inherently anticapitalist but could be the basis for a less radical multiclass counterhegemony favoring the popular masses. Because the strategy was at least partially complementary to parliamentary democracy, Communist leader Álvaro Cunhal proclaimed in a speech at the end of the PCP's Seventh Extraordinary Congress in 1974 that "the democratic revolution advances. We are going forward with the consolidation of liberties, towards the realization of elections for a Constituent Assembly, towards the edification of a democratic Portugal" (Cunhal 1975, 317).

The radicalism of 1974–76 touched the PCP's intrinsic ambiguity regarding the tradeoff between parliamentary democracy and Socialist change. While espousing the importance of elections and civil liberties, it also seized upon that part of the MFA program emphasizing an antimonopolist strategy, arguing that "either the monopolies and latifundistas will take control over political power, installing a new dictatorship, or the democratic forces [will be able] to construct a democratic Portugal [and] put an end to the economic power of the monopolies and latifundistas" (PCP 1974, 30).[3] During the course of the transition, this essentially meant that the PCP changed the focus of its strategy from a broad national democratic revolution to one that would support the initial steps in the transition to socialism. Consequently, this change suggested that a smaller social base would be targeted for mobilization and would necessarily be less amenable to the dynamics of party competition typical of parliamentary democracy.

The Socialists also shared some of the PCP's schizophrenia regarding the two strategies. Before the fall of the dictatorship, they, too, had engaged in revolutionary rhetoric, sounding similar to the Communists in their radicalism. Soares, in his lengthy tome *Portugal Amordacado*, mentioned that the Salazarist regime had been supported by "certain economic interests for whom [Salazar] doggedly served as a competent overseer." He emphasized that "above the People was situated the class of the rich which [Salazar] respected and efficiently served" (Soares 1974, 65). This perception of the dominant classes as instrumental to the retention of counter-productive policies and regime forms was to some degree shared by the PS and PCP leaders.

Moreover, the extent of Socialist change sought by these two parties seemed at times to coincide. The Socialist party program adopted in 1974 announced "the objective of the Socialist Party is the construction, in Portugal, of a classless society where workers will become associated producers, where power will be the expression of the popular will and where culture will become the work of the creative capacity of the whole society" (PS 1974, 1). Rather than acting as a force favoring the stabilization of capitalism, the party was to be an agent for change that repudiated "the way of those movements [that] while calling themselves social democratic or even socialist, end up keeping, in fact or deliberately, the structures of capitalism and the interests of imperialism" (PS 1974, 2).

Despite the revolutionary principles, the hallmark of the Socialists was not their desire for socialism but their defense of liberal democracy. While claiming that there could be no real separation between the pursuit of political liberty and socialism, the party's priorities in practice seemed clear. "We will never sacrifice liberty for socialism," party leader Soares declared (Soares 1979a, 20). Indicating the deepening chasm between the Communists and the Socialists regarding the country's path, Soares argued:

> What is at stake is the very meaning of the Revolution, the road to socialism. The latter will either be made by a democratic and pluralist method, *respecting the sociological givens of the real country* and its geostrategic insertion, or on the contrary, according to a classical Leninist scheme which implies the smashing of the State and the attribution of all power to a minority . . . which imposes itself thanks to its control over the

mass media, economic centers of power, implying the repressive application of policies. (Soares 1979a, 21), my emphasis.

Torn essentially between its role as democratic consolidator and change agent, the Socialist party formed a broad umbrella under which Trotskyists and Willy Brandt Social Democrats all found shelter at one time. In addition, the party was divided between the radical counterhegemonic route (which meant supporting only those parts of Portugal's sociological givens that would embrace democratic socialism) and a less confrontational route (which focused upon reconciliation and democratic consolidation but involved a vaster set of constituencies lacking much commitment to socialism). The revolutionary period made it obvious to key PS party leaders that the radical route meant an alliance with the Communists, an option that Soares rejected. Instead the party could gain immediate prominence by posing as antidictatorship, which made it appealing to large sections of the electorate who were motivated by both anti-communism and anti-fascism. Moreover, geostrategic concerns overlaid these considerations; Portugal's role in NATO would have made it hard for the Socialists to support much domestic radicalism.[4]

By the start of the democratic consolidation, each party was inclined to a different strategy despite internal contradictations resulting from the revolutionary transition. After the events of November 1975, the Communists realized there was no chance that the MFA-people alliance would provide the basis for an extraelectoral, counterhegemonic strategy. Therefore, they changed course and sought an alliance with the Socialists—a majority of the left. This was the only plausible course for the PCP, for it was unlikely to ever have enough electoral success to gain power alone. The Communists pursued this route but kept pressure on the character of the strategy that the left as a whole would follow, attempting to push the Socialists further toward radical counterhegemony. The unwillingness of the PS to accept the Communists as alliance partners led the PCP to direct much of its animosity at Socialist leader Soares, who was blamed for the absence of a left government. Only in 1990 was a partial alliance of the PS and PCP formed, with new Socialist leadership and only for the Lisbon local elections. While radical counterhegemony had some potential as a strategy for the left, it was never actively pursued.

For several years during the consolidation, the Socialists opted for democratic dishegemony as a party strategy. Despite increasing deradicalization, the PS maintained some commitment to the gains of the revolution. In its 1987 program, it continued to oppose the purely capitalist, neoliberal line of the intraregime softliners. On the key question of the state productive sector, for example, the party argued:

> Public monopolies have been violently criticized with the argument that they constitute a diversion from the logic of a competitive market and therefore produce global economic inefficiencies. What these arguments fail to point out is that in most cases, passage from public to private hands would not bring about a change from a monopolistic to a free market and thus gains in efficiency. What would be lost in terms of justice and solidarity would not be gained in improvements to the national economy. (PS 1987, 29)

The party's emphasis on justice and solidarity still resonated in the specific economic changes produced by the quasirevolutionary transition. It also sought to portray itself in terms more typical of contemporary Social Democratic parties under the postwar settlement—as a left modernizing party favoring greater citizen participation, political liberties, rationalization of the state, administrative decentralization, better social services, and environmental protection. Yet the PS still opposed a revision of the constitution that "would propose the ideological and programmatic reexamination of the strong social content of our Constitution and instead give way to an individualistic, dehumanized, and technocratic vision of the world and life" (PS 1987, 6). The Socialist party remained a left, dishegemonic, catchall party.

In part, the success of either strategy depended upon the soundness of electoral assumptions. Radical counterhegemony assumed three conditions: (1) the vast majority of agricultural and industrial workers supporting the left; (2) a disproportionately high mobilization of the working class compared to the rest of the electorate; (3) partial support from other social strata and categories, particularly the service sector. Democratic dishegemony involved a different set of conditions: (1) a more deradicalized working class, primarily but not completely concerned with traditional bread-and-butter improvement within capitalism, or a relatively low turnout among radicalized workers; (2) relatively large size and high rates of electoral turnout among other classes and groups uncommitted to retaining the left political economy. These two conditions would undercut the electoral viability of the radical route and reduce the political viability of the leftist structural changes. Even the Socialists required that a substantial part of the working class and other strata and categories be at least minimally committed to some key aspects of revolutionary change. Without them, the PS would be programmatically absorbed by the PSD, which straddled the line between social democracy and neoliberalism and dismissed many of the revolutionary gains as illegitimate and unproductive.

The right also faced fundamental strategic choices in the aftermath of the revolution. Its first option was rehegemony through bipolarization, the right-wing equivalent of radical counterhegemony. This strategic orientation included placing the Socialists and Communists in the same Marxist camp; arguing that the economic problems of the country could not be solved without fundamental changes in the constitution, stripping away many vestiges of socialism and suggesting a massive liberalization of the economy, and redirecting all right-wing votes into a single coalition or dominant party, thereby improving the odds for obtaining a majority of seats in Parliament.[5] This was the heart of the right's strategy during phase 2 of the democratic consolidation, a time when the Democratic Alliance obtained parliamentary majorities (1979–83), as well as during phase 4, when the PSD came to power.

The second strategy was a rightist version of the Socialists' preferred democratic dishegemony. It was less confrontational; did not necessarily assume that the right would be able to rule alone; and did not require quick, massive changes in the prevailing constitutional order. It was distinct insofar as it did not make peace with dishegemony but was a tactical move to gain time in anticipation of resurrecting the main elements of the first strategy. This typified CDS and PSD behavior during phases 1 and 3.

Electorally, six common elements were associated with the right's strategies: (1) the working class was either internally divided over the revolutionary political economy or ideologically sympathetic but likely to be won over by the right as the economy foundered; (2) working-class turnout, especially among the more leftist sectors, would decline over time; (3) service-sector elements would behave more like a new petty bourgeoisie than a new working class and would primarily support the right; (4) the rural petty bourgeoisie would provide unambiguous support; (5) both the service sector and the rural petty bourgeoisie would vote in disproportionate numbers; and (6) nonclass social categories such as Catholics and women would either provide consistent support or be swung over in sufficient numbers with high enough turnout rates to gain a majority. In general, the ideal scenario assumed that the right could effectively generalize its support across all groups and regions, building a multi-class, socially varigated coalition backing its hegemonic project.

The main differences in the two rightist strategies involved items 1 and 3. The assumption that both industrial workers and the service sector would gravitate to the right was partially based on the expectation that dishegemony was economically unworkable, inevitably leading to mounting contradictions between alternative models of accumulation. The confrontational strategy sought to blame the left and the Socialist constitution for the declining state of the economy but was only feasible when the left or the constitution could credibly be blamed for recent economic troubles. This was possible to some degree in 1979, when the constitution, the left, the MFA, and even the Communist-influenced CGTP could be portrayed as the cause of phase 1's relatively poor economic performance.[6] But at the end of phase 2, after four years of AD government, that argument could not be seriously presented to the electorate, resulting in recourse to the other strategy.

I use two complementary approaches to assess the relation between these party strategies and the social coalitions represented in their electorates. As in chapter 4, Eurobarometers provide a breakdown of the social support for each party over time. In addition, ecological analysis based on electoral results and census data refines some aspects left obscure by the survey data as well as provides estimates of electoral support when survey data are absent. The ecological approach also demonstrates the effects of contextual factors in shaping the behaviors of social categories in different regions. For example, it shows that the PSD's geographic nationalization of support was implicit in its electoral rise. Partly due to data limitations, my main focus is the mid-1980s when Eurobarometer surveys were conducted.

PSD: Hegemony by Overcoming Regional and Urban-Rural Cleavages

Portugal's complex social and economic topography has presented electoral obstacles to all political forces. Regional contexts have tended to concentrate party appeal to certain areas. During phase 1, the right gained most of its support from regions that reflected the confluence of several factors: a land-tenure system based on rural smallholdings, high levels of church attendance, and an industrial structure based on light and dispersed industries in the center and north of the country.[7]

Table 5.1 indicates the ratio of a region's share of the total electorate as compared to the regional percentage of a party's total vote.[8] The PSD started its electoral life as the largest party of the softliners by drawing disproportionate support in the north and the center coastal strip. Its relatively high standard deviation for the 1975 elections demonstrates the unevenness of its scores across the country. By the start of phase 2 in 1979, the right (AD) was able to broaden its support considerably, nearly halving its standard deviation. Despite a record vote in its favor by the fourth phase (1987), the regional structure of support for the right's major party, the PSD, did not undergo much further change, as revealed in the identical standard deviations for 1985 (when it received only 29 percent of the vote) and 1987 (when it obtained over 50 percent). This shows that by phase 4, the PSD and the right as a whole reached an equilibrium in which its electoral future was determined largely by changes in its overall national support rather than further relative gains in areas where it was historically weak. Should the PSD and the right in general falter in future elections, a reversal of the nationalizing trend may take place with a retrenchment of support to regions that were originally strong backers.

The right's strength in the north and center coastal regions reflects the general pattern of north-south differentiation associated with the country's formation as a nation-state. In brief, the nation-building impulse stemmed from the north and was based upon aristocratic, Catholic forces combating the Moors who had colonized the south. The need to conquer the south reinforced a pattern of land tenure characterized by large estates or latifundia, with towns existing as relatively defensible enclaves surrounded by vast fields.[9] Catholicism never advanced as an inherent part of southern mass culture, which explains very low rates of church attendance and a lessening of the church's local legitimacy. Overall, the south is characterized by a relatively irreligious, proletarianized labor force with a far greater propensity to support radical courses.[10]

In the north, land-tenure patterns have varied from feudal-like arrangements to highly fragmented smallholdings, with the latter predominant by the time of Caetano's fall. Furthermore, northerners are strongly tied to Catholicism and regularly look to the church for leadership, guidance, and charity. This pattern has contributed to the bipolarization of politics between a traditonalist, petty bour-

TABLE 5.1. Ratio of Regional Vote to Party's Total Vote

Region	1975	1976	1979	1980	1983	1985	1987
			Communist Party				
NC	0.52	0.42	0.58	0.62	0.63	0.67	0.65
Nint	0.26	0.14	0.22	0.28	0.26	0.33	0.26
CC	0.52	0.4	0.51	0.49	0.47	0.5	0.45
	0.98	0.98	1.07	1.03	1.01	1.0	1.0
SC	1.35	1.26	1.2	1.53	1.53	1.47	1.54
Sint	2.61	2.84	2.43	2.65	2.58	2.69	2.98
Standard Deviation	0.86	0.99	0.79	0.88	0.86	0.87	1.0
			Socialist Party				
NC	0.82	0.93	1.09	1.1	1.13	1.11	1.23
Nint	0.82	0.78	0.98	0.78	0.83	0.98	0.84
CC	0.56	0.59	0.62	1.01	1.05	1.11	1.05
Cint	1.18	1.1	1.03	1.07	1.01	0.9	0.95
SC	0.79	0.78	0.72	1.01	0.97	0.93	0.91
Sint	0.95	0.88	0.67	0.69	0.7	0.78	0.71
Standard Deviation	0.2	0.17	0.2	0.17	0.16	0.13	0.18
			Social Democratic Party				
NC	1.39	1.31	1.14	1.08	1.05	1.06	1.07
Nint	1.68	1.4	1.37	1.38	1.41	1.32	1.25
CC	1.43	1.134	1.19	1.19	1.27	1.24	1.15
Cint	0.72	0.75	0.93	0.93	0.98	0.95	0.94
SC	0.6	0.75	0.86	0.81	0.77	0.82	0.86
Sint	0.25	0.37	0.5	0.56	0.59	0.57	0.57
Standard Deviation	0.57	0.42	0.31	0.29	0.31	0.28	0.24
			Center Democratic Social				
NC	1.79	0.13	—	—	1.16	1.18	1.12
Nint	1.86	1.7	—	—	1.54	1.79	1.49
CC	0.97	1.13	—	—	1.15	1.18	1.22
Cint	0.64	0.99	—	—	0.83	0.73	0.88
SC	0.56	0.56	—	—	0.78	0.71	0.74
Sint	0.32	0.38	—	—	0.34	0.28	0.47
Standard Deviation	0.66	0.49	—	—	0.41	0.53	0.36

Key: NC=Northern Coastal, Nint=Northern Interior,CC=Center Coastal, Cint=Center Interior, SC=Southern Coastal, Sint=Southern Interior

geois north and a more secular, proletarian south. Table 5.2 shows the relationship among land tenure, class structure, and location through a factor analysis based on *concelho*-level census data (N=275) in which the patterns I have described line up as two contrasting factors. The specific variables are (1) farm size, (2) percentages of self-employed farmers and agricultural workers, and (3) geographic location (in this case, the variable of "southerness"). Table 5.3 identifies the weight of each of the eighteen districts for the two factors, demonstrating again the north-south character of the rural ecological context.

TABLE 5.2. Factor Analysis of North-South Contrast

	Factor 1	*Factor 2*
Self-employed farmers	0.054	0.821
Agricultural workers	0.814	0.369
Farm size	0.639	-0.136
Location	0.482	-0.445

*Note:*This is the varimax rotated factor matrix based on 1970 INE data.

This long-standing pattern was further reinforced in the postwar period. Sagging growth rates in agriculture constrasted with rapid growth in the service and industrial sectors.[11] The *cintura industrial* around Lisbon emerged as a pole of economic development for the country as a whole. New industries such as steel, shipbuilding, cements, petroleum refining, and chemicals emerged to draw rural proletarians from the south (as well as northerners) to industrial towns. With nearly ideal sociological conditions for working-class organization and the post-Caetano appeal of proletarian activists (given the history of political repression), workers in the suburbs of Lisbon were especially likely to develop proletarian consciousness.

Workers in the heavily industrial centers around Lisbon and Setúbal were predisposed to challenge bourgeois hegemony, especially in the immediate aftermath of the dictatorship's fall. By contrast, in the north, despite an early tradition of urban anarchism, the prevalence of dispersed light industries and semi-proletarianization due to the interspersing of rural smallholdings and factory life was much less favorable to the left. Combined with the cultural effect of the Catholic church, the region was more inclined to accept the appeals of reformist or right parties.[12]

A basic condition for the right's strategy of rehegemony through bipolarization was its ability to redirect votes into a single coalition or dominant party. This was theoretically possible because both the PSD and CDS had essentially a similar regional, social, and electoral base. The AD demonstrated that by managing votes carefully, the right could obtain a parliamentary majority. Given the electoral overlap between the two former AD partners, there was a possibility of obtaining a single-party majority; the PSD-CDS distinction applied to no intrinsic cleavage structure. Figure 5.1 shows that these two parties were highly correlated, gaining support in the same electoral districts.[13] Thus, by the mid-1980s, under Cavaco Silva's leadership, the PSD pursued the elusive single-party majority necessary to overcome the continuing dishegemony of phase 3.

TABLE 5.3. District Scores for Factor Analysis of North-South Contrast

Region	District	Factor One		Factor Two	
		Mean	*Sigma*	*Mean*	*Sigma*
NC	Aveiro	-0.46	0.27	0.47	0.79
Sint	Beja	2.34	0.43	-0.05	0.34
NC	Braga	-0.54	0.16	0.89	0.68
Nint	Bragança	0.19	0.79	1.72	0.45
Cint	Castelo Branco	0.82	0.66	0.83	0.63
CC	Coimbra	0.30	0.45	0.84	0.53
Sint	Evora	2.42	0.63	-0.40	0.44
SC	Faro	0.55	0.28	0.30	0.72
Nint	Guarda	0.26	0.54	1.30	0.63
CC	Leiria	0.28	0.46	0.49	0.68
SC	Lisboa	0.31	0.60	-0.10	0.76
Cint	Portalegre	2.34	0.81	-0.12	0.35
NC	Porto	-0.65	0.19	0.17	0.49
Cint	Santarem	0.92	0.81	-0.10	0.46
SC	Setúbal	0.88	1.34	-0.62	0.41
NC	Viana do Castelo	-0.71	0.26	1.72	0.61
Nint	Vila Real	0.28	0.74	1.31	0.51
Nint	Viseu	0.28	0.74	1.31	0.51

Figure 5.1. 1987 PSD Party Correlations

- —9—8—7—6—5—4—3—2—1—0—1—2—3—4—5—6—7—8—9 +

PCP '83   PRD '87   PS '87 PS '85   CDS '87   PSD '83

PCP '85   PRD '85   CDS '83   PSD '85

PCP '80   PS '83   CDS '85

PCP '87

To pursue this strategy successfully, the PSD needed to secure its base of support in the north, transfer CDS voters to itself, and encroach upon those parts of the south least likely to support radicalism. After the brief period of the PS-PSD grand coalition, followed by the minority Cavaco government from 1985 to 1987, the time was right for pursuing the bipolarizing strategy. As in 1979, previous austerity could be blamed on the Socialists and to some extent on the constitution and revolutionary structural elements, possibly leading to greater divisions within the working class, lower turnout among left sympathizers, and a higher turnout among right stalwarts such as smallholders and Catholics. The ever-sensitive service sector would most likely be irritated by the Socialist government and favor the Cavaco minority government and the better economic times associated with it. The PSD further neutralized some of the ideological antagonism of center-left voters by accentuating the modernizing character of its goals, which were compatible with both the Social Democratic and neoliberal strands within the party and more likely to tap the centrist ideological majority. This posture appealed to urban, better educated elements likely to benefit from economic development and further incorporation within a European-inspired model of modernity. By portraying itself as a competent political force able to forge a single-party government, the PSD sought to supplement and perhaps supplant its rural, less modern social base, forging a multiclass coalition and definitively overcoming the dishegemonic impasse. The results of this strategy appear in tables 5.4–5.7, which present ecologically based regional data and estimates of party electoral support from different social categories over time.

Table 5.4 compares the combined vote of the CDS, PSD, and PRD in 1985 with the total in 1987. The small differences between the total gains by the PSD and the combined losses by the CDS and PRD suggest that a crossover of voters defecting from the other two parties contributed decisively to the PSD's victory. Moreover, the PSD expanded its vote both in its northern and central strongholds and in the south where it had previously been weak.[14]

The PSD's entrenchment in the north was partly a reflection of its prominence in rural, traditional areas. In 1983, the party received only 26 percent of the vote from densely populated areas but 30 percent from low-population areas, which include the antirightist southern region. By 1987, the difference between the rural and urban areas had been reduced, although the rural zone still disporportionately favored the Social Democrats (55 versus 52 percent).

TABLE 5.4. CDS, PRD, PSD Regional Vote, 1985, 1987

Region	1985				1987				PSD PSD Gains	CDS- PRD Losses	Gains minus Losses
	CDS	PRD	PSD	Total	CDS	PRD	PSD	Total			
NC	13	16	34	63	6	3	56	65	22	20	2
Nint	18	9	38	63	7	2	63	71	24	19	5
CC	11	14	38	63	5	3	59	67	21	17	4
Cint	7	21	26	55	4	7	45	55	19	17	1
SC	5	20	22	48	3	7	41	50	18	16	2
Sint	3	13	16	32	2	6	28	36	12	7	5

How did the PSD compare to other parties from a regional and demographic perspective? Given prior election returns, only the Socialists could lay a claim to having electorally based hegemonic aspirations. Unlike the PSD, the PS was unable to gain a PSOE-like presence in government due to an inability to secure a strong, stable base in the countryside that could be supplemented with fortuitous urban votes or a solid urban vote supplemented by a sizable rural vote. When the PS vote was balanced between urban and rural areas, as in 1985, its *overall* vote decreased. In 1983, when the PS garnered over 36 percent of the vote, it had a strongly disproportionate urban vote. With the rural votes monopolized by the right in the north and the Communists in the south, the Socialists had to rely heavily on their urban base of support, which could not provide enough votes for a single-party majority.[15]

Social Basis of the PSD's Victory

Overcoming the limitations of a rural electoral orientation was a part of the PSD's efforts to recast the terms of Portuguese party politics. The forging of an electoral multiclass coalition was essential to creating a mass base for the policies associated with a resurrected bourgeois hegemony. I use ecological and survey data to assess the character and breadth of the coalition created in 1987 by the PSD.

According to calculations derived from the 1980 census, the work force had distinctly modernized. At 39 percent, the number of those occupied in the secondary sector had reached European levels. The service sector reached 40 percent, a bit below first-world standards due to the relatively large percentage of workers remaining in the primary sector (nearly 17 percent). Given this occupational structure, no party could hope to succeed in the long term as a rural, agrarian party; Salazar's bucolic utopia had been forever set aside. For the PSD, the persistence of a rural bias would limit its electoral strength. Even if it received all the votes from rural self-employed farmers and farm owners, it would not reach much beyond 10 percent of the electorate because the politically unreliable agricultural proletariat made up the rest of the primary sector. Instead the PSD needed to appeal to other social categories in more urban areas to modernize its electorate and create a hegemonic majority. This electoral majority would have to come from the service sector and industrial working class as well as other nonclass social categories such as retirees, housewives, students, and so on. I examine the voting behavior of some of these categories later in the chapter.

The service sector has been subject to considerable discussion regarding its class propensities. For example, Nicos Poulantzas makes the following argument in reference to the new petty bourgeoisie:

> The reason why these agents do not belong to the working class is that their structural class determination and the place they occupy in the social division of labor are marked by the dominance of the political relations that they maintain over the aspect of productive labor in the division of labor. Their principal function is that of extracting surplus-value from the workers—that is "collecting it." They exercise powers that derive from the place of capital, capital that has seized hold of the control function of the labor process; these powers are not necessarily exercised by the capitalists themselves. (Poulantzas 1987, 228–29)

For Poulantzas the service sector is noted especially for its managerial and technical-supervisory roles, yet in Portugal these roles constitute a very small part of the labor force (about 12 percent, depending on where occupational lines are drawn). Two-thirds of the service sector is composed of a lower component, ranging from waiters to bus and taxi drivers to salespersons. This electorally significant segment might be considered a new working class in terms of the "political relations that they maintain over the aspect of productive labor in the division of labor." Because they exercise no dominance over the production process but are exposed to many working-class conditions, although not in the industrial sector, one might expect their political inclinations to be somewhat similar.[16] This makes the service sector a hotly disputed electoral terrain because they might have some proletarian instincts despite strong internal stratification.[17] The PSD's modernizing right-wing social democracy could prove tempting under favorable circumstances such as those in 1987.

TABLE 5.5. Ecological Vote Estimate for Service Sector

	Year		
	1983	*1985*	*1987*
Party			
PCP	34	26	22
PRD	—	27	9
PS	37	18	22
PSD	15	20	41
CDS	10	5	3

Source: Based on 1980 INE census data and STAPE election returns.

Table 5.5 shows that according to ecological estimates, the tertiary-sector workers were at one point much more proletarian than petty bourgeois. In 1983 and 1985, the PSD-CDS only managed to gain 25 percent of the sector's vote, with the PCP, PS, and PRD as the greatest beneficiaries. By 1985, however, the rise of the PRD undermined in particular this segment's support for the Socialist party, whose 1983 vote was halved that year.

The decay of the PRD by 1987 did little to reverse the trend. The PCP's share of the service sector continued to decrease, while the PS regained only a small part of what it had lost in 1985. The PSD-CDS chiefly benefited from the left's defections. Dislodged from traditional voting habits by the PRD, these voters became available in the crucial 1987 elections.

I derived my analysis from ecological sources. To what extent do the Eurobarometers confirm this trend? According to Eurobarometer 26 (1986), for example, a nearly identical proportion of respondents—35 percent—had occupations in the white collar service sector (excluding nonclass categories from the "occupational" variable). By adding the 2 percent who claimed to be professionals, this nearly equaled the census figure of 40 percent for the service sector as a whole.[18]

Table 5.6 shows the pattern of white-collar support for the various parties over the years.[19] Unfortunately, because no Eurobarometer data exist before 1985, the swing from 1983 cannot be determined. The ecological data suggest that the service sector lined up strongly behind both the PCP and the PS in the earlier election. For 1985, the ecological estimate of the service-sector vote for the PSD was 20 percent as opposed to the 28 percent registered by the Eurobarometer. The latter nearly reversed the percentages claimed by the Socialists and Communists and gave the PRD a lower percentage. Nevertheless, the global percentages for left and right did not vary much: the ecological estimate of the combined PCP-PS-PRD vote was 71 percent; the Eurobarometer yielded 65 percent. It would not be surprising if the ecological estimates for 1983 were basically accurate in attributing the service sector's vote mainly to the PCP-PS camp rather than the PSD or CDS. The vote totals for the right did not change from 1983 to 1985 (around 40 percent), the PRD vote taking the greatest toll on the PS-PCP. This confirms the proposition that the service sector did in fact transfer its votes from the traditional left parties into the PRD, setting up the later movement to the PSD. Both methods of analysis point to the fluidity of the sector's vote and the likely doubling of the PSD's share in 1987. The sharp rise in the PSD's percentage indicated in Eurobarometer 28 (October–November 1987) may have been due to lingering campaign effects, again suggesting that the PSD as a political organization was particularly efficient in conveying its message.

The PSD was able to bring the service sector over to its side, but to what extent did it achieve a solid multiclass coalition, taking with it at least some parts of the industrial working class? Rehegemony through bipolarization assumed that the working class was internally divided along political and ideological grounds: those with more leftist leanings would be less likely to vote over time, and others would probably be won over when the party campaigned against the Socialist austerity governments. The Eurobarometers only partly substantiate this expectation. The sharp drop in overall working-class support for the left from October 1985 to April 1986 highlights a deradicalization of the class, accentuating political and ideological divisions that were already present. Table 5.7 shows that revolutionary zeal, as expressed in support for the Communist party, was never particularly impressive. The Communists were not able to get more than about one-quarter of the working class to support it electorally, with that percentage descending to under 10 percent at times. The Socialists could probably claim to be the party of the working class better than any other. They consistently gained pluralities of support, especially after the PRD disappeared as a serious contender. The left as a whole averaged nearly two-thirds of working-class support. Nevertheless, the right was able to gain a majority precisely during the 1987 electoral period. Proletarian instincts were apparently submerged by many of the same factors that swung other social categories around to the PSD.

TABLE 5.6. Eurobarometer Estimates of White-collar
Vote by Party, 1985–89

| | Eurobarometer | | | | | | | | |
	24	25	26	27	28	29	30	31	Mean
Party									
PCP	18	9	11	6	2	6	7	6	8
PRD	18	7	6	8	2	2	3	0	6
PS	30	39	31	31	30	40	31	38	34
PSD	28	41	46	48	60	49	54	49	47
CDS	6	4	6	8	6	3	5	7	6
Left	66	55	48	45	34	48	41	44	48
Right	34	45	52	56	66	52	59	56	53

TABLE 5.7. Eurobarometer Estimates of Working-class Vote, 1985–89

| | Eurobarometer | | | | | | | | |
	24	25	26	27	28	29	30	31	Mean
Party									
PCP	27	11	15	16	7	13	10	19	15
PRD	14	4	7	5	1	0	2	0	4
PS	31	41	44	40	40	39	51	43	41
PSD	23	35	30	35	49	44	31	33	35
CDS	5	8	4	5	3	4	4	5	5
Left	72	56	66	60	48	52	63	62	60
Right	28	43	34	40	52	48	35	38	40

The ecological estimates produced a stronger working class left bias. Table 5.8 shows the right obtaining less than one-quarter of the vote until 1987 compared to a somewhat higher number from the Eurobarometers. Both ecological estimates and Eurobarometers highlight the gains made by the PSD-CDS in 1987. In 1983, the year of relative Socialist ascendency, the PS alone obtained over half of the industrial workers' vote according to the ecological estimate. Consistent with prior findings, the PRD appears to have chopped PS working-class support in half. Yet if PS, PCP, and PRD figures are summed, the total is exactly the same as in 1983 for the combined PS-PCP total. Both the Eurobarometers and the ecological data agree with the overall trends: the left generally captured between half and two-thirds of working-class votes, with the right narrowing the difference considerably by the 1987 election. As was the case with the service sector, PRD-induced defections from the PS probably set the precedent for the PSD's success in 1987.

These trends point to the existence of some key conditions for right ascendancy. The fact that both the service sector and the working class proved vulnerable to similar patterns of wavering electoral support for the left allowed the PSD to gain its 1987 majority. But it would be inaccurate to say that the working class was nearly as unproletarian as the service sector. While working-class leftist instincts were not strong enough to enable it to resist PSD overtures in 1987, table 5.7 shows that after a sharp initial drop, the working class tended to remain more firmly committed to the left. The service sector wavered most, providing the right with a new and critical urban social basis of support. The left lost its industry-service worker coalition; the new working class became a new petty bourgeoisie politically. The left also saw the working class abstain in greater numbers in 1987, probably further imperiling its electoral fortunes.[20]

TABLE 5.8. Ecological Estimate of Vote by Workers in Secondary Sector

	Year			
	1983	1985	1987	Mean
Party				
PCP	16	14	11	14
PRD	—	27	6	11
PS	56	27	34	39
PSD	17	21	42	27
CDS	5	5	2	4
Left	72	68	51	64
Right	22	26	44	31

Right Ascendency among Rural Classes

The ecological data suggest that many PSD or CDS adherents were from rural society. Indeed, the right's strategy of rehegemony through bipolarization *depended* upon having a stable base of support in the countryside. Other than large landowners, two classes comprised most of the rural social structure: the smallholders and the agricultural proletariat. After the 1974 coup, the large landowners cemented a coalition with smallholders, who provided key mass support against revolutionary forces during that period by staging various mass demonstrations and attacks on PCP headquarters in Santarem and Braga. Smallholders strongly attached to their farms perceived the agrarian reform as deeply threatening, despite policies that focused upon collectivization of large landed estates in the south. An apparently irreversible link between the right and the smallholders was forged during the revolutionary period.[21]

As table 5.9 shows, the strength of the smallholder-right tie resulted in a statistical flaw in the ecological estimates of party support, which defied the logical limits of potential support for the right (PSD+CDS), exceeding 100 percent for those two parties in 1987. Conversely, for the Communists, the estimated smallholder vote was negative, again defying the logical minimum of possible support.[22] I conclude that smallholders gave overwhelming support to the right, forming a consistent kernel of electoral support.

TABLE 5.9. Ecological Vote Estimate for Self-employed Farmers

	Year		
	1983	1985	1987
Party			
PCP	-31	-22	-21
PS	17	21	10
PSD	69	67	94
CDS	33	32	12

This conclusion was also generally supported by the Euro-barometer surveys, which unfortunately do not distinguish between smallholders and agricultural workers.[23] Table 5.10 presents the various Eurobarometers and shows that on average the right garnered about two-thirds of the rural vote. Variance in the scores, however, with the scores for the Socialist party especially volatile, makes clear interpretation difficult. The small number of respondents (N=+/- 60) was probably a major cause of unreliable or questionable scores.[24] The small sample presumably deprived Communists of rural support because electoral successes in the Alentejo have actually depended upon many votes from the rural proletariat. The surveys do show that the right was again able to shift rural voters en masse to its camp during the 1987 election period, when over three-quarters of this social category claimed to have voted for the right.

The ecological estimates on table 5.11 emphasize relatively significant rural support for the left among agricultural workers. A quarter of the national rural proletariat voted for the PCP, making sense of the historically high vote total obtained by the Communists in the southern noncoastal zone of latifundia where they are especially concentrated. The PS, as an urban-oriented party competing with the Communists (who had a major commitment to land reform), picked up relatively few voters. Nevertheless, the PSD and to a lesser extent the CDS also found large numbers of followers, particularly in areas where the minifundia was the dominant farm structure. In this case, the north-south regional schism strongly penetrated the political predispositions of the same class, the agricultural proletariat.

TABLE 5.10. Primary Sector Vote Based on Eurobarometers

	Eurobarometer								
	24	25	26	27	28	29	30	31	Mean
Party									
PCP	6	9	14	0	6	0	0	0	4
PRD	19	0	0	5	3	0	0	0	3
PS	19	43	25	41	17	17	34	32	29
PSD	26	43	47	54	72	76	42	64	53
CDS	29	6	14	0	3	7	24	4	11
Left	44	52	39	46	26	17	34	32	36
Right	55	49	61	54	75	83	66	68	64

TABLE 5.11. Ecological Estimates of Agricultural Working-class Vote

	Year		
	1983	1985	1987
Party			
PRD	0	0	0
PCP	23	26	23
PS	13	16	8
PSD	41	36	47
CDS	14	13	6

The changing class nature of the social coalition formed by the various parties has added a key factor to the resurrected and renovated right hegemony: the ability to forge a multiclass coalition with sufficient breadth to sustain the right in power. While the industrial working class did not massively support the Communists at any point, the general erosion of the PCP's standing made it progressively less likely that the gains of the revolutions could be defended. The Socialists' ambition as a left catchall party was never fully realized due to its inability to depend reliably upon any class. Unlike the right, which could expect the faithful loyalty of the agrarian petty bourgeoisie and much of the northern rural population, the PS did not have a solid pillar. And it seems that the PRD acted like Portugal's Ross Perot: it dislodged many voters from the incumbent party but could not deliver a viable political package.

By 1987, this process sent disgruntled and frustrated voters over to the PSD. They became known as Cavaco Socialists—those who once voted for the PS but were attracted to Cavaco Silva's Social Democrats. This fusion of disparate elements of the social structure behind a national-popular program combining neoliberalism and a tinge of social democracy, carried the PSD to victory in 1987 and 1991. While the degree of association between PSD ideological themes and public opinion remained questionable, the seeds of a hegemonic project with a relatively broad basis of support were sown during the latter half of the 1980s. Although it did not realize Sá Carneiro's dream of one president, one government, one majority (due to the presence of Socialist leader Mário Soares as president), the multiclass coalition backing one government, one majority countered the dishegemonic legacy.

PSD's Hegemonic Project: Attraction to Other Social Categories

The ability of the PSD to link broad sections of various classes combined good luck, campaign skill, and positive outcomes when in power. For the hegemonic project to be sustained, its appeal would have to be generalized beyond class forces; in a strictly quantitative sense, these were insufficient to determine election outcomes. Whatever the impact of classes in the context of organized conflict and as representative of broad interest-based governing alternatives, other social categories would also have to lend electoral support to any of these alternatives.

The Weberian cleavages closest to ownership classes involve differential life chances: income and education. The Eurobarometers provide data concerning the relation between party and these two variables. Table 5.12 shows the electorate divided by income quartiles and party vote estimated for the 1985 and 1987 elections.

The relationship between party and income was significant only for the 1985 election.[25] The PRD proved especially attractive to the lowest income group, 63 percent of which voted for either the PRD, PCP, or PS. The contrast with 1987 could not be sharper; both the PRD and PCP lost nearly all of their support from that category. The PS picked up only a small portion of what the other left parties lost while the PSD obtained almost two-thirds of low-income vote in 1987. Moreover, the right did quite well among the highest income earners, putting top and bottom together into an electorally successful coalition. The left was able to retain a larger share of the middle-income categories in 1987, although it lost support across all the categories when compared to 1985. The right was concentrated somewhat less in the middle class in comparison to the lowest and highest quartiles[26] Apparently the right was appealing to those with the most to lose or the most to gain.

TABLE 5.12. Income Quartiles by Party Vote: Eurobarometers 24, 28 (1985, 1987)

	Eurobarometer									
	24					28				
	Income Quartile									
	Low			High	Party Vote	Low			High	Party Vote
Party										
PRD	26	17	17	15	18	1	7	2	3	3
PCP	15	18	17	18	17	4	5	10	3	5
PS	22	27	29	30	28	29	39	34	32	33
PSD	33	29	28	29	29	62	48	49	57	55
CDS	4	10	10	7	8	4	1	6	6	4
Left	63	62	63	63	63	34	51	46	38	41
Right	37	39	38	36	37	66	49	55	63	59
Total (%)	15	23	33	30		28	16	24	32	N=498/502

TABLE 5.13. Education by Party Vote: Eurobarometers 24, 28 (1985 1987)

	Eurobarometer									
	24					28				
	Education Levels									
	Low			High	Party Vote	Low			High	Party Vote
Party										
PRD	17	17	21	16	18	3	3	0	83	3
PCP	17	18	14	16	17	6	4	3	0	5
PS	28	23	27	36	28	34	30	27	25	33
PSD	28	34	30	32	29	55	54	60	58	55
CDS	9	7	8	0	8	3	10	10	8	4
Left	62	58	62	68	63	43	37	30	33	43
Right	37	41	38	32	37	58	64	70	66	59
Total (%)	66	17	13	5		77	15	6	2	N=498/502

Education did not show a consistent pattern from 1985 to 1987 (see table 5.13). As with income, there was a sharp global decline of support for the left across all categories, although the lower education levels showed less decline than the others. This was rather fortunate for the left; about two-thirds of all respondents were in the lowest education level (stopped studying at age fifteen). The right pulled votes disproportionately from the more educated categories in 1987.

Gender-based patterns varied between electoral periods. In 1985, the PCP and PS were predominantly male parties, and the combined left did 10 percent better among men. The right had a masculine gender gap instead. By 1987, these differences all but disappeared. Among the two largest parties, the PS halved its gender gap among women, while the PSD nearly eliminated its deficiencies among men. There was virtually no difference between the left-right party scores and their support from men and women.

Age might be expected to produce political generations with distinct experiences. Younger voters might be least attracted to the left because they have endured little of the dictator ship's repression and might be unresponsive to anti-fascist appeals. By contrast, those whose early adulthood was shaped by the colonial wars and the revolutionary mobilization of the mid-1970s should consistently support the left. The oldest voters might also have suffered under the dictatorship but might be less decisively favorable to the left due to traditional attitudes and fear of political or economic instability. As table 5.14 indicates, the PCP in 1985 and the PS in 1987 did indeed receive disproportionate support from the revolutionary generation between ages twenty-five and thirty-nine. For both years, that age group was the most likely to vote for the left. The right was least successful with the group, garnering most of its supporters among those under twenty-five (especially in 1985) as well as among older generations.

TABLE 5.14. Age Groups and Party Vote: Eurobarometers 24, 28 (1985, 1987)

					Eurobarometer					
		24						28		
				Age						
			Over					*Over*		
	15–24	25–39	40–55	55	*Party Vote*	15–24	25–39	40–55	55	*Party Vote*
Party										
PRD	13	16	22	18	18	3	4	3	1	3
PCP	16	26	13	12	17	3	5	5	7	5
PS	29	31	22	29	28	37	41	28	28	33
PSD	39	21	31	32	29	52	45	60	60	55
CDS	4	7	11	9	8	5	6	3	5	4
Left	58	73	57	59	63	43	50	36	36	41
Right	43	28	42	41	37	57	51	63	65	59
Total (%)	16	30	27	27		13	27	29	32	N=498/521

The role of the Catholic church as a conservative ideological ally of the old regime implies that those expressing a strong attraction to religion should be drawn to the right. The Eurobarometers did not offer a consistent measure of religiosity. In Eurobarometer 24 a question about the importance of God was included and produced statistically significant values when crosstabulated with party. The PCP was very clearly the choice of seculars, obtaining the vote of nearly half of all such respondents (48 percent).[27] Conversely, the PSD was disproportionately represented among those who were most extreme in their positive evaluations of the importance of God (39 percent). The Socialists did not show strong tendencies in either direction. It was advantageous to have support among those claiming the strong importance of God because on a ten-point scale,nearly half of the voters (46 percent) gave themselves a ten. Those claiming lesser values were relatively few: only 17 percent were between 1 and 5 on the scale. Eurobarometer 25 directly asked, "How religious are you." The results were again statistically significant and reinforced the notion that the PCP and PS were especially attractive to seculars. The PSD and CDS were clearly favored by those claiming to be more religious.

Like the rural petty bourgeoisie, religious believers formed a base of loyal support for the right. Even if the left could claim the overwhelming adherence of true seculars, their relative scarcity made them of lesser value. These results were essentially similar to ecologically derived relationships, which showed a very strong relationship between the right vote and the percentage of churchgoers within a *concelho*. The combined left was negatively correlated with churchgoers (r=-.72). Table 5.15 shows that there was little change in the basic structure of cleavages underlying the party vote across three distinct elections. Among several correlations between a number of ecological variables and the left-right, the "churchgoer" variable had the most consistently high values.

TABLE 5.15. Ecological Variables and Left-Right, 1975, 1985, 1987 (correlation coefficients)

	Tendency							
	Left				Right			
	1975	1985	1987	Mean	1975	1985	1987	Mean
Variable								
Churchgoers	-.87	-.72	-.70	-.76	.87	.71	.69	.76
Value of industrial prod.	.48	.46	.46	.46	-.42	-.42	-.04	-.41
Birthrate	-.65	-.44	-.43	-.57	.66	.43	.43	.51
Pop. Density	.21	.09	.10	.13	-.16	-.05	-.01	-.07
Southerness	.72	.57	.54	.61	-.75	-.58	-.59	-.64
Smallholders	-.66	-.67	-.62	-.65	.59	.62	.55	.59

CONCLUSION

During the mid to late 1980s, the right was able to make itself more attractive to all social categories, although certain strengths stand out. For the 1987 election, the right overcame its male gender gap, equalizing the proportion of men and women voting for it. Given the right's tendency to emphasize religion and traditional values and roles, its ability to draw men in equal numbers to women was notable, perhaps indicating the new right's (and specifically the PSD's) presentation as a modernizing force as well as a defender of traditionalism. Generational factors remained less uniformly favorable to the right because the left could still draw upon a revolutionary generation to act as a base of support. As new generations enter the work force, however, the left will find its antidictatorship claim less relevant; the right has already attracted the youngest cohort group in 1987. This suggests that the left will have to rethink the ideological and political basis for its popular appeals as older themes lessen in salience over time.

With respect to income and education, the right was able to forge a trickle-down coalition between low- and high-income earners, whose endurance in the face of distributive conflicts will prove a test of political imagination and effective macroeconomic management. Similarly, among educational groups, the right tended to do well with more educated groups, leaving the left an opening for a populist appeal in the face of an economic downturn.

For many years following the 1974 coup d'état, Portuguese elections did not create the basis for either a leftist counterhegemony or a rightist resurrected and revitalized hegemony. Nevertheless, soon after the start of democratic consolidation, the right was in favorable position to institute its sweetened neoliberal policies as evidenced by the early AD victories in 1979 and 1980. These were precursors of the eventual PSD majority in 1987. By contrast, the left did not present itself as a viable governing alternative.

The long-standing impasse on the left was partly due to the pattern of cleavages, which gave the right a key advantage electorally from the highly reliable support of smallholders, religious believers, and northerners. But, the formation of a durable, broadly based, multiclass coalition only became a reality for the PSD in the mid-1980s. Key segments of the working class in both the secondary and tertiary sectors shifted from the left to the right in the 1987 election, due especially to the dislodging effect of the PRD, which made possible a realignment of the Portuguese electorate. Perhaps the PSD would have obtained its majority in any case, given the frustration with the Socialist austerity governments; but what little partisan loyalty might have existed for the PS was undermined first by the PRD, then by the PSD.

The transformation of the party system created a new dynamic among the parties, in particular between the PS and PSD. Programmatically, neither of these parties represented dramatically different models of society. Both were committed to a class compromise between elements of a dominant class saved from revolutionary overthrow by softliners and subordinate classes unable to find a viable political strategy for establishing and maintaining an alternative hegemonic project. Nevertheless, the PSD found the social and electoral support for asserting itself as the agent of change. Party hegemony and electoral success would not in itself assure the creation of a workable social settlement, such as the neocorporatist aspirations held by softliner advocates of the "northern solution." In fact, despite strong electoral backing for the PSD, the multiclass coalition proved more elusive among organized interest groups, as chapter 6 reveals.

SIX

LABOR AND THE SEARCH
FOR A SOCIAL SETTLEMENT

The dishegemony prevalent during the democratic consolidation involved the roles of labor and capital within the Eurocentered accumulation strategy that had been encouraged by all governments since 1976. Unlike the Spanish labor movement, which was sharply constrained by the terms of consociational democratization engineered by the political elite, Portuguese labor was catapulted into an intense battle over the terms of a post-transition social settlement. This battle involved working out clear sets of rights and obligations between workers and employers, many of which were legally inscribed in the 1976 constitution. Organized capital never fully resigned itself to the priorities enshrined there, joining with the political right in an anticonstitutional pogrom for much of the consolidation period. Organized labor, ideologically and politically divided, split over the broad parameters of the evolving political and economic model. As in the party arena, the relative unity of capital and the disunity of labor meant that the latter had little chance of successfully defending counterhegemonic goals. In the end, the Europeanization of Portuguese class relations meant that a class compromise had to be worked out that would be minimally acceptable to capital and labor.

PRELUDE TO CHANGE: CAETANO'S FAILED LIBERALIZATION

When Marcello Caetano took over from Salazar in 1968, intraregime softliners hoped that a transition from authoritarian to voluntary corporatism would take place. Decree 49-058 allowed workers to present their own candidates for union elections, and decree 49-212 forced firms to bargain in good faith.[1] These laws granted workers' organizations more autonomy from the state and allowed them—and (to a lesser extent), the Catholic church—to be one of the few institutions escaping total state domination.[2]

Yet the regime's faltering fortunes in the multifront colonial war diminished its tolerance for domestic opposition. The dictatorship's commitment to liberalization proved to be short-lived; it was reversed by 1970, eliminating some of the unions' brief liberties.

Unlike the immediate postwar years, greater industrialization coupled with international détente meant that despite the brevity of the liberalization, it was possible to form an elected interunion commission called the Intersindical on 1 October 1970. The commission was largely composed of metalworkers, bankers, retail clerks, and wool-products unions. The Intersindical became a coordinating executive committee for the opposition union movement. In January 1971, only four months after its creation, it already included forty unions and it persisted more or less intact despite regime persecution from 1970 to 1974. In its brief existence, the Intersindical managed to evolve organizationally, setting up work groups on union-related subjects, holding reunions with union delegates, and, by November 1973, decentralizing its operation on a regional basis. The *Secretariado* remained the executive organ responsible for presenting proposals and organizing meetings (Lima 1975, 14). By the time of the dictatorship's fall, the Intersindical could claim to be a nucleus for a new trade-union confederation to unite all workers under a single umbrella. Nevertheless, their history of struggle against repressive political conditions gave the independent unions added political and social militancy. When tied to the role played by revolutionary parties and unionists, this militancy produced a radical, counterhegemonic orientation during the revolutionary period. The union movement that struggled against the dictatorship was more part of the extraregime opposition hardliners than the Caetano-inclined softliners.

THE LABOR MOVEMENT DURING THE REVOLUTIONARY PERIOD

Despite the Intersindical's inroads upon the regime's corporatist unions, when the dictatorship's fell, the bulk of the unions were still led by elements appointed or approved by the corporatist regime. After the coup, the workers occupied the unions and typically expelled union leaders faithful to the old regime. This process highlighted the importance of the Communist party, whose members claimed a special right to lead the new unions. As Kohler (1982, 217) remarks, the Communists' "presence in numerous factories and professional fields made it easy for them to ensure that many of the newly formed executive committees were filled with their nominees." PCP success in this process reinforced its control over the Intersindical and ultimately any new trade-union confederation that might develop from the occupied unions.

Divisions within the left regarding the proper role and organizational principles for the trade-union movement crystallized during the revolutionary period.[3] Predictably, the Communists emphasized the consolidation of the trade-union organizational apparatus. This both continued previous Communist practices as well as reflected the PCP belief in fostering a radical trade-union apparatus to help the party's political goals. The Communists' union efforts stimulated the political forces to the right and left to challenge the new union leadership. Amid dramatically escalating demands—for higher wages, a national minimum wage, the expulsion of PIDE agents (ex-secret police), and even the nationalization of industries—the trade unions could not be expected to fall into the PCP's hands without fostering considerable opposition.

Opposition to the Communists took three basic forms. First, there was the syndicalist or far-left opposition that wanted to use the union movement to press for revolutionary demands, culminating in the formation of a decentralized popular democracy. This opposition took advantage of decentralized authority structures that replaced the rigid centralized control exercised by the authoritarian regime. The far left saw special promise in a parallel workers' movement based upon the formation of workers' councils (Comissões de Trabalhadores). From a historical perspective, the Communist strategy, which focused upon the union apparatus rather than the more decentralized organizations at the point of production, reflected the long-standing division between revolutionary syndicalists and the Communists.

Second, the softliners (both intra- and extraregime) favored reformist, cooperative trade unionism more amenable to a neocorporatist framework. Although this opposition had left and right wings and thus may have accepted a policy of greater or lesser confrontation with recalcitrant employers, both wings wanted to avoid Communist dominance of the trade-union movement and excessive trade-union radicalism.

Last, employers were concerned with both the long-term ideological and more immediate economic effects of Communist control. Political conditions during the transition made employers' associations prone to party fights over the paradigmatic struggle of the revolutionary period, with the major advocates for responsible unionism coming from the reformist Socialists and Social Democrats.

From April 1974 to November 1975, clashes among the revolutionary syndicalists, Communists, and reformists had profound long-term regime implications. A central issue facing these contending factions was unity of the trade-union movement. On 30 April 1975, the Revolutionary Council approved laws granting the Intersindical the commanding role over the union movement.[4] The law recognized the Intersindical as the only legitimate national organization of Portuguese labor unions and prevented new unions from being established in any region where one already existed. In effect, the Intersindical could now legally seek to shelter all industrial and craft unions under its umbrella; it seemed that the single trade-union confederation was to be the one most influenced by the PCP.

The first Trade-union Congress occurred during the hot summer of 1975. Compared to its competitors, the PCP was best able to exert control over events. It secured a majority in the newly elected Secretariat, although it made room for the representation of other elements and tendencies as well. It was able to contain challenges by parts of the revolutionary left who denounced the PCP-endorsed MFA-people alliance as an effort to limit the goals and militancy of rank-and-file workers.

The elimination of the far left's military support following the events of 25 November 1975 meant that the Communists could now enjoy greater overall control of the Intersindical, even if at a certain cost in terms of a changed, more conservative balance of forces at the national level. With the ouster of COPCON commander Otelo Saraiva de Carvalho, the far left's major advances in the workers' committees as well as within the military (SUV) were either eliminated or had lost government support. While the workers' committees were not liquidated, the trade unions became increasingly more important.[5]

As the radical and populist forces lessened in importance, the trade unions' role in defense of the gains of the revolution increased. But, the unions were unable to perform the political functions of restoring working-class power at the national level. Unlike political parties, they could not be truly hegemonic agencies but were inevitably drawn into narrowly economic struggles. Many strikes during 1976 were primarily over economic issues, as workers attempted to consolidate wage gains in light of escalating inflation.[6] Defense of the revolution simply could not depend chiefly upon the trade unions.

The weakening of the far-left challenge to the Communist party caused the conflict between the PCP and the Socialist-Social Democratic opposition to heat up. The law recognizing the Intersindical as the sole confederation was subject to acute criticism from Social Democratic and Socialist quarters. The Communists were seen as wanting to cement their historic legations to the trade unions through legal decree and thereby preempt any possible counterorganizing efforts. This dispute reached a head at the beginning of 1976 with the publication of the Open Letter (Carta Aberta). The Open Letter was a petition primarily signed by sympathizers of the Socialist and Popular Democratic (PS, PPD/PSD) parties, and it focused upon the imposed unity of the trade-union movement. The Socialists wanted different ideological tendencies to be explicitly represented within the trade unions. From their perspective, this could mean either the establishment of a single democratic and independent union central open to competing political perspectives or, failing that, the erection of parallel unions and ultimately a competing confederation, in obvious violation of decree 215-b/75.[7]

The Communist response was predictably defensive. They called for the independence of the trade unions from the government and political parties, insisting that splitting up the workers' movement along political and ideological lines could only lead to its weakening.[8] Cunhal said:

> Union pluralism would cause the creation of competing unions, each with its own internal life subordinated to the party tendency dominating that union, where true class freedom would be quelled by the sectarianism animating the formation of the union. Union Freedom can only be assured by

unity [unicidade]. . . . The essential point regarding union independence is the independence of a class. Union pluralism
would signify the absolute domination of the unions by the
parties . . . in the concrete conditions in Portugal today, the
independence of the unions can only be assured by unity. (as
cited in Lima 1975, 37)

The reformists argued that workers' unity could not be legis-
lated from above; that the Communists only supported such unity
because they controlled the Intersindical; that there was insufficient democracy within the Intersindical to assure the representation of minority views; and that in a country with many parties,
there should naturally be many unions. Moreover, PS leader Mário
Soares has argued that the PS even proposed in the aftermath of the
1974 coup a common program of the left that might conceivably
have led to a widely shared counterhegemonic strategy. According
to Soares, the PCP undermined all prospects for reaching such an
agreement by "privileging its alliance with the MFA, linking itself
to pseudounitary movements like the MDP/CDE and seeking to
expel socialists from the union movement" (Soares 1979a, 14).

Cesar Oliveira and others have pointed to the fact that this
split reflected the ideological differences between the PCP and more
reformist parties and that also represented a social cleavage. Unions
that signed the Open Letter included an overwhelming number of
organizations in the service sector; only two of sixteen were not
from that sector.[9] A regional pattern was also evident because Communist strongholds were generally not supportive of the Open Letter movement. No unions participated from industrial Setúbal or
the land-reform areas of the Alentejo. Conversely, areas of Socialist
support such as Faro and Coimbra were visible as were the more
conservative zones prone to right-wing (as well as Socialist) sympa-
thies such as Aveiro, Vila Real, and Bragança. While the Open Letter
movement did not explicitly aim to cement an institutional cleavage within the labor movement, the presence of key social and geographic divisions made such an evolution all but inevitable
(Oliveira 1978, 20).[10]

THE LABOR MOVEMENT DURING THE
DEMOCRATIC CONSOLIDATION

The impossibility of creating an effective counterhegemonic
trade-union strategy during the period of democratic consolidation

became increasingly evident. In mid-1977, the Congresso de Todos os Sindicatos (Congress of All Unions) was held. Meant to be a symbol of solidarity for workers and unions, its results were contradictory. On the one hand, the Socialists failed to organize the congress on the basis of political tendencies. In fact, Socialist protests notwithstanding, some of the party's own members participated in the congress and obtained important posts in the elected Secretariat (for example, Kalidas Barreto and Santana e Costa). On the other hand, the congress could not realize its long-term aim of preventing the formation of an alternative trade-union confederation.

These contradictory results relate to the Communists' political strategy: the belated formation of a majority of the left government, which naturally meant some accommodation with the Socialists on trade-union matters.[11] The Communists were willing to compromise to a certain extent on the membership of the Secretariat, which in any case bolstered the nascent confederation's image of class unity across party or ideological lines. The revolutionary syndicalists similarly obtained some representation at the national level as well, finding strength in the Union of Textile, Woolens, and Clothing Workers of the South.[12]

Ultimately, however, the Open Letter movement was a precursor to the formal split between Communist and reformist (PS, PPD-PSD) tendencies within the Portuguese trade-union movement.[13] The dissenting unions left the CGTP and formed its primary competitor, the União Geral de Trabalhadores, in October 1978. The minority Socialist government had made this possible by revoking the various laws guaranteeing a single trade-union confederation.[14] Under Minister of Labor Maldonado Gonelha, the PS sought to break the spine of the Intersindical by complicating the way in which dues were collected, making the matter largely a union responsibility, with dues no longer deducted automatically from a worker's paycheck. Trade-union matters were hotly political, with the attacks upon the CGTP simply another component of the hostility between the hard- and softliners among the political parties.

The left failed to develop a coherent counterhegemonic strategy that could blend direct democracy, an organization labor movement, and parliamentary aspects of democratization. The intraregime softliners tantalized the Socialists by offering to join in a Euromodeled hegemonic alternative that would be especially attractive to them. The social settlement proposed by reformists sought to counteract the historic tendency of southern European countries to gravitate toward the conflict model of industrial relations. The inspirational ideal was clearly not traditional state-dominated corporatism but the northern model of a cooperative regime. Voluntary corporatism meant that an inclusive process of consultation between social partners would replace both anticapitalist radicalism and entirely decentralized market mechanisms. Macroeconomic policies and objectives such as growth rates, employment, inflation, and income distribution could be subject to negotiation.[15]

The emerging split within the trade-union movement during the first years of the democratic consolidation pit the Communists and other radical leftists lacking electoral support but deeply involved in union affairs against reformists with electoral support but fewer roots in labor organizations. What was at stake was the model of social settlement: would radicals cause Portugal to inevitably fall to the conflict pattern typical of southern Europe, or would a neocorporatist and cooperative model result from reformists' control of government?

In chapter 1 I mentioned several conditions characterizing the neocorporatist postwar settlements. Portugal can be evaluated in terms of these conditions as a means of anticipating the likelihood that the reformists' northern aspirations would be successfully incorporated into the overall hegemonic project.

- The union movements had to organize a high proportion of the working population.
- They needed well staffed and financed bureaucratic bodies to allow national union leaders to exert reliable centralized control over rank-and-file members and follow through on tripartite agreements.
- Under neocorporatist arrangements, the ideal union movement was composed of a single peak organization or several bodies with a history of cooperation or nonideological competition.
- The role of Communists needed to be limited, especially when there were several peak organizations.
- Employer organizations resisted broad ideological attacks upon the rights and legitimacy of organized labor.

Union Membership, Density, and Structure

How has the Portuguese union movement evolved regarding its ability to organize a high proportion of the work force? Overall membership information has never been very reliable because published union membership figures presumably have been inflated. Membership criteria have been broadly and variably defined, even changing from union to union. One union official mentioned that a worker is still counted as a member even if he or she has not paid dues for six months.[16] Generally, members must formally resign in order not to be counted (Kohler 1982, 241). These circumstances have made the clear identification of members problematic, not to mention the differentiation between active and conscientious as opposed to unenthusiastic members by default. Apparently, some laxity in counting members was true for unions adhering to the CGTP as well as the UGT.[17]

Using journalistic and other published sources, it is possible to estimate union membership.[18] Castanheira (1981) states that in 1981 the CGTP included the majority of organized workers: around 1.5 million of the 3.5 million in the work force (43 percent).[19] This figure was quite close to that claimed by the CGTP itself: 1.6 million (45 percent). Castanheira estimates the UGT total as closer to 300,000 (9 percent). Kohler, however, suggests that the UGT figure was much higher because "the CGTP-IN is twice as strong as the UGT" and cites a figure of 600,000 UGT members in 1979 (1982, 219–20). Castanheira (1985) eschews any precise percentages, saying that based on results in the votes for workers' commissions, the CGTP represented the majority of organized workers.

Other data sources are not much more help. Eurobarometer 30 (1988) included an item on union membership but inexplicably did not code responses to distinguish between affiliation in a CGTP or UGT union. As far as overall membership levels were concerned, the Eurobarometer 30 indicated that only 11 percent of all households had a union member, and only 6 percent of actual respondents claimed to be a union member. Broken down by recoded occupation (variable 710), 8 percent of those in the working class and 13 percent of those in the middle class had someone in the household who claimed to be a union member.[19] Interview and sampling bias might explain the exceptionally low figure for unionization, although Castanheira (1985) admits that unionization rates have gone down during the 1980s. Mário Pinto, a long-time observer of Portuguese trade unions, has concluded that the "real union rate is less than 40 percent, but it is hard to determine it any more accurately than that. It is universally acknowledged that in the last few years the overall unionization rate has declined. The UGT, however, is still growing" (1990, 252). If about half the work force was organized, this would constitute a relatively high percentage in Europe as a whole and a very high percentage among southern European countries, where union density has remained low.[20]

Because it is difficult to pin down the percentage of the work force organized by the labor movement, it is hard to say whether Portugal has met the first prerequisite of the neocorporatist model. The country had a history of involuntary corporatism, so there was a high probability of a carryover effect during the initial years of the democratic consolidation. Whether this effect endured into the 1990s is more uncertain.

Another organizational precondition for neocorporatism concerns the organization, staffing, and financial condition of the trade-unions. The presence of centralized structures that could oversee local unions and rank-and-file movements was necessary in order to make the union confederation a trustworthy social partner. In Portugal, these characteristics have been affected by the history of the dictatorship, which did much to structure the unions that emerged after the coup.

In part, Portuguese unionism resembles that of other European countries, with members organized along industrial and geographic lines. Nevertheless, because many of the current unions were based on the inherited structures of the dictatorship's official unions, it was natural for them to take up some of the particular characteristics of the latter. Specifically, the dictatorship's official unions were heavily based upon occupations and professions rather than industries or sectors and tended to be fragmented along geographic lines. Only a few occupational groups (especially liberal professions) were exempt from the legal obligation to form a union by district rather than for the country as a whole. Within a single plant, workers with a distinct professional status were organized into a multiplicity of unions, making collective action very difficult. The combination of professional rather than branches-of-industry criteria and district rather than national jurisdictions meant that the unions were small and limited. Pinto remarks, "As the unions had a reduced number of members and territorial breadth, it is not unlikely that they would, as a rule, have great financial fragility . . . and, as a consequence, also an accentuated organizational weakness" (Pinto 1973, 11). Thus, the organization of unions under Salazar was meant to limit the scope and impact of workers' demands.

Both major confederations have attempted to deal with this problem of organizational fragmentation and weakness.[21] Specifically, unions have sought to establish vertical structures that would include all of a plant's workers in a single union and thus avoid crisscrossing occupational categories to reduce union bargaining strength. In the UGT, a special effort to verticalize structures met with some success, particularly where it was possible to establish a new union based on individual membership. But major opposition to verticalization was found among preexisting regional sections, even among UGT unions.

Local unions, organized by either profession or branch of industry, may group themselves into national federations—railways, merchant marine, metalworkers, and so on. While federation structures have been similar to the occupationally oriented local unions, there have been attempts to create branch unions. As the CGTP has stated, "The evolution [of the federations] is moving in the direction of an association organized along industry branches rather than individual professions" (CGTP 1981, 66). Within a district or smaller local area, unions may participate in a *união de sindicatos*—that is, a coordinating unit where issues are discussed that concern the labor movement in the area.

The two confederations each exhibit specific characteristics. According to Castanheira (1981), the CGTP is composed of sixteen federations covering many sectors and industries: electrical, railways, hotels, tourism, merchant marine, metallurgy, cellulose, paper, printing, ceramics, cement and glass, commerce, construction and wood milling. These federations include 175 individual unions. They are concentrated in the secondary sector, branching into both light and heavy industry, and especially in the major nationalized industries. CGTP unions include a fair representation in the tertiary and primary sectors as well.

In contrast to the CGTP's 175 member unions, only forty four belong to the UGT. These are concentrated in the tertiary sector, particularly banking, insurance, offices, and commercial aviation. Some (between 20 and 25 percent) are parallel unions set up to compete with the Communist-influenced ones that previously existed. Like the CGTP, the UGT wanted to create more vertical unions, resulting in eight industry-based ones (Kohler 1982, 221). Unfortunately, the total expanse of the UGT in terms of industries and sectors was not detailed in the union's 1981 program, which simply stated, "Today, we are implanted in almost all economic sectors, making it important at the present to give maximum priority to the constitution of Democratic National Unions in the (few) remaining sectors where, until this point, it has not been possible to do so" (UGT 1981, 2). The UGT has not developed the network of federations that typified the CGTP because it lacked a sufficient number of constituent unions to justify this format.[22] The heart of its support has remained the banking, insurance, and office-workers unions.[23] In general, as Pinto (1990, 251) concludes "Portuguese unions are not highly centralized. . . . Collective bargaining is principally at the industry and also the company level." The history of collective bargaining has worked against centralized, tripartite formats, which depend more on confederation-level negotiations.

The strengthening of trade-union organizations as centralized bargaining agents depended not simply upon reorganization, but also upon the availability of resources to support training, publications, office staff, field agents, and so on. To a limited extent, the political parties and associated foundations have provided some of these resources; but the lingering fragmentation of the unions, relatively small staffs, and weak finances work against centralized bargaining. The need for organizational evolution among the unions, strengthening the unions and stabilizing or increasing their penetration into the work force, indicates the problems likely to be faced by neocorporatist arrangements in Portugal. Both the CGTP and the UGT have suffered from organizational handicaps insofar as the heritage of corporatism weakened their structures or the competition between confederations depleted resources and obviously resulted in less organizational centralization of the labor movement than is ideal for tripartite bargaining.

While a single representational monopoly would lend itself most easily to such bargaining, neocorporatism might succeed with several confederations as long as they have a history of cooperation or nonideological competition. The conflict regimes of the south have been especially prone to the appearance of trade-union confederations paralleling the European ideological spectrum. The Portuguese case, with its divisions between the Communist and reformist union confederations, fits the southern type well. The following discussion goes into greater detail regarding the political composition and ideological characteristics of the two unions to highlight the ideological nature of union competition. I assess some of the dynamics of that competition by examining the confederations' stands regarding the revision of the labor code, an issue that sparked much controversy during the 1980s.

Although the CGTP has demonstrated several political tendencies, the Communists have dominated the leadership structures. According to Kohler (1982, 241), of the thirty five members of the CGTP executive committee in 1980, twenty eight were members of the Communist party. Castanheira (1981) admits that "the

CGTP enjoys the support of diverse organizations: the PCP, UEDS, Base-FUP (defenders of self-managed socialism), UDP (pro-Albania [of old . . .], Marxist-Leninist), the PSR (Trotskyist) and diverse elements and leaders of the PS. . . . In any case, the PCP enjoys a hegemony at all levels of the organization." He also notes that "in a general way, the various political minorities (i.e. non-PCP) have a smaller representation in the leadership of the diverse structures of the CGTP than within the individual unions of which it is composed."[24]

The representation of the Communists and far left in the CGTP was reflected in the confederation's perception of its role during democratic consolidation. It argued that "the defense of the democratic regime and Constitution resulting from the April 25 Revolution is an integral part of the struggle for the rights and interests of workers and for the construction of a society without exploiters" (CGTP 1986b, 13). It favored "the struggle for the defense and consolidation of the conquests of the Revolution which form an integral part of the democratic regime" (CGTP 1986b, 14). In the UGT, the CGTP perceived an entity "whose constitution, program, and above all practice and position regarding the democratic-constitutional regime" have not made it "an organization which defends the interests of workers, but an instrument of division controlled by the right" (CGTP 1986b, 19). The prospects of collaboration between confederations were marred by competing perceptions of the hegemonic project, a replay of political divisions between the hard- and softliners among the old extraregime opposition during the dictatorship.

The shared party-union analysis led to a common counter-hegemonic strategy. Typical of many other Communist unions in capitalist countries, it placed a strong emphasis upon mass demonstrations, with the aim of creating a social momentum strong enough to affect legislation. The ultimate goal was to reestablish a working-class agenda at the national level rather than simply shape wage and employment conditions at the enterprise level. Castanheira (1985, 811) characterized the CGTP's approach in this way:

> First, [the confederation would offer] a sectoral critique, passing rapidly to a global critique of policies promulgated by the executive; second, after fighting specific policies, the struggle would turn against the government itself, ending with the demand for the fall of the government and its substitution. Depending on the situation, the CGTP would call for the inter-

vention of the President, or the realization of early elections, hoping these would produce an alternative political solution.

The politicized and counterhegemonic nature of the CGTP's agenda during the initial phases of democratic consolidation was expressed directly in its three declared general goals: "the struggle for Democracy, National Independence, and Socialism" (CGTP 1981, 11). It explicitly rejected neocorporatist arrangements, denouncing "practices of class conciliation, based on the acceptance of 'pacts' or 'social accords.'" The mobilization of workers was undertaken in the hope of "consolidating the constitutional regime and moving toward a society free of exploitation and oppression—socialism." Paradoxically, in the aftermath of the significant socioeconomic changes, the CGTP (like its party mentor, the PCP) became a conservative force, wanting to preserve the structural reforms and legal guarantees embodied in the 1976 constitution.[25]

If nonideological competition was a prerequisite to neocorporatist arrangement, the genesis and political roots of the UGT did little to improve it. The union's structure bore the marks of the softliner party pact from which it stemmed. By January 1981, the PSD had twenty four of the forty four unions, while the Socialists controlled the others—notably SITESE (office workers) and Sindicato dos Bancários de Sul e Ihas (southern bank workers), the most important unions. The executive was organized along party lines: the Socialists controlled thirteen seats, and the PSD held eleven. Over the years, the balance has changed somewhat; "the results of internal elections were accepted, and now the Socialists are slightly in the majority" among the unions (Pinto 1990, 250).[26]

The constituent parties imbued the UGT with a reformist orientation. The PPD-PSD had from the start argued that "it falls to the unions to constitute an autonomous project for the society of the future . . . because of this project's autonomy, it must express the aspirations of the workers during the course of their long historical experience, and this project cannot be confounded with any program of a political party nor should it submit to such programs" (PPD 1974, 67). While the unions could engage in action resulting "in social transformations through political legislation," this was still conceived as distinct from a "necessary independence from all those interests of parties that intend to direct or dominate the workers" (1974, 67). In short, the unions were conceived largely as a pressure group acting on behalf of workers, not another component of revolutionary change based on a party's counterhegemonic ideal. Ideally, unions were to be moderate but progressive bodies autonomously acting upon employers and elected governments to secure workers' interests.

The PS's perspective was rather similar. The party believed that the union movement was, along with political parties, an important cog in the formation of open and democratic society, in contrast to the PCP's totalitarian project. The Socialists had a specific conception of socialism that emphasized incremental working-class assumptions of positions of power within a globally capitalist economy. As one prominent Socialist leader wrote; "the intervention of the State in the economy constitutes one means for promoting socialization: it is the top-to-bottom component of the socialist process. The other means of promoting socialization consists of the progressive participation of the workers in the direction of the economy: this is the bottom-to-top component" (Cardia 1979, 77). For Cardia, this bottom-to-top process could occur both at the enterprise and the national levels. He argued that unions could have a national role insofar as the policymakers could be provided with "points of view of the social partners expressed institutionally in a national incomes and price council" (Cardia 1979, 80).

Socialists generally believed that unions should be among the actors involved in a national dialogue about economic policy but insisted that the unions were not political parties and could not therefore be expected always to agree even with Socialist parties in power: "a socialist policy doesn't signify systematic or habitual alignment with union demands" (Cardia 1979, 80). Tripartism involved three-sided bargaining among government, unions, and employers, bringing workers sufficiently into the process to have their demands and opinions aired.

These party conceptions oriented the UGT's program, which emphasized three broad goals: (1) the restructuring of unions (and the union movement) along different organizational lines; (2) encouraging the pursuit of a particular set of macroeconomic policies as well as a certain orientation to sectoral policy; and (3) stabilizing the democratic regime. The first goal depended on a conception of *democracia sindical*—union democracy—which the confederation perceived in terms of the experience of "other Democratic States in Europe," where unions "represent a counterweight to economic and entrepreneurial power." The UGT promised the organization of workers "in structures established uniquely to defend the class interests of its members." This was meant to "give the possibility for hundreds of thousands of workers currently dis-contented with the political orientation of the CGTP unions" to find a less politicized alternative (UGT 1981, 2).

In addition, the UGT recognized that divisions among member unions would undercut its effectiveness as a peak association. Therefore, it recommended the professional formation of trade-union officials so that they would emerge with a common apprecia-tion of the issues and foster an attitude of *cooperativismo* or collaboration among workers.

The goal of greater professionalization and centralization of control over the trade-union movement was linked to the confeder-ation's overall ambition of becoming a full social partner at national policy-making levels. The confederation's program featured many of the ideological predispositions of other labor movements in the neocorporatist European north: it called for a social partnership between employers and unions while concurrently issuing more radical demands for "the democratization of the economy," "indus-trial democracy" and "democratic socialism" (UGT 1981, 8).

The UGT emphasized collaboration not only among workers but among all social partners. According to the action program, eco-nomic progress depended upon "the global policy of prices and income[, which ought to be] consensual" (UGT 1981, 2).[27] Incomes policies were part of a general package backed by the union move-ment to improve the lot of the working class. This union confedera-tion acknowledged that overcoming economic crises required some short-term tradeoffs and that it would be willing to restrain its members' bargaining capacity for the national interest: "the condi-tions of crisis and the need to reanimate investment might, in some cases, impose temporary sacrifices which the democratic union movement . . . is predisposed to accept if they were accompanied by a reduction of inequalities and an increase in the participation of workers in economic decisions, both at the level of the enterprise as well as at the social level (1982, pt. 2, 2).

The participation scheme was intrinsically tied to the UGT's conception of democratic planning (*planeamento democrático*). This planning involved both substance and process. Substantively, it included the "satisfaction of the population's basic goals, includ-ing the right to labor within a perspective of full employment . . . [and] the bettering of the conditions of life, including a better distri-bution of income." Process goals focused on "the greater participa-tion of the workers in economic life pointing to the establishment of a true policy of economic Democracy" (UGT 1981, 3).

The economic crisis called for the development of a social contract "with the various social partners" and the definition of such targets as "the percent increase of the proportion of salaries within national income, employment policy, holidays, vacations, minimum wage" (UGT 1981, 4). Rejecting a class-conflict approach, the UGT insisted that consensus and negotiation rather than confrontation would better satisfy national and class interests: "we seek to find solutions to our [national] problems by consensus. Moreover, consensus will only be possible if all Portuguese [workers, employers, and government] recognize that we are all part of a single community of interests. Portugal will only find successful solutions for its problems if we find a general and genuine consensus between all our people and institutions" (1981, 3).

Centralized national bargaining was also a means for overcoming weakness in the labor market. Liberal, pluralist-style unionism with an emphasis on local, decentralized bargaining to the relative neglect of top-level tripartism would only help the employers, who "prefer freely decentralized bargaining, as they believe that the unions are weak when unemployment is high. Under these conditions, the UGT thinks that a global policy of prices and incomes is indispensable. [To this end the] voluntary negotiation between the State, Workers and Employers [must occur]" (1981, 16). The neocorporatist hue of the UGT was again reflected its 1987 document *Contracto Social para a Modernização*, a detailed discussion of many problems such as continuing inflation, unemployment, income distribution, and labor legislation. The document mentioned that while enterprise and sectoral negotiations have their roles, "national and interconfederation levels are important because macroeconomic policies, fiscal, income, prices . . . [have the] rules of the game defined there assuring a stable framework for those who have to negotiate at sectoral or enterprise levels" (UGT 1987, 23). The UGT continued to acknowledge the role of tripartism as a key element in its overall orientation to unionism in Portugal.

Despite its apparent readiness to bargain with employers, the UGT was aware of left-wing criticism, which claimed that the UGT simply sought a neocorporatist framework for controlling workers in order to stabilize the existing set of exploitative social relations, not unlike the Panitch's critique (1976) of similar efforts by the British Labour party. The program specifically argued against a notion of "a social pact that stabilizes and protects a given conjuncture of the economic system and limits the demands [*poder reivindicativo*] of the workers." Rather, the project that it favored would "define new contours of the contract, broadening the concept of collective bargaining, including new aspects and extending the negotiations in more general terms that can decisively affect the workers' lives and establish minimum national working conditions" (UGT 1981, 16).

A content analysis of the 1981 programs of both labor confederations reveals their different orientations. I evaluated them in terms of the comparative space devoted by each to major issues. Table 6.1 exhibits the percentages of the union's programs in terms of nine basic areas and shows that the CGTP was more concerned with ideological and organizational questions. The UGT stressed specific favored policies, social welfare concerns, and other bread-and-butter issues. More precisely, the CGTP spent four times as much program space as the UGT discussing union principles and organization. The UGT spent three times as much space discussing sectoral policies; twice as much on prices, wages, and economic policy; and slightly less on social welfare issues. The more explicitly political nature of the CGTP was implied by the fact that it devoted nearly 15 percent of its program discussing workers' rights as they were guaranteed in the revolutionary 1976 constitution; by contrast, the UGT mentioned this only 4 percent of the time. Although not shown in this table, the CGTP used some of its time discussing sharply political issues such as nationalization, agrarian reform, and the role of social property. The UGT did not directly deal with these topics except in its review of banking policy and its mention of *cooperativismo*.

TABLE 6.1. Comparison of CGTP and UGT Programs

Category	Actual Pages in Program		Percent of Total	
	CGTP	UGT	CGTP	UGT
Prices, wages, taxes, economic policy	8.1	18.1	11.5	25.6
Union principles, organization, strategy	24.4	6.1	34.6	8.6
Social welfare, education	7.8	13.3	11.1	8.6
Workers' rights	10.4	3	14.8	4.2
Sector policies	4.1	11.7	5.8	16.6
Political analysis	5.9	5.5	8.4	7.8
International issues	4	3.2	5.7	4.5
Economic democracy	2.2	2	3.1	2.8
Other issues	3.6	7.7	5.1	10.9
Total	70.5	70.6	100.	100.

Even where there was agreement regarding the importance of issues, the confederations differed over the proper positions to adopt. For example, in one area where the two confederations spent nearly the same amount of space discussing—international affairs— the contrasting ideological affinities of each were obvious. The CGTP denounced stabilization policies associated with the International Monetary Fund:

> The application of the International Monetary Fund's economic, monetary and financial policies which resulted from the 1977 accords, namely the depreciation of the escudo, the wage ceilings, the credit restrictions, the limitations imposed on the development of the public sector, the attacks and lack of support given to the UCP's [farm cooperatives] and other cooperatives and self-managed firms, the liquidation of small and medium enterprises, the liberalization of imports, and the permitting of uncontrolled speculation have caused the deterioration of workers' living conditions and put seriously into question the future of independent economic development. (CGTP 1981, 27)

The CGTP was clear about the political nature of such policies as they were "inserted in the strategy of capitalist recuperation" as part of "a policy of submission to large capital, both national and international." Opposed to such submission, the CGTP insisted upon goals such as the protection of the nationalized sector "as a primary objective of the Union Movement" (1981, 29); the protection of agrarian reform; the support of the social sector, the maintenance of '*controlo de gestão*' (control over management); and the reinforcement of state planning. These were conquests of the revolution that were now to be deepened and protected, not distant pursuits to be eventually realized or means for harmonizing intrinsically antagonistic class interests.

The UGT program was less specific about defining the conquests of the revolution and commented upon structural reforms such as nationalization and agrarian reform in technical rather than broadly ideological terms. In analyzing the country's economic difficulties, the UGT placed little direct responsibility upon any program of capitalist recuperation and did not blame Western governments and agencies. For example, in the initial passages of the action program, the UGT presented a scenario of economic troubles that made no direct mention of the role of international capital as a prime culprit: "The decade of the 1970s, starting with the oil crisis of 1973, was marked by a series of problems which are yet today unresolved, especially those referring to the worsening of inflation, the increase in unemployment, the instability of the international monetary system, the appearance of strong disequilibriums in the external balance of payments, and the worsening of unequal conditions with the countries of the Third World" (UGT 1981, 1).

The UGT was created as part of the hegemonic project favored by the softliners, whose views were not identical but still found much common ground. The CGTP was a product of both the historic Communist approach to labor movements as well as the specific circumstances of the Portuguese transition. For northern-style neocorporatism to have any chance of being adopted in Portugal, some CGTP acceptance of the softliners' hegemonic project was needed. This would have meant either a change in the basic ideological orientation and political analysis of the PCP or a separation between the union confederation and the Communist party.

Tripartite Convergence in the Final Analysis?

The last condition necessary for the installation of neocorporatist arrangements concerns the willingness of employers to avoid broad ideological attacks on the rights and legitimacy of organized labor. The revolutionary aspects of the transition to democracy unleashed what employers perceived as a generalized attack on their own rights and legitimacy. For a bourguoisie unaccustomed to open class conflict on a relatively even playing field (like that found during the transition), the entire democratization experience was traumatic. It would have been hard enough for employers to accept a Spanish-style consociational arrangement that ensured their basic interests; the presence of workers' commissions, nationalized factories, and a leftist constitution was an absolute role reversal from the norm under Salazarism.

Portuguese employers organized themselves into three primary organizations after the fall of Caetano: the Confederation of Portuguese Agriculture (CAP), the Confederation of Portuguese Industry (CIP), and the Confederation of Portuguese Commerce (CCP). This means that a reasonable degree of representational monopoly exists among employers despite the presence of long-standing regional trade associations (such as AIP—Association of Portuguese Industry) and employers' associations (north/Porto, south/Lisbon).

CAP and CIP have been vocal opponents of the post-transition dishegemony. The agricultural confederation has "strongly criticiz[ed] the collectivist approach to agrarian reform and the socialist guidelines laid down in the Constitution" (Pinto 1990, 253). The CIP has steadily denounced all traces of socialism and dishegemony. For example, a 1983 editorial in its magazine *Industria em revista* proclaimed that "all can see that the country's economic system, based on public initiative and limiting the capacity of private entrepreneurs, can't solve any of our great national problems." For the author, the dishegemonic character of the situation was obvious: "It will be necessary . . . to guarantee to each economic agent conditions like those which exist in the Europe with which we seek to integrate, for otherwise we will persist with a fundamental contradiction: we will have an economic system which continues essentially pointed towards socialism, while we want to participate in a community characterized by a market economy" (Industria em revista 1983, 5).

According to the CIP, all efforts to improve the performance of nationalized industries were hopeless unless "they kept in view the total privatization of the enterprises" (*Industria em revista* June 1988, 5). Structural reforms (making labor law flexible and privatizations) to eliminate "the last slices of the socialist economic model" were fruitless without a general revision of the constitution (*Industria em revista* May 1988, 5).[28] Pinto points out that nationalized industries were not represented within the CIP. Thus, "the representative strength of the CIP is not great. Perhaps this is why it has steadily maintained a very hard-line political position with regard to the rigidity of labour [/] legislation and to the socialist tendencies of the Constitution" (1990, 254). Whatever the reason, the industrialists' organization consistently made the policy paradigm an issue at the forefront of its agenda.

Along with privatization of industry, revision of the labor code was one of the prime requests of the CIP and employers who blamed the code for imposing impossible constraints upon the prerogative of employers to dispose of workers in response to market conditions. They argued that this structural rigidity was a prime cause of unemployment and a major contributing element to the absurd *salários em atraso*, the inability of economically ailing firms either to fire or pay workers for months at a time. A more detailed investigation of this issue will reveal relevant patterns in union, government, and employer relations.

Several attempts have been made to liberalize labor law: the AD governments in 1981, the PS-PSD grand coalition in the early 1980s, and the PSD governments in the mid and late 1980s. This issue has sparked active union resistance despite the ideological differences between the two labor confederations.

The reaction of the UGT to the Socialist-Social Democrat government's labor proposal highlighted a basic problem of the confederation: despite its ideological proximity to the executive, it could not consistently expect legislation to be easily defensible from a union point of view. In 1985, the UGT joined the CGTP in criticizing the government's *pacote laboral.* According to UGT general secretary Torres Couto, the government engaged in an "illegal and unconstitutional" process by not putting the package of proposed changes in labor legislation to public discussion. Despite the fact that the ruling coalition was composed of PSD and PS members, the proposed package—(according to Couto) and particularly the firing law—was even worse than that proposed by the AD government in 1981, which was composed of the PSD and the conservative CDS. The UGT was predisposed to engage in serious strike action in protest of this legislation, "if possible, in conjunction with the CGTP unions or independents." In a refrain that characterized the UGT, Torres Couto called for "coming to an agreement with the Government and employers in an authentic social pact for modernizing the economy, the only way in which we can confront with success the supranational challenge represented by the [entrance of Portugal into] the EEC" (*O Jornal* 1985, 22).

The CGTP's reaction to the government proposal was consistent with its general perspective on the political situation over the last few years. The CGTP consistently followed the same policy I have already outlined—that is, a defensive strategy to preserve the gains of the revolution. The proposed revision of labor legislation was inherently undesirable. The CGTP felt that after the great progress made during the transition, the current period and alignment of political forces could only take rights away from the workers, not enhance them. "Without prejudicing its permanent availability for dialogue and negotiation, the CGTP . . . will proceed by way of struggle, whose first step must be the dissemination to workers and public opinion in general its appreciation of such antidemocratic and socially backward projects" (*O Jornal* 1985, 22). For the CGTP, really there was little to discuss—compromise constituted an inevitable step backward from the advances of the revolution. For the UGT, compromise was desirable, but the other social partners were not accommodating: compromise came to be identified with unilateral labor concessions by employers, government, and unions. Oddly, employers as represented by CIP essentially agreed with the CGTP's reluctance to negotiate: compromise with the current system was a policy-paradigm problem not appropriate for tripartite bargaining, which required a legal framework acceptable to all social partners. For the CIP, creating a new paradigm was the issue rather than specific laws within the old paradigm.

The reformist parties and their union counterpart had attempted to institute neocorporatism without capital or much support from labor, starting the tripartite Permanent Council on Social Concertation (CPCS) in 1983. The CGTP viewed the CPCS "in the political and social context in which it was inserted, the forms it has taken, and its goals" to be "only an act of political propaganda" justifying the CGTP decision "to reject the seats offered to it . . . and denounce it as a political maneuver" (1986, 152). Among the social partners only the UGT wanted to negotiate within the dishegemonic policy paradigm. Even its participation, however, was predicated on political conditions such as the presence of the PS-PSD coalition in government during the first part of phase 3 (1983–85). With the PS out of government, Socialist militants within the UGT were less inclined than ever to go along with labor-code revisions.

The first version of the *pacote laboral* was introduced in January 1987 by the minority PSD government. The UGT refused to accept the government's proposals due to objections about the layoff policy; the CGTP remained outside the CPCS at that time and pursued its mass mobilization strategy of frontal opposition. When the July elections yielded a PSD majority and a revised *pacote* by November, the UGT was even more militantly against the proposal. The CGTP agreed, calling it "the most violent and destructive of the minimum guarantees of workers' protection and dignity ever drawn up in Portugal," especially because of employer discretion in determining just cause for firing decisions.[29]

The establishment of the CPCS was meant to provide a forum for resolving class antagonisms and agreeing on common goals and approaches. By centralizing acrimonious disputes over the labor code, the atmosphere was poisoned when other issues also proved contentious. During 1988, continuing controversies over the realism of the predicted inflation level, used as one base for determining wage settlements, combined with animosities arising from conflict over the labor code. Even after the government presented a third version of the labor code, the two union confederations found themselves united in opposition. The UGT proclaimed 28 March to be the date for a general strike opposing the government; the CGTP agreed with the concept and date as well.

The call for a general strike directed against the PSD government necessarily tore at the heart of the UGT, with PSD partisans markedly less enthusiastic about the planned event. The general strike took place as intended, but the PSD government passed the legislation anyway. Only the objection of President Mário Soares, elected by the combined efforts of the PCP and PS in 1986, prevented its implementation. The Constitutional Court, to which the legislation was sent, declared it out of conformity with the regime's constitution, forcing the PSD to rewrite it once more. In August 1988, the government passed the legislation again, only this time without further objections from Soares.

The trade union's experience in the CPCS in general and with regard to the labor-law revisions in particular set up a pattern of convergence between the two confederations. The CGTP, once wedded to an outsider's role in defense of radical counterhegemony, finally entered the CPCS in 1987 and moderated its principled opposition to national bargaining within a framework of emergent bourgeois hegemony.[30] Conversely, the tripartism-advocating UGT launched into militant opposition using political strikes and mass mobilization. While the party-based developments stimulated internal stresses within the UGT, the two confederations were still able to engage in a limited process of mutual recognition and agreement. This included further collaboration on a second general strike in the summer of 1989 and the acceptance of plans for summit meetings between the union leaderships.

AN UNCERTAIN MODEL OF INDUSTRIAL RELATIONS

The reconciliation between the two confederations occurred at a time of realignment in the power relations between dominant and subordinate classes. After 1986, when Portugal became part of the European Community, international pressure to conform to the postwar settlement model of labor relations (based on a capitalist accumulation strategy) expanded the relative power of severely weakened national capital and hastened the erosion of Portugal's recent history of counterhegemony and working-class power. The still tentative unity of the trade-union confederations was therefore *not* an expression of radical counterhegemony as much as an acknowledgment of working-class weakness in the face of PSD policy initiatives. Earlier, the social settlement of the European north had been used to foster the image of progressive Social Democratic neocorporatism in a context of democratic dishegemony. It was a hegemonic project whose insertion within Portuguese history was specific to the particular alignment of class forces, which had been tipped decisively against the dominant class, at least for an instant. When dishegemony was replaced by an ascendant PSD that was able to consummate the intraregime softliners' accumulation strategy, neocorporatism became a less important part of the hegemonic project.

That project has remained somewhat constrained by the absence of a PSD constitutional majority, the presence of former Socialist leader Soares as president, and the Constitutional Court. Thus, elements of the dishegemonic democracy remain because the PSD was not completely successful in monopolizing power and reshaping the class character of the state. The further revision of the constitution in 1989 did go a long way to dissipating dishegemonic residues and forming a less ambiguous policy paradigm. Whether the formation of a more distinctly bourgeois economic framework will be an added inspiration for the social partners to participate in neocorporatism remains to be seen. The events of the late 1980s show that at the same time that the labor movement was coming to accept elements of the neocorporatist viewpoint, the government was inclined to move away from it when it conflicted with key elements of the accumulation strategy.

The search for a social settlement in Portugal remains difficult in an era in which the postwar settlement throughout Europe has been subject to much internal change. In part, as Wiarda (1988, 281) has argued, the statist top-down legacy of Mediterranean culture has clashed with the liberalizing influences of the north. "At present the precise implications of this form of change for the affected countries [in southern Europe] are unclear." It does seem possible to discount one scenario advanced by Wiarda: "a full-fledged transition of growing corporate pluralism or neo-syndicalism to revolutionary socialism." Nor have "the demand and possibilities for an authoritarian solution [become] stronger." There is also little evidence that "a further fragmentation and disintegration of the social and political fabric" has taken place in which there is "almost complete subsystem autonomy, little attachment to a central core or consensual nucleus, virtually constant conflict, accelerating violence, morbific politics, competing group militias and the potential for much greater civil strife" (1988, 281).

Rather, the changing balance of class power has affected the predisposition of major social and political actors to pursue their interests through a given set of institutions. Neither neosyndicalism, narrow corporate unionism, radical political unionism, nor traditional neocorporatism have crystallized as a definite long-term pattern. In part, this paradigmatic ambiguity reflects the difficulties of reproducing the policies and governing arrangements of the core European countries in a country that remains a semiperipheral former imperialist on Europe's outer rim. Situational power as reflected in elections produced the possibility of ending much dishegemonic democracy through the PSD's governance. Institutions such as the CPCS were created to facilitate a northern social settlement. Yet the structural context of Portuguese capitalism continues to act as a constraint upon adoption of a neocorporatist order. Chapter 7 reviews the evolution of economic policy under dishegemonic conditions and ponders the effect of structural conditions upon the movement to a cooperative rather than a conflict-based regime.

SEVEN

THE POLITICS OF ACCUMULATION AND DISHEGEMONY

Much as the collapse of the old regime was a product of conflicting accumulation strategies, dishegemony during the democratic consolidation was a partial product of the ambiguous place of private capital within the post-transitional regime. In the aftermath of the hot summer of 1975, the country was faced with a complex set of property relations and accumulation imperatives. The nationalized industries constituted a significant nucleus of many capital-intensive firms in heavy industry (steel, cements, chemicals), infrastructure-oriented enterprises (electricity, transportation) and financial enterprises (banking and insurance). Through bank holdings, the state became a major owner in firms in many other sectors throughout the economy.[1] The private sector remained, however, the largest employer and had the largest number of enterprises given the preponderance of small and medium-sized firms in Portugal. Policies meant to help the country catch up to the standard of living in the rest of Europe were intrinsically hampered by a weak economic structure whose main comparative advantage was low wage labor.

This chapter will examine the attempts of governments and parties to deal with the interplay of electoral politics, which determined the political composition of governments, and the structural characteristics of the Portuguese economy, which set limits upon the range of accumulation strategies that could be followed. Briefly, the electoral argument states that immediately after the transition, elections affirmed dishegemonic economic policies as reflected in Socialist rule during phase 1. The Socialist government sought to find a middle way through policies promoting a regeneration of the private sector but without a sharp curtailment of the public sector. By phase 2, however, a gradual erosion of the middle way continued through the next phases, culminating in the PSD attempts at substantial reprivatization after EC integration.

Structurally, an analysis of the makeup of the Portuguese economy demonstrates that despite EC membership, the country faces serious obstacles in its quest to move from the semiperiphery to the core. The Portuguese bourgeoisie is poorly prepared to foster a high skill, high wage policy that would lead to rapidly rising incomes. Instead it must rely on an export-dependent accumulation strategy based on low-wage firms in key exporting industries. Major hurdles await democratically elected governments attempting to foster a new hegemonic project that can overcome the legacies of weak industrialization, susceptibility to external deficits, poorly defined firm ownership, social polarization, and political business-cycle constraints.

ECONOMIC POLICY DURING THE FOUR PHASES OF DEMOCRATIC CONSOLIDATION

During the four phases of democratic consolidation, economic policies were alternately directed at modifying or reversing basic structural changes produced by the 1975 hot summer or aimed at short-term macroeconomic stabilization (and quite often both). The former dealt largely with the scope and function of public and private sectors while the latter involved fiscal and monetary policy, especially as they were affected by balance-of-payment considerations. Political parties were obliged to deal with two coincidental transitions: from the colonial-protectionist accumulation strategy to a new European-centered one; and from a division of private and public sectors produced by revolutionary times to one compatible with the will of the Portuguese people as expressed through electoral mechanisms.

Phase 1: Contradictions of Dishegemony under the PS and Presidential Governments

The first elections for a postrevolutionary government occurred on 25 April 1976 and were somewhat inconclusive; the Socialists obtained an electoral plurality but not an outright majority. The PS had a strict policy at that time of eschewing formal alliances either to the left or the right. Because no other party or tendency could form a government, the Socialists agreed to form a minority executive based on understandings with the other parties.

During this period the Socialists embodied the essence of the dishegemonic situation they inherited from the revolution. Compelled to choose between contrasting social forces and their ideological emphases, their accumulation strategy was based less on abstract economic rationality than on political objectives such as social reconciliation. As Mário Soares wrote in 1977, the PS understood its mandate to be that of an intermediary between conflicting sides of Portuguese society: "The PS continues to think of itself as being a bridge of dialogue and the natural intermediary between different sectors of Portuguese society, whose divergence of camps and progressive radicalization, leading to violence, we fight against and fear" (Soares 1979, 183).

For the Socialists, this role as political stabilizer and guarantor of democracy meant that any proposed socioeconomic project had to avoid the excesses of the PCP's centralized and bureaucratic model as well as the conservatism of the right. They needed to "define a road to follow [consistent with] the Revolution of Carnations and the economic model desired by the majority" (Soares 1979, 190). The characterization of the model that Socialist leader Soares offered is worth quoting at length:

> After profound social transformations, which we have to almost always consider positive, and the wave of disorientation which touched the spirits of so many, convinced that collectivist totalitarianism had definitely won, we must win over the country, with serenity and firmness, for a national democratic project which is executable and progressive, which doesn't lose Socialism as its point of departure—understood as the equalization of opportunities, participation of the workers, and social justice, but also including Liberty, political Democ-

racy and economic efficiency, without having the real benefits attained by the working classes end up lost. (Soares 1979, 190)

Soares realized that his party faced the historic task of attempting to reconcile liberalism and socialism in the aftermath of great radicalization. But the excesses of *Gonçalvismo* had produced more socialism than liberalism, meaning that the Socialist interregnum was to be characterized mostly by a stress on liberalism.

Structurally, the dishegemonic character of the Socialists' postrevolutionary settlement was amply illustrated by the passage of a law dealing with the delimitation of private and public sectors (law 46/77). To an extent nearly unthinkable for most other capitalist countries, it attempted to delineate legally the areas in which private capital could be prevented from entering. For example, article 5, number 1 prohibited private enterprises from the following basic industries: armaments, petroleum refining, petrochemicals, steel, and cements. Article 3, section 1 stipulated that "private enterprises and other enterprises of a similar nature are prohibited from banking and insurance activities." Exemplifying the dishegemonic situation, laws also permitted the "activity of economic 'houses,' agricultural credit 'houses,' regional development companies, parabank institutions, specifically investment companies" (article 3, number 2). The sectors from which private capital were excluded were subject to government evaluation, which could "authorize enterprises that result from the association of the public sector . . . with other entities, specifically foreign" (article 5, number 2). Nationalized firms could even in some cases be managed by private capital, a genuine separation of ownership and control. Forty-seven other activities were left totally open to private capital, including such important sectors as beverages, textiles, clothing, some chemicals, paper, pants, soap products, pharmaceuticals, electric materials, vehicle assembly, cement products, wholesale trade, tourism, and many others.

The dishegemonic settlement was also evident in laws that applied to the agrarian reform. The controversial *lei Barreto* (law 77/77) reduced the scope of the land reform without directly eliminating it altogether. For example, the area affected by land-reform laws was restricted to a specific zone of intervention rather than the entire national territory; the manner of counting the total land owned was made more favorable to owners of dispersed holdings and others who could claim to be part of an agricultural cooperative;

and autonomous producers were guaranteed their land irrespective of total holdings.[2]

Similar dilution of laws introduced during the revolutionary period occurred in other areas: for example, the law of indemnization and the foreign-investment code. In each case, the laws were made more favorable to private capital. Although Soares insisted that the sum of these and the other previously cited laws "did not mean the resurrection of capitalism in the country, as communist propaganda has insisted, but merely to put the system in working condition, giving it economic viability and dynamism . . . without which democratic institutions, as consecrated in the Constitution and our own national independence would be seriously compromised" (1979, 190), the Socialists did not have the political weight to carry out this equivocal arrangement. Their fragile government, dependent on intraregime softliners inclined to do away with revolutionary changes and extraregime hardliners inclined to consolidate them, could not give consistent direction to the structural character of the economy. The *politica económica de transição* was neither the radicalism tending to authoritarianism of *Gonçalvismo* nor a right-wing social democracy that only ends up managing capitalism. The Socialist party had proposed a far-reaching plan for democratic socialism:

> a series of well defined steps with a controlled implementation, characterized by the extension and consolidation of the socialist mode of production; a radical transformation, but a necessarily progressive one, of the social relations of production; the planning of production, employment, productive resources and the distribution of income, subordinated to political objectives; and favoring the taking of power by the workers in relation to the means and organization of production. (PS 1975, 11).

Despite the apparent overlap between this program and many points expressed by the Communists, the PCP's call for a majority of the left, fell on deaf ears. For Soares, the PCP-PS majority in Parliament was not a *left* majority: "such a majority of the left doesn't exist now and has never existed" (1979b, 349). The historic impasse within the extraregime opposition had policy consequences due to the unwillingness of Socialists to entertain Communist participation in government. The Socialists were also reluctant to rely on the PSD or CDS for a parliamentary majority as this would undermine the uniqueness of the PS's autonomous project and result in the right's "complete domination of the country" (Soares 1979b, 273).

Apart from the issue of property ownership, the major problem that consumed the Socialists related to macroeconomic policies. Faced with a ballooning balance-of-payments deficit, the minority government felt compelled to pursue economic policies meant to curb domestic demand and reduce government spending. According to the Socialists' leader,

> to reduce the balance of payments deficit—an indispensable condition for us to continue our policies of national independence . . . we must limit our consumption and practice a policy of real prices. The cost of living rises necessarily, and given the limitations which weigh upon collective bargaining, real salaries diminish. If we alleviated this pressure by increasing salaries or subsidizing certain products to artificially reduce prices, it is certain that we could not reestablish essential financial equilibriums nor reduce the insupportable deficits in the balance of payments. (Soares 1979b, 173–74)

The PS was acutely aware that such policies would cause an erosion of support but pursued them because the positive results would be felt in the long term. Erroneously, the party was confident that given the absence of any other viable governing arrangement, it would remain in power long enough to take credit for improving economic conditions. But the momentary difficulties led to a wave of frustration and discontentment that made it increasingly difficult for the PS to play off the left and right.

Both sides of the political spectrum used the austerity policies to bolster their arguments in favor of a preferred structural model. For the Communists, any structural concessions to the right were unforgivable, especially regarding the land-reform program upon which the PCP had staked much politically. They insisted upon using the public sector as the motor of development; references in the 1976 constitution to "the socioeconomic organization of the Portuguese Republic, based on the development of socialist relations, through the collective appropriation of the principle means of production" were ceaselessly repeated. Dishegemonic policies involving Socialist concessions to the right were seen as heretical and illegal subversions of the constitutional order. The PCP sought to mobilize working-class opposition to the Socialists by continuing to stress that in the end there could be no pragmatically devised middle ground between accumulation models. It compared the salary increases gained during 1975 to the drops experienced since and emphasized that both the liberal structural policies and austerity measures were part of a generalized attack on working-class revolutionary gains (see table 7.1).

In addition, the Communist left was deeply cynical of the Socialists' pursuit of the country's entrance into the European Community. Unlike the Socialists, for whom entry into the EC was a vital precondition for political democracy and economic modernization, the PCP was inclined to see it as one more attempt to undo the leftist aspects of the revolution. As one Communist-inclined editorial put it:

> The objective of EC integration as an instrument for the destruction of the conquests of the Revolution is now openly being proclaimed. . . . The so-called readaptation of socioeconomic structures and labor legislation, in a manner which identifies it with that found in EC countries, is nothing more than the defense of the reinstallation of state monopoly capitalism which in those countries rules but which was liquidated in Portugal by the Revolution. (n.a. 1979, 3)[3]

Popular unhappiness with the austerity policies also gave the right a chance to make a general case against the entire structure of dishegemonic democracy. Internal struggles within the PSD prevented an immediate challenge to the Socialists as the dominant party but did not prevent the right parties from joining with the PCP to form a negative majority and bring down the Socialist minority government in late 1977.[4] This led to the formation of the short-lived PS-CDS government and finally to a series of presidentially appointed governments.

As events subsequently made clear, for the right to gain power and start dismantling dishegemonic democracy directly, it needed to remove the Socialists from power while reinforcing Socialist culpability for income-reducing austerity policies. By tying these to an illusory structural middle ground pursued by the PS, the right could point to the country's drift away from any comprehensive hegemonic project. As one PSD deputy remarked:

> We have passed from war to peace, from dictatorship to pluralist democracy with respect for human rights, from an anachronistic project to a European one, from an unjust situation to

the creation of certain conditions for more justice, more participation and the development of a free and just society. . . . It is
still important to recognize that we are today in a period of profound political, economic and cultural indefinition. (PSD
1978, 17)

In order for the right to present a distinct alternative that
maintained the Europeanist political elements and merged them
with more liberal economic ones, it sought to paint the PS as part of
a Marxist left, a partner in crime with the PCP in pursuit of a collectivist hegemonic project. Such bipolarization was given a major
impulse in September 1978 with the fall of the PS-CDS government.
Its collapse allowed the right to start forging greater political unity
and a coherent electoral strategy. By supporting the presidentially
appointed Mota Pinto government for a short period of time, the
right could reinforce the argument that a party-based political center did not really exist: the Pinto government's limited duration and
lack of party support meant that bipolarization of the political scene
was the only means for producing a stable governing configuration
with a clear direction.

Phase 1 of democratic consolidation demonstrated how tenuous the left's grasp was on any counterhegemonic or dishegemonic
strategy. The Communists were unwilling to acknowledge—
although they probably realized—that their revolutionary gains in
1975 could not be politically sustained afterward. Surely, if the PCP
had been serious about retaining as many of the gains of the revolution as possible, it would not have followed the strategy of concerted attack upon the Socialists during this time. Despite its
concessions to the right, the PS was all that stood between an
intraregime softliner victory and the advanced democracy that
emerged from the revolution. The PCP's vote ending the first PS
government laid the seeds for an irreversible period in which the
left's ability to sustain Socialist policies in *any* form declined. While
the Communists argued about the nuances of Socialist structural
policy and its Europeanist aspirations, what ultimately confronted
the PCP was a future of governments directly hostile to both the
structural reforms and general imagery of *Abril.* In the final analysis, the PCP's actions were directed largely at preserving its specific
strengths in the trade unions, the Alentejo, and its status as a party
wedded to Marxist-Leninist principles. The party clearly overplayed
its hand in thinking that it could leverage the Socialists into form-

ing a united left without serious changes in Communist policies and principles.

For the Socialists, phase 1 demonstrated their political vulnerability as a minority party trying to mediate between hostile sides. Left and right were able to seize upon the uncomfortable effects of austerity to attack Socialist equivocation on structural policy. The PS was forced to pay the political price for the inevitable backlash against declining economic conditions, as demonstrated in the 1979 elections in which both the PCP and the PSD-CDS (as the AD) improved upon their 1976 performances at the PS's electoral cost. Democratic dishegemony, while proving sound as a strategy to avoid fundamental conflict, left its main proponent painfully open to challenge.

The presidentially appointed governments that followed the PS-CDS coalition were composed of independents with no strong ideological convictions regarding the primacy of the public sector and the need to circumscribe the power of the private monopolies. President Eanes had no declared Socialist leanings; two of his prime ministers—Nobre de Costa and Mota Pinto—represented the *bloco central,* Pinto becoming leader of the PSD for a brief period during phase 3.[5] Only the explicitly caretaker Pintasilgo government had a more leftist tinge. The tenuous party support received by these Eanes-inspired governments meant that they could not undertake any decisive restructuring of private and public sectors. Due to the absolute primacy given to overcoming the external deficit, the focus of economic policy was short-term and not structural, relying upon the traditional policy instruments of stabilization: exchange rates, interest rates, credit ceilings, and so on. Although the politics of stabilization took precedence over those of rehegemonization, the result was a steady dilution of the counter-hegemonic changes. With the gradual atrophy of the radical message of *Abril,* the stage was set for a resurgent right ready to offer a sharper vision and greater political stability.

Phase 2: The Decline of the Postrevolutionary Settlement under the AD

While the terms of dishegemony tilted increasingly to the right, they were not decisively altered during phase 1. Only with the start of the second phase and the election of the first AD government in 1979 was a concerted, ideologically driven attack on the postrevolutionary settlement made. For the gains of the revolution it was the formal beginning of an end that was already partly implicit in the Europeanized character of the new hegemonic project supported by all the non-Communist parties.

CDS president Diogo Freitas da Amaral singled out the following goals for the Democratic Alliance: to provide a stable and cohesive government that would be faithful to its program but also respect the parliamentary opposition; restore order out of the anarcho-populism of the revolutionary period; eliminate the excessive changes and collectivist measures stemming from the revolution; and resume the original democratizing process.[6] Antistatism, reprivatization, and markets became the mantra of the AD. The structural policy of the alliance was limited by the constitution, the Revolutionary Council, and the AD's lack of control over the presidency.

The top priority for the newly elected AD government in 1979 were policies meant to address difficult economic conditions. Cavaco Silva was the minister of finances in the first AD government headed by PSD leader Francisco Sá Carneiro. He summarized the economic circumstances facing the newly elected AD coalition (Silva 1982, 17–18).

- Slow growth rates
- Rising unemployment
- Stagnant or declining investment, especially in construction and the private sector generally
- Worsening inflation
- A continuing fall in real wages resulting in increasing income inequality
- A sharp rise in oil prices
- A drop in demand in external markets
- Limits on financing due to balance-of-payments difficulties in other major countries

The only positive note was the steady decline in Portugal's balance-of-payments deficit, which had shrunk under previous governments from $1.5 billion in 1977 to nearly nothing by 1979 due to austerity policies, increasing exports, tourism, and emigrant remittances.

These circumstances offered the possibility for expanding internal demand to take up the slack created by declining foreign markets. This was partly desirable insofar as it would prevent more unemployment and help stimulate investment. More revealing were Silva's acknowledged political concerns: "Another important element of a political nature . . . was the realization that in the coming October [1980] elections, voters would judge the AD based on the ability of the government to resolve the major social and economic problems of the country and respond to popular aspirations for progress and justice by the concrete results achieved in the short space of ten months" (Silva 1982, 19). It was clear to him that the thin AD majority could be imperiled by the "opposition parties, the President of the Republic, the Council of the Revolution and the Intersindical who would do everything possible to ensure the failure of the AD's policies and have it defeated in the next elections" (1982, 19).

With elections clearly in mind, the AD government set forth economic policies meant to have both procapitalist structural and positive short-term, electorally oriented effects. The expansion of investment was to be guided by the AD's desire to relaunch the private sector by encouraging more private investment, expanding the number of private exporters, and reinforcing market mechanisms. The strategy was to create a "climate of investor confidence" and to "demonstrate to entrepreneurs that the policies adopted were correct, producing a high probability that the AD would be reelected, thus creating a perspective of long term governmental stability" (Silva 1982, 34). The government was to give its "unequivocal support to private enterprise and its role as the motor of economic development." Changes in the system of planning were to make the state itself more compatible with the needs of private capital.

The alliance optimistically forecast that rather than the stagnant economy anticipated by the OECD, a strong growth rate should be set (6 percent). In order to have positive short-term electoral effects, the package included an anti-inflation program meant to reduce inefficiencies and the need for subsidies in the public sector, using negotiations in the latter to set the tone for collective bargaining agreements in the private sector. To stimulate demand and investment, increases both in government entitlements and public investment were targeted. Given the intrinsic susceptibility to growth-induced balance-of-payments deficits, this program was only possible because of previous improvement in the balance-of-payments situation. This permitted the AD government to conclude that "a deficit in the balance of payments could be favorable if associated with an intensification of investment, while it would be viewed negatively if joined with economic stagnation" (Silva 1982, 22). A deficit of more than one billion dollars was judged acceptable "if justified by an expansion of investment."

The AD also used the favorable current-accounts situation to lower inflation by curbing the devaluation of the escudo.[7] This meant that although Portuguese exports would be more expensive, imports would be relatively cheaper, prompting a decline in the rate of inflation. As long as the AD focused on a short-time horizon, a domestic miniboom fueled by rising real incomes, expanding investment, and selective government pump priming would attain the key purpose of securing a long-term AD majority in the next elections. The only probable casualty in the plan would be the balance-of-payments deficit, a price the AD government was admittedly willing to pay. It was a kind of *Gonçalvismo* of the right, coupling a boost in demand with a reinforcement of the private sector in an effort to use the popularity afforded by expansion-oriented macroeconomic policies to solidify a preferred accumulation model.

The short-term results of the first AD government's policies were impressive because several economic goals were attained. As shown on table 7.1, 1980 was an exceptional year. Gross domestic product increased at nearly double the 1979 rate (6.1 versus 3.4 percent) as did domestic demand (6.6 versus 3.1 percent). After three years of stagnation, total investment was up. Real wages, in decline for several years, increased by 6.6 percent. Inflation decreased from nearly 24 percent to less than 17 percent. Even unemployment dipped below the 8 percent mark where it had been hovering for the last couple of years. While not spectacular, the first AD government was able to claim significant turnarounds in many macroeconomic indicators. As anticipated, the major blemish was the balance-of-payments deficit, which jumped from only $52 million in 1979 to $1.251 million in 1980.

The October 1980 election confirmed the economic-electoral strategy developed by the AD: it returned a larger AD majority and seemed to assure the coalition a full term to implement their structural reforms. But with the accidental death of PSD leader Sá Carneiro just before the 1980 presidential election, the coalition lost its charismatic leader. The new AD government was led by Francisco Pinto Balsemão. The minister of finances and plan in the Sá Carneiro government, Cavaco Silva, was removed as part of a general change of cabinet personalities.

What remained of the first AD government was its legacy: the ghost of Sá Carneiro hovered as a dark cloud around the shoulders of Pinto Balsemão, who had a difficult time asserting his authority over his party and the coalition. More important, the government's economic performance was subject to constant invidious compar

Table 7.1. Principal Economic Indicators, 1977–91

Indicator	1977	1978	1979	1980	1981	1982	1983	1984	1985	1986	1987	1988	1989	1990	1991
Government balance as a percent of GDP	-3.4	-8.3	-8.1	-8.6	-10.6	-7.6	-10.1	-7.1	-7.4	-6.4	-7.3	-5.9	-3.1	-5.4	—
GDP	625.8	787.3	993.3	1,256.1	1,501.2	1,850.4	2,303.7	2,814.8	3,523.7	4,418.4	5,173.6	6,001.7	7,127.6	8,487.9	—
GDP percent real change	5.6	3.4	6.1	4.5	1.6	2.1	-0.2	-1.9	2.8	4.1	5.3	3.9	5.4	4.2	2.5
Domestic demand	6.6	0.4	3.1	6.6	3.4	2.2	-5.7	-6.7	0.9	8.3	10.4	7.4	4.2	6.2	4.2
Gross fixed capital formation at 1985 prices	12	7	-0.9	10.3	5.5	2.3	-7.1	-17.4	-3.5	10.9	15.1	15	8.3	7.3	3.5
Nominal salaries	16.4	16.5	16	24.4	21.7	17.9	17.8	18.1	20.4	20.2	16.2	9.8	12.6	17.3	17.7
Real salaries	-8.5	-4.5	-6.6	6.6	1.4	-3.6	-6.1	-8.7	1	4.1	5.4	0.1	-0.4	3.4	5.6
Prodctivity	6.7	2.7	3.5	3	1.1	2.2	-4	-1.8	3.3	4	2.6	1.2	3.1	1.9	-0.5
Perunit cost of labor (percent change)	14.1	15	15.6	22.5	20.2	19.8	19.8	18.3	19.5	16.9	12.9	10.2	11.2	15.2	18.3
Disposable income (family)	3.4	5.1	4.6	3.6	0.8	4.6	-3	-3	1.7	3.4	3.1	3.1	3.1	4.5	3.9
Inflation (year average)	27.3	22.5	23.6	16.7	20	22.4	25.5	29.3	19.3	11.7	9.4	9.7	12.6	13.4	11.4
Unemployment	7.5	8.1	8.2	7.8	7.7	7.5	7.9	8.6	8.7	8.6	7.1	5.8	5.1	4.6	—
Balance of payments	-1.5	-0.8	-0.05	-1.25	-2.5	-3.1	-0.8	-0.5	0.4	1.1	0.4	-1	0.2	-0.2	—

Sources: OECD Economic Surveys of Portugal, 1985/1986, 1991/1992; O Jornal, 21 August 1992,7, UGT 1987, 224.

isons with its predecessor. Unlike the first AD effort, which lasted only ten months, the Balsemão-led AD coalition had a much longer period to prove itself. Hampered by a less favorable international conjuncture, the Balsemão governments struggled with a ballooning balance-of-payments deficit, paying the bill for a year of political business-cycle macroeconomic engineering.

The government, in a move certain to bolster its ability to condemn the public sector even if it undermined the viability of major firms in the short term, used public enterprises to deal with the external deficit. These enterprises were obliged to obtain foreign loans, resulting in an increase in their foreign debt from $2 billion in 1978 to $7.7 billion by 1982. By the end of the AD's term in 1982, the comparisons with the 1980 miracle were politically catastrophic. The growth in GDP dropped from 6.1 percent in 1980 to 1.3 percent in 1982. Inflation increased from 16.7 to 22.4 percent. The balance-of-payments deficit tripled from $1,251 billion to $3,245 billion. Worst of all, real wages, which rose 6.6 percent in 1980, dropped 3.6 percent in 1982. Overall, the Balsemão governments were commonly perceived to have failed in managing the economy. Moreover, the private sector kept up pressure, saying, "We don't believe that we can get out of the current crisis through the current system" (*Industria em revista* 1983, 5). Robbed of the legitimacy gained by short-term policy successes and unable to meet rapidly the expectations of the private sector, the AD coalition unraveled. In late 1982 the AD government dissolved, leading to new elections in April 1983 and the start of phase 3: the emergence of the PS-PSD grand coalition.

Phase 3: From the Grand Coalition to Political Fragmentation

The formation of the PS-PSD government was predicated on the notion that only a broad national consensus could provide the necessary political cover for the coming austerity policies. As he had in the minority PS government, Mário Soares became a prime minister embattled by the need to impose unpopular policies without a Socialist parliamentary majority. The PS, having learned a lesson from phase 1, refused to tackle alone the serious problems facing the new government. Soares remarked, "To repeat the experience of a minority government would be completely unrealistic if not suicidal. It would be a government to liquidate in only a few months" (Soares 1984, 7). The PSD would have to take some responsibility for the inevitably unpopular policies that were to follow.

The magnitude of the problems left by the AD was impressive. In his initial speech to Parliament upon formation of the new government, Soares said: "As everyone knows, the country has found itself paralyzed for many months. The economy is unregulated. Major public and private enterprises employing thousands and thousands of workers are on the brink of bankruptcy, asphyxiated with losses totaling millions of contos, living artifically from subsidies which the State can no longer afford to provide" (Soares, 1984, 18). Particularly pressing was the balance-of-payments problem. As the prime minister noted, "the total external debt went from seven billion dollars in 1979 to thirteen billion dollars by the end of 1982. . . . Interest on the external debt has risen to $1.2 billion for this year. The deficit in the balance of current accounts was $3.2 billion in 1982, while it was only $52 million in 1979" (Soares 1984, 19). He offered "18 months of short-term emergency policies" involving the need to "take restrictive measures which would necessarily affect the Portuguese standard of living" (1984, 194). He expected the program passed by Parliament in June 1983 to be respected for four years. This time it seemed, the PS would not only be blamed for austerity but also be credited with the recovery that a four-year cycle would likely produce.

The need for harsh austerity policies was driven by the depth of the crisis, which was in some ways even more serious than the one in phase 1. As table 7.1 shows, while GDP growth had been modest in that period, it turned negative in 1984 and 1985. Driven by a need to redress the balance-of-payments deficit, a depreciating currency contributed to an escalating inflation rate, which reached nearly 30 percent in 1984. Unemployment jumped to historic highs; real salaries in 1984 dropped nearly 9 percent. Investment dropped by about 18 percent from 1983 to 1984, finally bottoming out in 1985. Interest rates rose, as did some taxes. These restrictive policies did manage a sizable decrease in the external debt, reducing the deficit in the balance of current accounts from 13.5 percent of GDP in 1982 to under 4 percent in 1984. The government's deficit was also reduced as a percentage of GDP, from 11.5 percent in 1982 to about 9 percent in 1984. Exports rose each year from 1983 to 1985, while imports decreased in volume.

Table 7.2 compares several economic indicators over the various phases of the democratic consolidation, separating phase 3 into

Table 7. 2. Economic Indicators Averaged over Each Phase

Presidential Govts.	Phase 1 1977–78 PS, PS-CDS	Phase 2 1979–82 AD	Phase 3 1983–84 PS-PSD	Phase 3 1985–86 PSD Minority	Phase 4 1987–90 PSD Majority
Government balance as a percent of GDP	-5.9	-8.7	-8.6	-6.9	-5.4
GDP	706.6	1,400.3	2,559.3	3,971.1	6,697.7
GDP percent real change	4.5	3.6	-1.05	3.5	4.7
Domestic demand	3.45	3.8	-6.2	4.6	7.1
Gross fixed capital formation at 1985 prices	9.5	4.3	-12.3	3.7	11.4
Nominal salaries	16.5	20	18	20.3	14
Productivity	4.7	2.5	-2.9	3.65	2.2
Per unit cost of labor (percent change)	14.6	19.5	19.1	18.2	12.4
Disposable income (family)	4.3	3.4	-3	2.6	3.5
Inflation (year average)	24.9	20.7	27.4	15.5	11.3
Unemployment	7.8	7.8	8.3	8.7	5.7

Source: Derived from table 7.1.

two parts in order to highlight the contrast between the softliners' grand coalition and the PSD minority government. For the years that the Socialists (or presidential governments) were in power, relatively high inflation and major reductions in real wages were the rule. In all AD-PSD periods, inflation was lower, and real wages fell less or rose. The grand coalition period (1983–84/85) was clearly the harshest; the misery index (unemployment and inflation) was the highest, while GDP growth, investment, real wages, and productivity stagnated or declined.[8]

Despite the brevity of the grand coalition, there were several major policy and institutional innovations, most of which reinforced the Euromodel of political economy and further diminished the counterhegemonic residues of the revolutionary period. The coalition passed a law redefining the delimitation of sectors, allowing private banks to compete with nationalized ones. This was partly to stimulate competition in the banking industry but also to attract foreign banks and capital. It opened other sectors to private enterprise, such as insurance, cement, and fertilizers. The state's public enterprises were subject to a major review, with the aim of improving their operations and closing down hopelessly uncompetitive ones. The government broached other sensitive issues such as increasing the flexibility of labor laws, liberalizing rents, financing local government, and even installing a domestic investigatory arm to combat internal subversion and terrorism usually attributed to the radical group Forças Populares-25.[9] Negotiations with the EC continued, and the tripartite CPCS was created. While some of these measures had paradigmatic implications, the period was largely characterized by the extreme harshness of the austerity policies. The political consequence was to pin the major responsibility for hard times on the Socialist party, despite the fact that the PSD had been a willing accomplice.

The Transition from Phase 3 to Phase 4: Economy and Politics under the PSD Minority and Majority Governments

The alternation of bad times with good was only partially broken with the formation of the PSD minority government in 1985. Previously, one or two boom years (1975–76, 1980) were followed by busts for four to five years (1977–80, 1981–85). For a seven-year period, starting roughly from 1986 and continuing through 1992, Portugal avoided a serious economic downturn. The sensitivity of the electorate to apparently successful macroeconomic policies was implied in the single-party majorities given to the PSD in 1987 and 1991.

The PSD benefited by an improving international conjuncture. By 1986, declining oil and raw material prices, a cheaper dollar, and a reduction in international interest rates curbed inflationary pressures. The relatively low inflation rates were also attributable to notable rises in productivity during the first two years of PSD rule. The biggest political reward probably came from the sharp rise in real wages by 3.7 and 5.4 percent in 1986 and 1987. The fact that incomes were going up after a long period of decline meant that the Cavaco-led government could claim to have undertaken policies that showed the wisdom of its programmatic orientation.

Whether by luck or design, the PSD was able to profit by the timing of the next political business; economic performance peaked in 1987 when legislative elections were scheduled. The following two years featured negligible gains in real salaries, although overall growth rates remained positive. Inflation jumped two percentage points, rising to nearly 14 percent by 1990. The next turn of the cycle was 1991, however, when the government was obliged to stand for election again. Real salaries started going up again in 1990 and peaked in 1992. Inflation dropped four points, again partly benefiting from timely international events. The 1991 election gave the PSD a nearly identical majority. Less clear was the probability that the PSD could sustain high growth, low unemployment, and moderate inflation into the future. By 1991, several years of growth had produced a much tighter labor market and a growing divergence between real salaries and productivity growth. Either a continuation of favorable international conditions or the reinvigoration of incomes policies was needed to prevent an eruption of high inflation; otherwise, political death was assured by the need to impose austerity policies.

In order to pursue its neo-AD policies, the Cavaco governments also needed further revisions of the constitution and again had to depend upon the PS for a qualified two-thirds majority. Several elements of the constitution were changed to reduce the residue of revolutionary changes, although many radical sounding elements were left in place. Part 2 of the newly revised 1989 constitution dealt with economic organization and listed six basic principles:

■ Subordination of economic power to democratic political power

- Coexistence of public, private and cooperative, and social forms of property in the means of production
- Collective appropriation of means of production, the earth, and natural resources in accord with the public interest
- Democratic planning of the economy
- Protection of the cooperative and social sector
- Democratic intervention of the workers

Despite the leftist tone of many of these general principles, they corresponded to the continuing dilution of the original 1976 constitution's Socialist content. Whereas that version made a priority of collective property forms, the second revision diminished collective ownership to situations that accorded with the public interest. This left the determination up to the political leaders of the time rather than maintained a principled constitutional stand. With respect to the nationalizations undertaken during the revolutionary period, which had been irrevocable in the original constitution, article 85 (section 1) of the 1989 document read, "The reprivatization of title or rights of exploitation of means of production and other goods nationalized after April 25, 1974 can only be effectuated in terms of a framework law approved by an absolute majority of Deputies currently holding office." Section 2 said; "Small and medium enterprises indirectly nationalized and situated outside of basic economic sectors may be reprivatized under terms established by law."[10] Both these measures enabled the standing government to have much more flexibility in handling state enterprises. The state was restricted from further intervention into private enterprises except for "cases expressly stated by law" (article 87, section 2). The revision also left to legislation the identification of those basic sectors in which private enterprises would be prohibited (article 87, section 3). The revisions generally left sectoral decisions to be determined by the current alignment of political forces and thereby much more susceptible to the liberalizing economic plans of the PSD.[11]

With its parliamentary majority, the Cavaco government proceeded to reprivatize nationalized firms. This was a contentious move not just for the left, which might have had basic ideological opposition, but also for the old owners, who felt entitled to compensation based on current values rather than values determined at the time of the nationalizations. The basic terms of the nationalization and the compensation of old owners had been set in 1977. As PSD Finance Minister Miguel Cadilhe (1990, 50) put it, no other legislative proposal came forth in the Assembly. . . . [I]t would probably be a tragic error for the stability and progress of the country to want to radically correct the indemnities which were fixed long ago. What it amounts to is a *redistribution of wealth* and income between those who had nothing to do with the nationalizations and those who were victimized by it. . . . [But] it doesn't seem that Portugal in 1990 should respond to the political earthquake which shook the country in 1974/75.

The government put banks and breweries on the auction block, with specific shares set aside for potential purchase by current employees. Other percentages were devoted to citizens rather than foreigners. Because old owners were by and large not able to recoup their assets, the Cavaco government sought to recast its dominant class in terms of those agents who were financially able to purchase shares at that time. Obviously, this gave the government a much larger cash flow, which it could use for other purposes. As Cadilhe mentioned, "the receipts of privatization were to be applied to the early amortization of the heavy public debt . . . a large part of which came from the investment needs and losses of nationalized enterprises" (1990, 50). In this sense, the state exerted autonomy from the incumbents of the pre-1974 capitalist class, while simultaneously acknowledging its dependence on capital as a whole. The specificity of the state's interest led to a controversial reprivatization that reconfigured the Portuguese capitalist class.[12]

By 1992, the democratic consolidation as nurtured by the PSD had disposed of many aspects of dishegemony. Politically, the outcome was incontrovertibly Europeanist: a multiparty democracy reigned, and the authoritarian regime was largely a nightmare of the past. The social settlement had changed as well. The state sector diminished substantially; a neocorporatist organ for macroeconomic consultation was created in which even the CGTP participated; the constitution was liberalized economically; and integration into the EC was accomplished. The major alternative model of accumulation admired by the PCP (Soviet-style socialism) succumbed completely, lessening further the sense of viable alternatives to the Euromodel. The scope of politics moved increasingly from paradigmatic contention to normal politics, involving not radical proposals but increasingly incremental adaptations of structures and legal framework to the emerging hegemonic choice.

The PSD's Social Settlement and the Structure of the Bourgeoisie

While the political victory of the PSD culminated from the steady dilution of revolutionary challenges to the softliner hegemonic project, the Social Democrats' ability to remain politically attractive depended on their capacity to forge a new social settlement. PSD governments were based on the premise that procapitalist structural changes would be combined with positive short-term outcomes. Together these would lead to a historic compromise in the style of a postwar settlement in which property claims against the bourgeoisie would be renounced in exchange for effective economic management and social concessions. This compromise assumed that the Portuguese dominant class was structurally capable of leading the path of modernized democratic capitalism—or could be made so. A sound accumulation strategy could overcome the historic weakness of the Portuguese bourgeoisie and make democratic capitalism work well.

Increasingly, the accumulation strategy that became a distinct part of government policy combined a strong export orientation with a degree of import substitution. The growth of exports was vital to solving the vexing balance-of-trade problem as well as a means for attracting foreign capital and spurring greater internal competition. Throughout the consolidation period, export markets were redirected to reflect the greater incorporation of Portugal within the European regional division of labor. Table 7.4 presents the geographical breakdown of foreign trade from 1977 to 1988. Portugal had historically concentrated its exports to OECD Europe, the United States, and the previous escudo area. Europe remained its largest customer, taking nearly 70 percent of its exports in 1977 and gradually increasing to 80 percent by 1986, the year of Portugal's entry into the EC. The share to France nearly doubled, while the UK percentage dropped somewhat. Spain became a more significant trading partner as well. The previous escudo area and other non-OECD countries took a smaller share of Portuguese exports. Overall, the country's exports became more closely tied to European markets as the softliner consensus regarding the external direction of the Portuguese economy was implemented.

Table 7.3 shows the import pattern over the same range of countries and years. Despite many similarities, import patterns did not exactly match those for exports—due especially to the growing bill for oil imports, which nearly doubled from 1977 to the mid-

Table 7.3. Geographic Distribution of Foreign Trade: Imports (in percent)

Area	1977	1978	1979	1980	1981	1982	1983	1984	1985	1986	1987	1988	1989	1990
OECD countries	73	77	73	69	69	69	70	67	67	78	82	84	84	83
OECD Europe/EC	58	60	57	53	45	47	45	43	46	59	64	67	68	69
Germany	12	14	13	12	11	12	12	10	12	14	15	15	15	14
France	8	9	9	7	8	9	8	8	8	10	11	12	12	12
Italy	5	5	5	5	5	6	5	5	5	8	9	9	9	10
UK	10	10	9	9	8	8	8	7	8	8	8	8	8	8
Spain	—	—	—	—	7	6	5	7	7	11	12	13	15	14
Other European OECD	21	22	21	20	6	7	7	6	6	8	9	10	11	12
United States	10	12	12	11	12	11	14	14	10	7	5	4	4	4
Other OECD countries	5	5	5	4	12	12	11	10	11	12	13	13	11	10
Non-OECD countries	27	23	27	31	31	30	30	33	32	21	18	16	17	17
OPEC	11	12	14	—	19	20	19	19	18	9	6	5	6	7
Previous escudo area	1	0	1	0	0	0	0	1	1	1	0	0	0	0
Total (billion escudos)	190.7	230.1	331.9	465.8	631.3	809	949.2	1,195	1,282	1,400.1	1,956	2,597.8	3,035.8	3,462.6

Note: OECD Europe percentages as listed in OECD Economic Surveys, 1983/1984 Portugal for 1977–78, 1985/1986 Portugal for 1979–80. OECd EC is different (excludes EFTA) as listed in OECD Economic Surveys 1991/1992 Porgugal, used from 1981 to 1990. The EFTa countries were moved to "other OECD countries." Spain was included starting in 1981. Other 1977–80 data from 1983/1984 and 1985/1986 Surveys; subsequent data from 1991/1992 Survey.

Table 7.4. Geographic Distribution of Foreign Trade: Imports (in percent)

Area	1977	1978	1979	1980	1981	1982	1983	1984	1985	1986	1987	1988	1989	1990
OECD countries	79	81	81	81	78	82	83	84	85	89	91	91	91	91
OECD Europe/EC	69	71	72	73	57	61	63	62	63	68	71	72	72	74
Germany	12	13	12	14	13	13	14	14	14	15	15	15	16	17
France	8	9	10	10	13	13	14	13	13	15	16	15	15	16
Italy	4	6	6	6	4	5	4	4	4	4	4	4	4	4
UK	18	18	18	15	15	15	15	15	15	14	14	14	12	12
Spain	2	2	2	2	3	4	4	4	4	7	9	12	13	14
Other EC	—	—	—	—	10	12	13	13	14	14	14	12	13	12
United States	7	7	6	6	5	6	6	9	9	7	6	6	6	5
Other OECD countries	3	3	2	2	16	15	14	13	14	14	14	13	13	12
Non-OECD countries	21	19	19	19	20	16	16	15	13	10	8	8	8	8
OPEC	2	1	2	—	4	3	4	3	3	2	2	1	1	1
Previous escudo area	6	6	5	6	8	5	5	4	4	2	2	3	3	3
Total (billion escudos)	77.7	106.4	176.1	232.2	268.2	356.7	538	796.6	951	1,055.5	1,304.8	1,598.8	2,037.1	2,252.6

Note: OECD Europe percentages as listed in *OECD Economic Surveys, 1983/1984 Portugal* for 1977–78, *1985/1986 Portugal* for 1979–80. OECd EC is different (excludes EFTA) as listed in *OECD Economic Surveys 1991/1992 Porgual*, used from 1981 to 1990. The EFTa countries were moved to "other OECD countries." Spain was included starting in 1981. Other 1977–80 data from *1983/1984* and *1985/1986 Surveys*; subsequent data from *1991/1992 Survey.*

Table 7.5. Imports by Main Commodity Group, 1977–90 (in percent)

	1977	1978	1979	1980	1981	1982	1983	1984	1985	1986	1987	1988	1989	1990
Food and beverages	15	13	14	12	14	11	11	12	11	11	11	10	10	10
Basic material and Semi-finished goods	28	27	31	34	33	36	37	42	39	25	19	16	18	17
Manufactures	56	60	54	54	53	53	52	46	50	63	70	74	73	73
Chemicals	11	12	12	11	10	9	10	10	10	11	11	10	9	9
Goods classified chiefly by material	16	16	14	15	13	13	12	12	15	18	19	19	20	20
Machinery and transport equipment	26	28	25	25	27	26	26	21	22	29	34	38	37	37
Miscellaneous	3	4	3	3	3	4	4	3	3	5	6	6	7	8
Unspecified	0	0	0	0	0	0	0	0	0	1	0	0	0	0
Total in millions of U.S. dollars	4,963	5,142	6,529	9,271	9,787	9,541	8,257	7,975	7,650	9,454	13,966	17,885	19,043	25,334

Source: OECD Economic Surveys, 1985/86 for 1977–80, 1991/1992 for subsequent data

Table 7.6. Imports by Main Commodity Group, 1977–90 (in percent)

	1977	1978	1979	1980	1981	1982	1983	1984	1985	1986	1987	1988	1989	1990
Food and beverages	15	14	13	11	10	10	10	9	8	8	7	8	7	7
Basic material and Semi-finished goods	14	12	11	17	18	15	16	15	14	12	12	13	14	13
Manufactures	69	71	74	71	70	73	73	75	76	78	80	79	79	80
Chemicals	5	5	6	6	6	8	8	8	7	6	5	6	6	5
Goods classified chiefly by material	33	34	36	32	31	30	29	28	28	26	25	25	24	23
Machinery and transport equipment	15	14	12	13	13	14	15	17	16	16	17	17	19	20
Miscellaneous	16	18	21	20	20	21	21	22	26	30	33	31	30	32
Unspecified	2	2	2	1	1	2	2	1	2	1	1	0	0	0
Total in millions of U.S. dollars	2,013	2,426	3,478	4.633	4,147.1	4,173.3	4,601.4	5,207.5	5,685.4	7.204.9	9,318.3	10,989.7	12,797.7	16,415.5

Source: OECD Economic Surveys, 1985/86 for 1977–80, 1991/1992 for subsequent data

1980s, only dropping in 1986. Generally, the import pattern for goods other than oil did not undergo much change, with Spain rising a bit and the UK declining.

The geographic concentration of Portugal's markets formed one component of a more general pattern of interdependency among economies within a regional and global division of labor. The position of the Portuguese economy within Europe was also illustrated by changes in the import-export mix of major commodity groups. The late and reticent industrialization fostered under the dictatorship determined much of the country's economic profile, which was not unlike that of a newly industrializing country. Table 7.5 shows that the Portuguese economy emphasized raw material, semifinished, and heavy machinery and transport equipment as its major imports, reflecting its relatively underdeveloped heavy manufacturing and its role as an assembly point for products within the international production strategies of several large multinational corporations (for example, Toyota, Renault, Citroen). Food products also constituted a major share of imports, as did goods classified mainly by material. Overall, the import pattern has pointed to the historic weakness of agriculture, the relative scarcity of key raw materials (including oil), and the need to import capital equipment and sophisticated machines, with the latter becoming especially prominent during the Cavaco boom years.

Exports to some extent reflected the intermediate stage of industrialization typical of the country. As indicated on table 7.4, exports increasingly shifted to manufactured goods, rising from 69 percent in 1977 to 80 percent by 1990. Miscellaneous products represented a significant and growing share of total exports. Machinery and transport equipment exports were slightly less than one-half as significant a share of exports as they were of imports, partially revealing the dependent character of the Portuguese economy.

The concern over the balance-of-payments problem meant that the government was obliged to provide incentives for producers to encourage import substitution as well as export-led growth. The austerity period during much of phase 3 magnified the export drive, with export values increasing steadily even as import values declined. This was reflected in manufactured exports, which were only 49 percent of manufacturing imports in 1977 but rose to well over 100 percent by the mid-1980s.

In its *Program for Structural Correction of the External Deficit and Unemployment*, the PSD government identified a host of plans for the major sectors of the economy in light of the trade deficit and impact of EC integration (Finance Ministry 1987). It identified areas in which the country's individual sectors had either natural or acquired comparative advantages. Some of the main points summarized here give a sense of the structural obstacles faced by the country as it tried to implement its Europeanist accumulation policy.

In agriculture, domestic policy was shaped to accommodate EC demand for the crops most likely to be intrinsically price competitive or whose upgrading might eventually result in competitive production. The implementation of this policy was hampered by the dismal rural sociology associated with Portugal: only 15 percent of farmers were under forty (in 1979) over 30 percent were illiterate; many farms were either too large or small for optimal production and timely adaptation to changing market conditions. Out of the 4,700,000 hectares devoted to agriculture, only 2,259,000 hectares were in fact suited to productive farm use, resulting in "vast areas of marginal land, with low productivity" (Finance Ministry 1987, 3). To cope with entry into the EC, government policy needed to overcome these conditions and get farmers to consider greater and more efficient use of machinery, fertilizers, new crops, and other modern techniques. At the end of the transition period delineated in the Adhesion Treaty between the EC and Portugal, the government will be forced to curtail price subsidies while Portugal's borders are opened to agricultural imports. A sociostructural policy combining EC and national government aid for expanding irrigation, draining, roads, electrification, technical aid, and reforestation would help agriculture adapt better. Participation in the EC meant that the global productivity of Portuguese agriculture would have to rise without a concomitant increase in overall capacity. This would reduce the proportion of the work force employed in agriculture, making workers available for other more productive economic sectors while reducing the marginal land under cultivation.

Overall, Portugal faced a serious challenge adapting to the more advanced agricultural bourgeoisies elsewhere in Europe because the postwar efforts to modernize agriculture in countries such as France and Italy were not echoed under Salazar. Long years of low private investment, poor land-tenure patterns, and insufficient state-provided infrastructure to expand markets under the dictatorship were not aided by the political uncertainty of the transition to democracy. The government might have stimulated greater investment and productivity among the rural latifundia had a decision been made to support the cooperative farms in the south while actively fostering the rationalization of land holdings, equipment use, and marketing in the north. But support for the cooperatives was politically unattractive given the domination of the area by the PCP.

Efforts to transform the land-tenure patterns in the center and north were somewhat unappealing for the PSD and CDS because both parties depended on the votes of a conservative, religious, rural petty bourgeoisie. PSD changes in attitude regarding agricultural policy were partly an unavoidable concomitant of EC integration. But it was also the case that the PSD's broad success in both rural and urban areas in 1987 and 1991 gave the party more confidence that it—like other postwar centrist parties—could convert its rural middle-class support to an urban equivalent. This might explain the priority placed by the PSD on maintaining a high level of general employment: it could build up its long-term urban social support while implementing plans to rationalize agricultural production and reduce the size of its most electorally loyal class, the rural small holders.[13]

In manufacturing, the long period of relative isolation during Salazar's reign had already given way to the split between the Europeanist and colonial political lines within the Portuguese dominant class. The dilution of Portuguese capital occurred because of the need for a faster pace of development to pay for the colonial war of the 1960s. This resulted in the entry of foreign capital as well as greater dependence upon foreign technology and patents (Rolo 1977). Nevertheless, the nationalization of the monopolistic groups probably delayed the increasing internationalization of Portuguese capital by placing assets under government control without the possibility of share purchases by foreign (or domestic) private capital for over a decade. The closing of some sectors to private investment also forestalled the entry of foreign capital. The liberalization of the investment code as well as the sale of nationalized firms should subject Portugal's reconstituted bourgeoisie to the pressures of internationalization that EC integration implies.

After the transition, industrial capital was divided between the state and private sectors, with both a foreign and domestic element in the latter. Despite the dishegemonic nature of this arrangement, manufacturing steadily increased its share of GDP, as shown on table 7.7. Having lost their ties to the colonial-protectionist accumulation strategy, manufactures also became a progressively larger part of the export picture (table 7.6). With the denationalization of the state entrepreneurial sector, a new dominant-class coalition composed of foreign capital, a domestic bourgeoisie triggered by foreign investment, and a national bourgeoisie located in large and especially small and medium enterprises was formed.

Does this mean that the Portuguese bourgeoisie had finally become Europeanized? As the government's discussion of each sector shows, industry still suffered from many of the historic frailties that kept Portugal a semiperipheral country in the past. Traditional industries still dominated the economy: food, textiles, clothing, wood products, cork, and furniture represented 38 percent of gross value added, 50 percent of employment, and 48 percent of manufactured exports in 1980. The country lacked entrepreneurial resources because of insufficient managerial skills and the tardy adoption of new technologies that have been "in large part dependent on direct investments" and require the payment of royalties abroad (Finance Ministry 1987, 60). Total research and development as a percentage of GDP was quite low (0.3 percent), compared to 2 percent for most countries in the OECD. Low skill levels and the lack of training for personnel partly explain the lack of technology, which requires a more talented labor force to operate. Much of the Portuguese work force has been concentrated in occupational categories associated with the lowest professional training.[14]

Table 7.7. Gross Domestic Product by Kind of Activity, 1977–86 (in percent)

	1977	1978	1979	1980	1981	1982	1983	1984	1985	1986
Agriculture, forestry and fishing	12	12	11	10	9	9	9	9	9	9
Industry	26	26	28	29	29	29	29	30	30	31
Electricity, gas, and water	2	2	2	2	1	2	2	2	2	2
Construction	8	7	6	7	7	8	8	6	6	6
Services	53	53	52	52	54	52	53	53	53	52
Public administration	11	11	11	11	11	12	12	11	11	11

Source: Anuário Estatistica (INE 1987); *OECD Economic Surveys, 1985/1986 Portugal.*

The lack of investment, organization abilities, and work-force training was also reflected in sizable disparities between Portugal and other EC countries regarding levels of productivity. Despite some important bursts of productivity during certain years, "the global productivity of Portuguese manufacturing represents a level between a third and a quarter of the average productivity in the EC, which creates competitive disadvantages in the majority of industrial sectors" (Finance Ministry 1987, 61). Some sectors most heavily involved in exports registered the lowest levels of global productivity, making them competitive only on the basis of low labor costs. This was typically the plight of traditional industries, which also tended to have firms of smaller size (under fifty workers). Given the lack of comparative advantages stemming from natural resource and topographical endowments, Portuguese industry has faced a crisis of structural adaptation to a more modern paradigm of production, management, and marketing.

By using a 1986 government study of Portuguese industry (which measured a specific industry's market, comparative advantage, performance, and impact on the commercial balance along with some other industrial statistics published by the National Institute of Statistics), a closer examination of the structure of the Portuguese economy is possible. In table 7.8 the lefthand column measures industries in terms of their viability as determined by government indicators of market, performance, and effect on trade balance. Industries are grouped by category into viability thirds (rather than the taking the number of firms of workers and dividing into thirds). This accounts for the fact that the righthand column does not produce even groupings of firms, workers, or capital value. The table is then divided on the basis of two categories: monopoly and competitive. Those industries where few firms complete are placed in the monopoly camp, while other industries featuring many firms are grouped under the competitive category. The table makes it possible to duscuss the broad characteristics of industries based on their level of concentration and likely persistence into the future. By noting the number of firms, workers, and capital value, we can also assess the weight of the sectors in the overall economy.

Tables 7.8 and 7.9 reveal that there were relatively fewer workers and firms in the monopoly (19 and 8 percent) sector than in the competitive one (81 and 92 percent).[15] Predictably, a larger relative share (30 percent) of the gross capital value was in the more concentrated sector, which included such capital intensive industries as steel, machine tools, train bodies, tires, and cement. While the number of firms in the monopoly sector varied from four to thirty six, the competitive sector showed a much wider range, with as few as thirty seven firms (fish canning) to 1,087 (carpentry). Overall, the

Table 7.8. Monopoly and Competitive Sectors: Viability, Firms, Workers, and Capital Value

Viability by Industries	Characteristic	Value	Overall Percent
	Monopoly Sector		
Top Third	Firms	211	1.9
	Workers	29,429	4.8
	Capital value	152,746,026	8.2
Middle Third	Firms	332	2.9
	Workers	42,946	6.9
	Capital value	162,283,021	8.8
Bottom Third	Firms	315	2.8
	Workers	44,960	7.3
	Capital value	244,284,312	13.2
Sector Totals	Firms	858	7.6
	Workers	117,335	19
	Capital value	559,313,359	30.2
	Competitive Sector		
Top Third	Firms	3,697	32.7
	Workers	223,246	36.1
	Capital value	446,629,388	24.1
Middle Third	Firms	4,757	42.1
	Workers	124,246	20.2
	Capital value	436,281,343	23.5
Bottom Third	Firms	1,979	17.5
	Workers	153,568	24.8
	Capital value	410,840,287	22.2
Sector Totals	Firms	10,433	92.4
	Workers	501,627	81
	Capital value	1,293,751,018	69.8
Grand Totals	Firms	11,291	100
	Workers	618,962	100
	Capital value	1,853,064,377	100

Source: Tables 7.8–7.10 are derived from Finance Ministry (1987) and INE (1987).

Table 7.9. Summary by Viability Thirds

	Categories	Number	Percent
Top Third	Firms	3,908	34.61
	Workers	237,302	38.34
	Capital value	567,577,697	30.63
Middle Third	Firms	5,089	45.07
	Workers	167,759	27.1
	Capital value	598,564,364	32.3
Bottom Third	Firms	2,294	20.32
	Workers	198,528	32.07
	Capital value	655,124,599	35.35

great majority (81 percent) of firms were in the top two viability levels, although a much larger proportion (36 percent) of the monopoly firms were in the lowest tier than was the case in the competitive sector (19 percent). Furthermore, a very significant percentage of firms with the highest gross capital value in the monopoly-sector firms were in the lowest tier (44 percent), compared to a small number (32 percent) in the competitive sector. These facts underscore the vulnerability of the monopoly sector.

The political consequences of greater weakness in the more concentrated sector are suggested by comparing the average wages between monopoly and competitive sectors. In the monopoly sector, wages were nearly one-third higher than in the competitive one in equivalent lowest viability thirds (see table 7.10). Over 38 percent of all workers in the monopoly sector were found in the lowest third, compared to only 31 percent in the other sector. Lowest tier average firm size was almost 76 percent greater in the monopoly sector. Thus, the most vulnerable sector was a high-wage, large-firm operation—precisely the kind most likely to be organized by unions and important in local communities.

Table 7.10. Competitive and Monopoly Sectors: Economic Traits (medians)

Sector/	Workers per Firm		Wages per Firm		Capital Form/Firm		Value Added/ Firm		Value Added/ Worker	
Viabil.	Comp	Mono	Comp	Mono	Comp	Mono	Comp	Mono	Comp	Mono
Top	69	150	394	611	5,322	13,620	49,436	109,549	804	1,238
Middle	35	121	473	505	2,888	7,461	34,673	75,407	752	843
Bottom	42	74	452	599	4,045	9,631	30,170	123,000	667	1,231

The monopoly sector seemed to benefit from larger firm size. On all the other indicators, the middle third displayed lower values than the lowest third. The upper third had the highest number of workers and level of capital formation per firm. The relation between viability and wage rates was not direct; wages were highest in the upper third (only 2 percent over the value for the lowest third) as was the value added per worker. There was a positive statistical relationship between the number of persons employed per firm and wages (r=0.31) as well as value added (r=0.32). It is possible that the lowest third had an industrial structure that was overly dispersed and prevented sufficient economies of scale given the kinds of markets in which those firms competed. Moreover, effective competition for the lowest third may imply a greater spread between value added and wages than in the upper third. This suggests that the accumulation strategy appropriate to bolstering the monopoly sector is that of industrial concentration and lower relative wages. This would confirm Portugal's comparative advantage as a site for low-wage labor given a certain level of productivity.

In the competitive sector, larger firm size was also a key distinction between the top and other viability levels. Unlike the pattern in the monopoly sector, however, the top third paid wages that were 13 percent less than the bottom third (and 20 percent less than the middle), but value added per firm and per worker were much higher (63 and 20 percent higher). Capital formation was higher as well (by 31 percent). Over 60 percent of all competitive-sector workers (and 45 percent of all workers) were in the bottom two-thirds. As in the monopoly sector, these patterns suggest that low relative wages must be a key component of a successful accumulation strategy because low-wage, high-productivity firms appear to do best.

If these findings are accurate, government policy that seeks to improve the competitiveness of Portuguese industry should pursue a combination of goals: (1) further develop industries in the monopoly sector so they pay higher overall wages, especially those in the upper third because wages there were 55 percent higher than those in the competitive sector's upper third; (2) encourage greater concentration of firms because that appears to be correlated with viability, higher wages, and more value added; (3) ensure that the wages paid to Portuguese workers remain relatively low, especially in the competitive sector, which seems to thrive on a combination of high productivity and low wages.

In the long run, such policies would recast the Portuguese economy by leading to fewer and larger firms, particularly in those industries with adequate domestic and foreign markets. Given that relatively few firms are in the viable parts of the monopoly sector and that the relatively low-wage competitive sector has a large number of viable firms, it is hard to argue that the monopolistic segment of capital possesses uncontested hegemony. Rather, the politics of the resurgent Portuguese bourgeoisie will surely focus on the conflict between the needs of the larger, more capital-intensive firms in the monopoly sector and those in the competitive sector. The conflict over accumulation strategies that undermined the dictatorship was only partly resolved by jettisoning the colonies and accepting the EC. Conflicts now reflect the fortunes and interests of firms within the Europeanist scheme of things.[16.]

CONCLUSION

This chapter has examined how political parties competed to overcome the contradictions of dishegemony after the transition. The Socialists failed to become the Portuguese PSOE due to the difficulties of defining a Europeanist, but Socialist, alternative to the vision presented by the right. The PS was hampered by inopportune timing, always finding itself imposing austerity policies or being blamed for economic crises. Advocates of a leftist neocorporatism but administrators of policies constrained by balance-of-payment deficits and weak governing coalitions, the PS remained the democratic opposition as the PSD formed executives during phase 4 of the consolidation.

Conversely, political relations on the right were typically more cooperative than on the left. Having seen its choices narrowed with the end of the colonial accumulation option and radicalized after the attacks on private property during the transition, the right could focus on the overcoming dishegemony and securing capitalism in Portugal. But there was nothing automatic about the process by which dishegemony was ended. The problems in the second AD government, which paid the bill for the electorally inspired economic policies of the first, did not inevitably assure the ascendancy of the PSD. Had the international conjuncture during the early part of phase 3 been more forgiving, the Socialists might have been rewarded for adroit management of the economy. This might have slowed the pace of reprivatization and generally continued dishegemonic policies for a longer period.

In the long run, without a basic agreement on the left about fundamental questions, dishegemony was destined to be overcome. The recomposition of internal relations among the segments of the dominant class was a process that fell largely to the PSD, the party that controlled Parliament during the last half of the 1980s and engineered the privatization of the old monopolistic groups.

The empirical analysis of monopoly and competitive sectors demonstrated that an accumulation strategy narrowly directed at the monopoly sector was intrinsically insufficient. While some parts of the monopoly sector were quite competitive and productive, many firms were not. By contrast, while there were many weak firms in the competitive sector, a significant number were viable. In terms of total employment, number of firms, and total capital value, the top two-thirds of the competitive sector vastly surpassed their counterparts in the monopoly sector.[17] A single-minded emphasis on the monopoly sector could have devastating middle-term consequences for Portugal's competitive position in the international division of labor given the preponderance of viable firms and workers in the competitive sector.

The sheer weight of the competitive sector ensured that at least two distinct if overlapping options hampered the ascendancy of a single hegemonic class segment and corresponding accumulation strategy. The competitive sector was less productive but paid lower wages, which enabled it to remain competitive internationally. While government policy could have tried to increase productivity through restructuring of firms and industries and provide better access to markets among firms there, the viability of the sector was strongly driven by low relative wages. Politically, this option might be compatible with neocorporatism, which could ensure full employment in exchange for wage restraint. Conversely, another approach could base itself on union attacks, greater employer flexibility over the labor force, and a looser labor market as a constraint upon wages. Such a set of options would seem to split a possible social settlement in post-dishegemonic Portugal into left and right variants.

By contrast, the monopoly sector provides another option for government policy: accentuating higher productivity and wages. This would blend well with the Europeanist hegemonic project because many of the firms in that sector are directly or indirectly tied to foreign capital. Politically, a left neocorporatism undertaken by, for example, a predominantly Socialist government might seek to link wages closely to productivity increases in the monopoly sector, whose higher initial productivity would conceivably help close the gap between Portugal and Europe more quickly. The hegemonic capacity of this approach would still be confronted by the vaster size of the competitive sector and the low-wage dynamic that has operated there.

During the late 1980s and early 1990s, PSD governments were faced with the dilemma of reconciling these alternative approaches. The maintenance of the emerging alliance between newly re-created private groups, both domestic and foreign, with the more typical domestically owned competitive firms would depend upon the government's ability to smooth out the differences between the sectors. The government's popular legitimacy will be predicated upon positive outcomes such as maintaining employment through high growth rates while not allowing wage drift and excessive inflation.

The PSD has managed the economy effectively in this regard for much of phase 4's but by the early 1990s, it was unclear how long this would continue. Despite Europeanist aspirations, Portugal remains on the southern fringe of the continent, lacking a decisive sector of high-wage, high-productivity enterprises that can serve as the fulcrum of accumulation. It continues to rely too heavily on low-wage consumer services linked to tourism rather than high-wage producer services. Its politics will continue to reflect the difficulties of establishing bridges between competing accumulation strategies associated with different segments of the capitalist class. These structural conditions of the Portuguese economy provide the parameters within which party competition and union-employer bargaining shape the country's social settlement.

EIGHT

PORTUGAL AND DEMOCRATIZATION IN THE LATE TWENTIETH CENTURY

Has Portugal joined the late twentieth century, a time in which cold war divisions have purportedly thawed to a point where conflicts between left and right, dominant and subordinate classes, imperial and peripheral states have been overshadowed by a growing global consensus on some version of democratic capitalism? Has the country managed to eliminate the vestiges of its colonial-corporatist past and exceptional transition to democracy to find its destiny among the modern European states?[1]

Richard Morais (1992), in his article "Welcome to the 20th Century," has suggested that the answer is yes. Morais argues that Portugal's recent economic performance means that "Portugal has come full turn in a relatively few years, from economic basket case to economic miracle." Specifically, the country "has grown at an average annual rate of 4.3 percent, very near the top of the entire Organization for Economic Cooperation and Development list. Its 4 percent unemployment is the lowest in the European Community, bar Luxembourg." Moreover, "labor productivity [has] increased at an average annual rate of 2.6 percent during the last five years of the 1980s." The revolutionary transition had inspired anarchic worker uprisings, and "for almost a decade [afterward] the economy stagnated." The rise of Cavaco Silva and the PSD to power made it possible to "adroitly [mix] privatization with infrastructure investment, deregulation with EC 'convergence' subsidies" and "set Portugal on course." This modernizing capitalist attitude has meant that "direct foreign investment has been doubling every year," and major firms like automakers Ford and Volkswagen have collaborated to produce a "next generation plant, a $2.8 billion factory for minivans" in Setúbal, part of the red industrial belt. Considering the country "a very attractive point of entry for the EC," PepsiCo Foods International decided to build a $150 million state-of-the-art snack-food factory, tapping $20 million in government and EC subsidies, and plans to spend "a half billion dollars in Portugal over the next ten years." Other foreign firms such as Pacific Telesis Group, which is investing $250 million over the next five years to set up a mobile phone network, have also become convinced that Portugal is now part of the modern capitalist world. At this point, foreign capital accounts for 14 percent of industrial employment and 42 percent of total industrial production.[2]

Throughout this book, I have argued that major elements of the colonial-corporatist and transitional legacies have been supplanted by an emergent Portuguese hegemonic project mixing a European identity; liberal political institutions; and a capitalist, somewhat dependent economic model strongly shaped by the country's relatively low-cost labor force within the EC.[3] But the impact of past events continues to "weigh like a nightmare on the brain of the living."[4] While attempting to emulate its more developed European counterparts, "Portugal's transition to European normality is not complete" as Fred Halliday (1992) wrote not long ago. The country's underdevelopment—expressed in low wages, 80-percent adult literacy, and high infant-mortality rates, among many other indices—and residual transitional elements make it different.

Portugal's tendency to feature high inflation rates along with its strong record of growth means that it needs to institute "wage restraints [and] tighter fiscal policies" (Double 1992, 14); yet the role of employers' associations, the state, and organized labor—still divided between Communist and reformist federations—in national collective bargaining remains in flux. Fiscal pressures may oblige governments to cut back on the incipient welfare state, which despite the many leftist incantations of Portuguese constitutions remains in many ways a dim reflection of those elsewhere in Europe. The government's privatization efforts have been proceeding steadily, but in 1993 many large firms still remained at least partially in state hands—Banco Português do Atlântico was one important example.[5] Furthermore, some privatizations have reconstituted elements of the monopolistic groups that predated and possibly forestalled the democratization process, with the once nationalized Banco Espírito Santo back under the control of the Espírito Santo family, "Portugal's best-known banking dynasty." Proving that even old *comprador* capitalists have now accepted the Europeanist accumulation strategy, the banking family is now "spinning a web of alliances abroad" and expanding into new financial services markets domestically in anticipation of banking law reforms that "will ensure that Portugal's banking system complies with European directives by the end of the year. That will make it easier for other European banks to set up shop in Lisbon" (*Economist* 1992, 97). The old must now act like the new under changed historical circumstances.

In part, as Halliday argues, "the instrument of conformity [to European semiperipheral capitalism] was not war, as it had been for [postwar] Germany and Italy, but the EC" (1992, 25). But the specific course of Portugal's expanded democratization process played a critical role in setting the stage for a degree of Euroconformity insofar as it linked political changes with the elimination of the colonial-protectionist accumulation strategy. In addition, after the fall of the dictatorship the process altered the social and political bases of support for the new regime by reducing the influence of antidemocratic or radical elements both among the ruling circles as well among the popular masses.

Dishegemony corresponded to an interlude between the repudiation of the hegemonic project of the old corporatist authoritarian regime and the progressive installation of a hybrid Europeanist model of political economy, a process that is by no means complete. Tensions continue between left and right—for example, between rightist control of the executive and leftist defense of a constitution that still embodies some of the gains of the revolution. Former Socialist leader and now the Republic's president Mário Soares has used his power to refer controversial legislation to the Constitutional Tribunal thirty times since 1986 and succeeded two-thirds of the time in obliging the PSD government to redraft important pieces of its legislation.[6] The May 1994 local elections confirmed that a coalition of Socialists and Communists would control Lisbon's government with opposition from a weak, fragmented right. Indeed, to the extent that those elections may have illustrated current sentiment about national party choices—always a risky proposition given the importance of local personalities and issues in municipal elections—the results resurrected the 1983 party situation, with the

PS the plurality party, the PSD a close second, and the CDS and Communists strengthened somewhat in comparison to the 1991 election results.

In the Alentejo, candidate lists without the backing of the big four parties have confronted the political status quo. In Evora, a PCP stronghold, a movement called "Citizens for Evora" has issued a manifesto declaring its "regionalist outlook, in the context of the construction of a Europe of Regions" and wishing to contribute to the "appearance of new [political instruments] that . . . remove from the Alentejo false mistrusts."[7] Dissidents from the larger parties have also formed such lists elsewhere in the Alentejo. In 1991, the National Solidarity party with a platform focused on the needs of the elderly managed to elect a single deputy to Parliament. Despite the conquest of national power by the PSD, the *estado laranga* and post-transition political establishment have shown fissures.

Moreover, the period 1992–93 was "the darkest year of the PSD government's rule" according to the Portuguese weekly *Espresso* (17 July 1993). Rising unemployment, bankruptcies, unpaid wages, accusations of high-level corruption, deep controversies over education, health and agricultural policies all reduced the credibility of the PSD government. Yet with the government managing the infusion of billions of ECUs and the opposition unable to present a credible national alternative, the electorate may have no choice but to continue its support for the PSD and the outline of its hegemonic project.

Dishegemony was notable for more than its results, the fluid but discernible outlines of a partial combination of the southern conflict and northern cooperative regimes. Expanded democratization and the dishegemony that followed produced an extraordinary process: political and social actors had to compete under conditions of relative structural indeterminacy to find an electorally acceptable combination of features resulting in a more legitimate hegemonic project. For this reason, the Portuguese experience is particularly relevant to similar cases of centralized dictatorship in which the incremental or consociational approaches for democratization are not available, as in many parts of the former Soviet bloc.

This chapter underscores the key factors that decisively shaped the Portuguese experience and compares six alternative forms of democratization. These routes are then used to characterize the pattern of change in the former Soviet bloc. It also explores the dilemma of semiperipheral democratization in a context of broad changes in capitalism, which has made models of democratic capitalism acquired during its organized phase less attainable now for democratizers at Europe's edge. Important changes in the character of Europe's advanced political economies have made the typology of conflict regimes of southern Europe and neocorporatist ones in the north less relevant for both aspiring democratizers and those countries to which they were initially applied.

KEY FACTORS IN PORTUGUESE DEMOCRATIZATION

The first variable explored in chapter 2 was the absence of a leading segment of the traditional dominant class that could provide a viable resolution for key economic policy differences and guide the democratization process. For incremental democratization to succeed, intraregime softliners, including key segments of the dominant class and the political elite, must take precedence in the policy debate and force hardliners to accept or resign themselves to the leading segment's softliner hegemony. This hegemony not only implies a greater tolerance of dissent and willingness to entertain genuine parliamentary rule, but an acceptance of these political changes as part of a larger package of policy and institutional reforms.

In Portugal, a fissure between softliner Europeanists, more inclined to free markets, foreign investment, and a general redirection of economic attention toward Europe, and hardliner colonial protectionists, who wanted to retain the colonies and sheltered markets, sharply divided the dominant class and set intraregime softliners against hardliners within the political elite. These strategic differences did not correspond to structural splits that might have neatly divided the Portuguese bourgeoisie into contending segments, each seeking to impose a clear direction upon the political economy. Rather, overlaps and contradictory interests within the bourgeoisie made it prone to indecisive policy stands and only weakly hegemonic. Therefore, it was hard for softliners to sustain Caetano's liberalization in the face of rising labor agitation and self-organization and diminished enthusiasm for the single dominant policy stand that might have fostered a controlled democratization from above: the end of the colonial wars. As a result, neither the dominant class nor policy advocates among the political elite could resolve these strategic dilemmas, making them unable to lead the democratization process. Before the MFA's action in 1974, the rise and fall of the liberal softliners symbolized the inconclusive character of the softliner-hardliner struggle among the regime's political elite and dominant class.[8]

In the absence of a civilian revolution from above, democratization could still occur through some combination of actions by other state institutions, (primarily the military) and the popular masses. In the event that institutional actors (military, political parties) have taken power in an instance of relative state autonomy and weak hegemony, the second key factor shaping the democratization process concerns the range of available coalition options and the policy directions associated with them. When the Portuguese military took action in the face of prolonged immobility among civilian leaders, its propensity to look outside the traditional elite for allies multiplied the prospects for radicalization and a basic questioning of the nature of the social settlement to follow.[9] Not only were intraregime softliners included within the coalition, but extraregime soft- and hardliners as well. This opened the door to the broad range of social and political choices that characterized the dishegemonic period.

Particularly important in this regard was the role and ideology of the extraregime opposition.[10] In Portugal, the division between soft- and hardliners within the extraregime opposition was partly camouflaged by the growing radicalism during the Caetano years as the colonial wars dragged on. In the struggle against fascism the opposition seemed to reflect less the conflicting pulls of ideology and social cleavages and more a common purpose in defeating the old regime and replacing it with a generally leftist, if democratic, alternative. Yet in the aftermath of the 1974 coup, a more distinct differentiation between the hardline revolutionary opposition and the reformist softliners appeared. The difficulties of creating a common program for the left remained a singular trademark of both the transition and consolidation. The extraregime soft- and hardliners found common cause largely as an anti-fascist opposition to the old regime rather than as leaders of a new counterhegemonic program united around a common conception of democracy, capitalism, or socialism. As I noted in chapters 3 through 5, the electorate was divided between the parties of the left along various sociological and attitudinal lines, reinforcing if not determining a longstanding split between Communists and Socialists along ideological and organizational lines.[11]

Conversely, throughout the consolidation period, the most impressive trait of the intraregime softliners was their ability to overcome partisan differences and unify around a common basic model of political economy. From an early point, the PSD became identified as the party of liberal softliners under whose leadership most significant intraregime reformers could unite to overcome the association with the defunct corporatist regime. The hegemonic project of these softliners was essentially that of the Europeanists, now sheared of the pernicious conflict with the colonial protectionists. This project was largely a deepening of structural patterns developing throughout the 1960s, coupled with the adoption of requisite political institutions for EC membership. In this sense, it was intrinsically more concrete and tailored to the imperatives of the larger political and economic context surrounding Portugal rather than competing ones from the left that were divided over the ideal concepts of socialism and democracy. Because the right's model was more straightforward, the issue became less the message than the strategic choice of the PSD as the ideal messenger.

The ability for the right to adapt its message and manage its political divisions illustrates what Nancy Bermeo (1992) describes as political learning. She defines this as "the process through which people modify their political beliefs and tactics as a result of severe crisis, frustration and dramatic changes in environment" (1992, 274). She argues that "political learning is most important during the second phase of the redemocratization process—at the critical moment between the crisis of the old order and the consolidation of the new one" (1992, 273). Bermeo does not discuss types of democratization in any detail, essentially limiting her concerns to the narrow aspect of institution building, and focuses upon elite beliefs along lines of authoritarianism, anti-authoritarianism, prodemocracy. As useful as this approach is, the learning concept can also help us focus upon the capacity for political actors not simply to endorse some or all dimensions of parliamentary democratic institutions, but also learn lessons about how to manipulate such nascent institutions to better impose their concepts and policy paradigms upon society as a whole. Peter Hall (1993) has developed the concept of social learning as a means of discussing the emergence and durability of policy paradigms in his examination of economic policy-making in Britain. A combination of both types of learning seems most appropriate when discussing the transition from expanded democratization to a more stable hegemonic project. In these situations, the identification of key policy concerns and the discovery of successful strategies for their realization within newly constructed political arrangements may strongly reinforce prodemocratic institutional attitudes, at least among those obtaining favored outcomes.

In Portugal, lessons about the relationship among authoritarianism, democracy, and economic strategies or models are better understood if attributed to elements differentiated along a left-right scale. The right included much of the post-transitional dominant class, an important part of the political elite, and relevant support classes or social categories (for example, smallholding farmers, religious elements in the working class, and parts of the urban petty bourgeoisie). For the right, the lessons of the dictatorship grew increasingly clear with the passage of time: authoritarianism was incompatible with the long-term political and economic interests of the dominant class due to its limitations as a model of accumulation (that is, rejection of the colonial-protectionist line and authoritarian labor relations) as well as its weakness as a specific political arrangement (that is, insufficient popular legitimacy and unacceptable to EC). The lessons of the transition reinforced some classic right principles such as anti-Communism and an aversion to challenging established authorities, but they also limited the right's attraction to military intervention into politics. Over the course of the dishegemonic consolidation, the right effectively perceived the costs of political division, resulting in more viable political strategies (massive support for the AD and PSD) and a honing of its modern message. The remarkable strategic voting of the right electorate for the AD-PSD suggests that this lesson was not confined to the elite but was shared by other classes and social categories.

The extent of political and social learning on the left was less impressive. This was especially true for the PCP, which failed to embrace the reforms needed to help it overcome the limitations of its centralizing, vanguardist, Leninist party organization and Soviet-style hegemonic project. PCP changes in a Eurocommunist direction might have made the party more amenable to the PS as a potential coalition member and possibly more appealing as a populist party of the left. By combining short-term dissatisfaction with economic conditions and emerging post material issues such as those of ecologists, the PCP might have become a serious electoral actor in its own right. But the Communists could not adequately address the paradigmatic implications of the failure of Leninism, making its openings to the PS (as with the Lisbon coalition) or its alliance with ecologists implausible avenues for significantly gaining a share of national power in a democratic way.

For the PCP, the legacy of dictatorship taught it much about political survival under fascism; the collapse of the dictatorship and the MFA's role as vanguard demonstrated that revolutionary reforms from above coupled with Communist directed class support from below were the best ways to reach socialism. Given the scope of change under the transition and the reversals experienced under the dishegemonic consolidation, the lesson of vanguard-induced change was too readily confirmed. It reinforced the intrinsic ideological predispositions and historic experiences of much of the PCP's leadership. The history of coalitions with small electorally inconsequential parties, electoral decline, and even the breakup of the Soviet Union during the consolidation produced few lessons of adaptation and renewal as the party ejected its internal critics and pursued only the blandest reforms.[12]

The experience under the dictatorship generally reinforced the Socialists' antipathy to dictatorship and was a critical reason for their opposition to PCP-MFA vanguardism during the transition. But their adaptability during the dishegemonic consolidation was also limited by the transitional experience and other long-standing attitudes. The party's historical anti-Communism, bolstered during the transition, made it completely hostile to the PCP and narrowed its coalition options to a point where it lost leverage in its dealings with the right. Despite evidence that it would not become the majority party, the PS did not adapt its coalition strategy; it refused alliances with both the PCP and later the PRD. It never found a means for broadening political responsibility for austerity to the right and failed to anticipate the PSD's defection from the grand coalition in 1985. These factors combined to reduce the scope of coalition options and eventually made the resurgence of the right more likely.

Conversely, PS support for a Europeanist policy paradigm was learned not only from the days when its members were in the illegal extraregime opposition, often abroad in democratic Europe, but also after the fall of the Caetano regime, when Europeanization became quickly identified with the success of democratization in the face of vanguardist alternatives. As the party's many policy zigzags have revealed, it has been hard for the Socialists to pin down the exact boundaries of their favored political economy; their espousal of socialism adapts to circumstances as much as principle. More than anything, the Socialists and their allies in the UGT have retained the view that possible socialism is the realization of an idealized version of a northern cooperative regime—a Social Democratic postwar settlement adapted to Portuguese conditions at the outer border of mainstream Europe.

Democratic consolidation in Portugal was also greatly facilitated by another major factor: the relatively rapid introduction of a coherent institutional model—a stable four-party electoral democracy. This made it possible for democratic political institutions to channel intra- and interclass conflicts into a nonviolent political arena. Within the ruling circles these were mostly translated into alternatives between the CDS and the more liberal PSD. Similarly, narrowing differences within the left to those expressed by the PCP and PS made it possible to steer national debates regarding the character of any new hegemonic project into distinct party choices.

The rapid rise to prominence of the parliamentary system reinforced the link between electoral success and executive control, making the political system a vital arena of choice in the face of structural indeterminacy and impotent traditional leadership. The relatively autonomous state was able to elicit guiding messages from the parties, making the process of establishing a new hegemonic project a better fusion of national aspirations, party leadership choices, and structural constraints.

Given the heightened importance of the political system's leadership functions, the emergence of a widely accepted hegemonic project depended upon the timely link between short-term economic circumstances and a party or tendency's presence in office. The short-term success of a government reinforced the image of a coherent and plausible hegemonic project. As short-term gains multiplied, the broader programmatic lines represented by the reigning political forces became institutionalized and set the structural limits of a new social agreement. The fact that the Socialist party was faced with the need to govern during periods of economic crisis and austerity contributed to its declining popularity and a diminished prospect of a leftist slant to the emerging political economy. Conversely,the timing of the general upswing in the global economy during 1986 meant that the PSD was in the right place at the right time, benefiting from the reality and perception of improving economic conditions. The party's short-term popularity boost could then be converted into support for its long-term structural choices. In this way, the termination of dishegemony was accelerated by events only partially under the control of the actors themselves. Although these events gave the right an opportunity for long-term political success, the parties had to cement the link between short-term improvements, stable governing options, and the long-term options they represented. For the right, this meant consolidating support behind the AD in 1979 and the PSD in 1987 while reinforcing the perception of the PS as the only viable alternative, but also as an excessively leftist overseer of bad times.

Portuguese democratization has moved from a stage that could be characterized as passive revolution to one of expansive hegemony. According to Jessop, the former imposes "the interests of the dominant forces on the popular masses through a war of position which advances particular popular interests (if at all) through a mechanical game of compromise rather than their organic integration into a 'national-popular' project" (Jessop 1983, 103–5). This description seems entirely appropriate *in reverse* to much of the transition, which was an attempt to impose the interests of the popular masses on the dominant forces through a game of compromise in light of the weak counterhegemony established by the left. Dishegemony was characterized by policies of compromise between essentially incompatible models of political economy—incomplete privatization of firms and cooperatives; partial reversal of the leftist constitution, workers' rights, and the like. Nevertheless, the nature of the passive revolution gradually was transformed in the 1980s to correspond better to Jessop's initial formulation. Eventually, an "expansive hegemony in which support of the entire population is mobilized through material concessions and symbolic rewards" was created. This was expressed by the PSD's electoral victories in 1987 and 1991, which coincided with perceptions of improvements in the economy, the functioning of democracy, and life satisfaction.

Working-class integration into policy-making through neocorporatist arrangements was increasingly accepted as part of the process of reestablishing capitalist structural limits to policy. As the gains of the revolution eroded, both unions and employers found greater utility in working as social partners through the council on social concertation. With the decline of broad counterhegemonic alternatives, the calculus of cost and benefit within the bourgeois hegemonic project progressively replaced paradigmatic debates.

Forms of Democratization

Portugal's experience with expanded democratization may be used to establish a framework for characterizing forms of democratization, ranging from one extreme in which factors essentially preclude it to another in which democratization is far-ranging and multifaceted. My purpose is not to generate a theory that follows a deterministic logic—starting with economic crisis and inevitably resulting in a democratization process. As Markoff and Baretta (1987, 440) have suggested in their examination of Brazil, an independent variable such as "economic crisis may be a major spur to political movement, but actors intent on rejecting democracy and those intent on dismantling authoritarianism may equally draw energy from their sense of the political solutions to the problems they confront." Any case-specific examination of the political effects of economic crisis must deal with the contextual circumstances of economic crisis, singling out how different sectors of the state and society are affected and the power or resources that they may bring to bear in favor of alternative political strategies.

Historic institutional conditions may also influence the transitional options that ruling circles use, as Foweraker (1987) has claimed in examining the role of corporatist institutions and democratization in Spain. An effort to understand the inclination of soft- and hardliners to favor centralized bargaining, peak associations, and the twin use of parliamentary and neocorporatist representational forms must recognize that corporatism is "always a state strategy which will be inserted differently into the institutional ensemble of the state and contribute differently to the structuring of state-civil society relations in distinct forms in specific historical moments" (Foweraker 1987, 57). Roniger's (1989) study of democratization notes that the global context, not simply the domestic environment, provides its own set of incentives for domestic actors to entertain certain political strategies that are not just intrinsic manifestations of indigenous interests. Schwartzman's (1989) study of the first Portuguese republic has underlined the constraints posed upon the choice of contending accumulation strategies by Portugal's semiperipheral status and dependence upon British imperialism.[13] Like many other topics, the study of democratization can easily pose the problem of "too many variables, not enough cases" (Lijphart 1971). Karl and Schmitter (1991, 282) have accurately remarked:

> Since the Portuguese "Revolution of the Carnations" in 1974, one autocratic regime after another has given way to some type of democracy—first in Southern Europe, then in South and to a lesser extent Central America and, most recently, in Eastern Europe. These transitions can all be considered part of the same process in that each successive one has contributed to

the likelihood of the next. Despite these diffusion effects, in most cases the changes were deliberately confined to the realm of political authority alone; in others they involved a simultaneous and compound transformation of political, social and economic relations. The actual means whereby these regime changes were accomplished has varied a great deal.

Generalizations must deal not simply with the variable *means* by which democratization has occurred, but also with the variable *scope* it entails. This further complicates efforts at theory building, the dependent variable is no longer simply a question of a qualitative change in forms of political authority, but also one of expanded democratization extending to variable social and economic domains. Because the transition as well as the consolidation periods are of interest to our investigation of the concurrent processes of political institution building and the redesign of hegemonic projects, we must include scope and form over time. Stretching the dependent variable may well entail an expansion in the number or character of the independent variables: political and social learning might be extended to apply to broad social strata rather than confined to political elites; concern with the structure of cleavages in the electorate and short-term incumbent party effects complicate analysis further.[14]

The cases grow more dissimilar with the addition of post-Communist political economies, and concept stretching further dilutes the meaning of key terms in an effort to extend a relatively parsimonious set of variables to increasingly disparate cases. Because this study has focused on a single case, any attempt to extrapolate key variables, patterns, and conditions cannot be strictly theory building as much as hypotheses generating.[15] With these caveats in mind, I offer a framework that classifies forms of democratization in a manner faithful to the tone and logic used to describe and explain elements of the Portuguese transition.[16]

Table 8.1 identifies six forms of democratization arranged in terms of the degree of discontinuity with the preexisting regime. The first form, continuity without democratization, represents a condition in which virtually no democratization is likely; policy conflicts within the ruling circles are not deep and generally reconciled within authoritarianism. Cries of dissent from the opposition have little immediate impact upon the two-nations strategy that specifically pays disproportionate attention to a selected constituency and disregards all others.

Slow liberalization with possible democratization also represents continuity but with at least some degree of change. In Portugal, it was represented by Caetano's liberalization, which did make it possible for popular organizations and conflicting opinions to gain some autonomy from the regime. This form of democratization also corresponds to the doubtful leadership of softliners, who may easily succumb to conservative pressures from hardliners to crack down and reverse course. In Portugal the failure of this option eventually led in the direction of dishegemonic democratization, but it might have resulted in a more controlled democratic opening like that depicted by the softliner-led alternatives.[17]

The two forms of democratization led by softliners represent evolutionary processes of liberalization and democratization without broad social confrontation. As in Spain, they constitute situations in which intraregime softliners gain the upper hand over the hardliners and make overtures to the extraregime softliners who may be needed to resolve policy differences or to help institutionalize potentially destabilizing social conflict. They differ largely in the degree of control exerted by intraregime as opposed to extraregime softliners.

The last two forms are variants of dishegemonic democratization, differing mainly in terms of the success of reformist or revolutionary elements within the extraregime opposition in imposing their political economic conceptions upon society. Under revolutionary dishegemonic democratization there is the possibility that political democratization may succumb to the radical pretensions of extraregime hardliners and thereby eclipse Western-style democratization altogether.

The pretransition degree of dominant-class division initially defines each option. This variable calls attention to the severity of contention among intraregime advocates of differing accumulation strategies. It is assumed that democratization will rarely if ever be simply the product of pressures from below in the absence of fissures at the top and that the impact of mass pressures will be greater as those fissures expand. Conversely, mass pressures may be one important element exacerbating strategic divisions among the ruling circles—perhaps nationalist, protectionist, or labor-repressive policies versus Europeanist, open-economy, neocorporatist alternatives. Mass pressures might still be present under continuity without democratization, but reliance on repression and the two-nations hegemonic project prevent them from being as effective. The tight bond between ascendant intraregime hardliners and softliners makes overtures by the extraregime opposition largely irrelevant. For many years in the aftermath of the overthrow of President Allende in Chile, General Pinochet's rule made distinctions between hard- and softliners appear negligible; in Portugal, divisions from the 1930s until the early 1960s were never deep enough to undermine the ascendency of hardliners within the ruling coalition.

Slow liberalization with possible democratization places the intraregime softliners in a more ascendant position over the hardliners due to the need to deal with minor controversies at the top and growing but manageable pressures from below. Nevertheless, the political opening to the opposition remains restricted. The 1993 presidential elections in Paraguay represented such an instance insofar as the military announced its hesitation to accept a non-Colorado party victory; the opposition was tolerated during the electoral period but never seriously expected to govern.[18] Depending upon the harshness of general conditions, a tendency for this intraregime hard- soft-liner coalition to rely upon a passive revolution rather than an organic national-popular project makes this option susceptible to decay into renewed authoritarianism or may yield to a dishegemonic transition should popular resistance or military action prove forthcoming, which occurred in Portugal after Caetano's failed liberalization.

The third form of democratization features the leadership of intraregime softliners who have managed substantially to lessen their dependence upon intraregime hardliners and instead reach out to the softliners in the extraregime opposition. Under this form, the choices facing the dominant class stir greater controversy, and policy options favorable to the intraregime hardliners seem globally dysfunctional. Because the regime does not face a deep crisis, democratization is an evolutionary process in which the intraregime softliners are able to dictate the limits to the policy paradigm and new institutional arrangements. Unlike the previous form, hegemonic options are soon tied more directly with national electoral choices. To the extent that national institutions or parties can frame broad alternatives short of expanded democratization, an expansive hegemony may be attained. This seems to capture the transitional process in Spain, where a series of compromises were struck limiting the reach of demands from below to those tolerated at the top. The expansive hegemony that followed depended less on the figures actually in political office and more upon the terms of the transition: the collapse of center-right parties by 1981 brought the leftist PSOE to power, but the party generally conformed to the

Table 8.1. Forms of Democratization

Key Variables	Continuity without Democratization	Slow Liberalization with Possible Democratization	Democratization Led by Intraregime Softliners	Democratization led by Extraregime	Reformist Dishegemonic Democratization	Revolutionary Dishegemonic Democratization
Pretransition degree of dominant class division	none	low	medium	medium	high	high
Mass pressures	limited	growing	medium	major	major	major
Pre-Transition degree of liberalization	none	low	medium	medium	minor or failed	minor or failed
Character of transition	none	incremental liberalization/democratization	evolutionary democratization	medium	Abrupt/expanded democratization	Abrupt, revolutionary expanded
Hegemonic project	two nations	passive revolution	expansive hegemony	reversed passive revolution to dishegemony	revolution moving	popular counter-hegemony
Coalitions	IR hard/IR soft	IR hard/IR soft	IR hard/IR soft	IR hard/IR soft	IR hard/IR soft	IR hard/IR soft
Electoral cleavages	Decisively support old order or irrelevant	Generally support old order	evenly balanced	evenly balanced	generally supports change	decisively supports change
Ideological divisions	predominantly traditionalist	predominantly traditionalist	predominantly centrist	predominantly left-center	predominantly leftist	predominantly leftist and radical
Organized class relations	corporatist, authoritarian	corporatist or liberal	neocorporatist or liberal	neocorporatist or liberal	left neocorporatist?	popular power/ authoritarian
Viability of new accumulation strategy	must keep unified D/C	must prevent minor divisions from growing	must overcome divisions		must decide among basic options	must pursue counterhegemonic option against resistance
Short-term success consolidation	low import/ irrelevant	medium import	medium import	medium to high import	high import	medium to high import

the leftist PSOE to power, but the party generally conformed to the policy limits agreed to during the transition.

Democratization led by extraregime softliners is distinguished by the emergence of severe splits at the top and an influential role for extraregime softliners during the transition and consolidation. It may also be combined with greater pressures from below for political and social reforms. These conditions lessen the prospects for a thoroughly accepted hegemonic project because pressures from below expand the scope of institutional and socioeconomic change and polarize the ruling circles. This constitutes a kind of reversed passive revolution in which ruling circles reluctantly accept the terms of transitional compromises without much threat of a major transformation of property relations and authority patterns. Brazil might have faced this option had the leader of the Brazilian Labor party, Luis Ignâcio da Silva, beaten the more centrist Fernando Collor de Mello in the 1989 presidential elections. Portugal itself might have followed this course had the Socialists been able to obtain a single-party majority in 1976 to the disadvantage the PCP and the revolutionary left. This would have given the party four years to shape the post-transition social settlement by implementing important reformist policies in areas such as land reform, labor relations, health, and education. Instead, the PS was forced to rule as a minority government facing competitive pressures from the left and right. The abruptness of democratization, the collapse of the intraregime elements, and the significance of the revolutionary hardline both electorally and ideologically made this form of democratization unlikely.

Dishegemonic democratization can occur in two forms. In the first, it is led by the extraregime softliners with some reliance upon revolutionary hardliners; in the second, the extraregime hardliners are predominant, with the softliners playing a diminished role. In both cases there is the presence of a more serious and unresolved crisis within the ruling circles. Democratization efforts flounder due to the top's lack of consensus on the terms of an internal agreement and the apparently unacceptable consequences of allowing popular pressures to structure institutional and policy outcomes from below. Hesitations within the ruling circles are reinforced when a revolutionary opposition seems likely to play a decisive role in a democratization process, which can be self-fulfilling if intraregime elements resist reform. In Portugal, labor activism coupled with antiwar pressures helped immobilize the regime and spurred the opposition to greater radicalism. The collapse of intraregime elements in leading the democratization process meant that the demands of the extraregime opposition established the limits of the process. The key struggle that emerged was within the opposition. The extent of expanded democratization that results from this struggle cannot be inferred without a case-specific understanding of the programs and strategies of the opposition's parties. The collapse of the old regime, the weakness of its supporters, and the illegitimacy of its principles make a broad assault on both traditional institutions and social settlements more likely.

Dishegemonic and expanded forms of democratization pose the special problem of balancing the power of the popular masses as expressed through their organizations—political parties, trade unions, residents' and workers' councils', and other popular movements—with the structural power of the dominant classes, who control capital, managerial knowledge, markets, and alliances with international capital and supportive states. Despite efforts to nationalize the commanding heights of the economy quickly, the mere transference of formal title does not ensure that an alternative accumulation process can be erected. Furthermore, it is precisely over the shape of any alternative system that divisions between extraregime soft- and hardliners are most likely to materialize; softliners such as the Portuguese Socialists proved unwilling to sacrifice parliamentary democracy to carry out an anticapitalist revolution. For extraregime hardliners to remain in charge of Western-style democratization, they need to develop a deep network of ties to the popular masses, alliances with key figures in the military, and broad electoral support for expanded democratization. This combination seemed to be in place for some time in Nicaragua under Sandinista rule. In Portugal, the Communists lacked electoral support for their counterhegemonic project; the Socialists had more electoral support but less organized popular support. Together, they played vital roles in producing a dishegemonic outcome: a leftist constitution and some major reforms along with continued competition and ideological fractures between the major left parties.

In each form of democratization, a set of sustaining conditions must be present during the consolidation period to ensure the continuity of events generated during the transition. To the extent that a specific case establishes a functioning, electorally based political system, electoral and ideological cleavages need to correspond to the coalitions established and ascendant during the transition in order for programs to continue. For intraregime softliner-led processes, traditionalist electoral cleavages encourage a slow pace of change and reduce the risk of electoral defeat or successful programmatic opposition. Without the strong assurance of electoral confirmation in a competitive democracy, liberalization might remain only partial and reversible at the first sign of trouble, as was the case for Caetano.

When the coalition guiding democratization expands to include extraregime elements, increasing electoral uncertainty for the ruling circles means that traditional interests may be undercut by the electoral process. When the opposition's program is not revolutionary, at least some intraregime elements should find democratization tolerable: if extraregime softliners should win an election, they will probably help resolve policy conflicts without undermining (and, indeed, they may bolster) the overall hegemony of the dominant class. To sustain these reformist democratizations, electoral cleavages ideally impede a decisive victory of either intra- or extraregime softliners and thereby force them into a formal or informal coalition while excluding the possibility of hardliners' electoral victory.

In dishegemonic and expanded democratizations, the extraregime opposition requires supportive electoral cleavages to provide the legitimacy needed to confront or transform the broad parameters of the accumulation model. Given that the newly ascendant (formerly extraregime) opposition typically lacks the structural power of the ruling circles, it cannot hope to sustain expanded democratization during the consolidation period without a steady electoral majority committed to change. In Portugal, the left won successive electoral majorities, which, despite the lack of coherent government, still hindered efforts by the right to claim an unambiguous mandate for its hegemonic project. In Nicaragua, the Sandinistas discovered the limits of their power after the UNO coalition's electoral victory in 1990. While that event did not result in a complete repudiation of their rule, the dishegemonic dismemberment similar to the AD's in Portugal was given popular legitimacy that Sandinista efforts ultimately lacked. In both Portugal and Nicaragua, an inability to rely upon a consistent leftist majority united around a common program meant that, over time, the structural weight and foreign support of the ruling circles, combined with the left's internal divisions, would reestablish the capitalist boundaries of the policy paradigm.

In the case of an anticapitalist form of dishegemonic or expanded democratization, the prospects for the former extraregime opposition to unite its electoral base and mobilize its organized allies in civil society during the consolidation are typically dim. Przeworski (1985) has noted several key constraints upon working-class, leftist attempts to go beyond the inherited framework of social relations. These can be summarized in nine points:

- Representative democracy creates an intrinsic fissure between political organizations such as parties and economic ones such as trade unions.
- Relations among individual workers are often competitive, easily reflected as political cleavages in elections that represent workers as citizen-voter/individuals and not as a class as a whole.
- Secondary cleavages based on religion, ethnicity, region, and so on may further undermine efforts to represent broad working-class interests.
- Parties seeking electoral majorities typically must aggregate interests to gain electoral majorities and therefore represent interests other than those of workers exclusively.
- Representation by leaders rather than direct mass action demobilizes the masses and results in a greater willingness to forgo revolutionary objectives.
- The political and union organization of workers produces a petty bourgeois strata of notables easily persuaded to give up broad counterhegemonic goals for a share of power.
- The acceptance of constitutional and legal processes results in responsible parties who are oriented toward partial improvements.
- Positing political democracy as an ends further limits the scope of counterhegemonic efforts because a broad array of personal and property rights must be respected, including some contrary to leftist attempts at socialization of production.
- As wage earners achieve partial improvements within capitalism, the popularity of counter-hegemonic ideas diminishes.

The historical division between Communist and Socialist/Social Democratic movements reflects differing conclusions about the trade-off between the scope of change and commitment to democratic processes. Before their conversion to Eurocommunism, Communists were inclined to defend broad socioeconomic change even at the risk of undermining electoral democracy; in Portugal, the PCP constantly vacillated between securing the gains of the revolution through mass action and participating in electoral processes. Socialists, concerned especially with electoral success and stabilizing parliamentary democracy, were much more willing to sacrifice Socialist goals in pursuit of an elusive electoral majority. To the degree that the Socialists were successful, many of the factors impeding working-class hegemony came into play (as I have already outlined). This underlines the fact that leftist versions of dishegemonic and expanded democratizations are inherently unstable, either tending to deradicalize as electoral democracy consolidates or radicalize as electoral democracy is bypassed.

In part, the inability to maintain the change-oriented transitional coalition during the consolidation period reflects Marx's faulty conclusion that the proletarianization process would strip away structural divisions among workers as well as undermine the saliency of secondary identifications and cleavages. As Marx said, "the proletarian movement is the self-conscious, independent movement of the immense majority" caused by the incorporation of other classes into the proletariat with the development of capitalist production (Tucker 1978, 482). "The lower strata of the middle class—the small tradespeople, shopkeepers, and retired tradesmen generally, the handicraftsmen and peasants—all these sink gradually into the proletariat . . . [which is] recruited from all classes of the population" (Tucker 1978, 479–80). Even the bourgeoisie finds that "entire sections of the ruling classes are, by the advance of industry, precipitated into the proletariat" (Tucker 1978, 481). Moreover, "differences of age and sex have no longer any distinctive social validity for the working class" while "modern subjection to capital . . . has stripped [the worker] of every trace of national character" (Tucker 1978, 481).

For Marx, proletarianization was a key product of the long-term evolution of capitalism. But Marx and other Socialists erred when they placed an emphasis upon the growing size of the industrial proletariat, claiming this immense majority's electoral representation would translate into Socialist transformation.[19] Even in Portugal, where the development of an affluent service sector (a move typical of advanced capitalism) was not comparable to that in other Western European countries, a completely solid electoral block of industrial workers united behind the left (unlikely in any case) could not provide an electoral counterhegemonic majority without allying itself with more class-ambiguous strata. Rather, the typical problem for leftist parties is one of broadening the social coalition to include the "lower middle class, the small manufacturer, the shopkeeper, the artisan, the peasant" who all "fight against the bourgeoisie to save from extinction their existence as fractions of the middle class" (Tucker 1978, 482) as well as the modern service sector that expands and matures directly as a by-product of capitalist development.

Alan Hunt points out: "Since the 1930s the general strategies of the Communist movement in Western Europe have revolved around the problem of class alliances. They have centred [sic] on the fundamentally Gramscian project of the realisation of the hegemonic influence of the working class, which encompasses both the realisation of that class itself and the extension of its influence and leadership over other social classes" (1977, 82).

Attaining the Gramscian project in the course of democratization requires a relatively solid electoral and social coalition composed of the popular masses, strongly unified around a counterhegemonic program. The noninsurrectionary nature of political democratization, especially after the initial transition period, implies that despite their intrinsic instability, strategic alliances with nonindustrial working-class elements must be forged if any aspects of expanded democratization are to be retained. The gains of the revolution face more serious challenges during the democratic consolidation when a leftist government feels the burdens of incumbency and the fraying of the counterhegemonic social base. The passage from expanded democratization during the transition to a broader leftist dishegemony during consolidation requires a program that prevents socialism from being associated with untenable accumulation models and impossibly narrow social coalitions. In an era when "the revolutionary way [to socialism] has been rejected," a counterhegemonic, leftist project must be more flexible and accommodating, as Giorgio Napolitano, a leader of the Italian Communist party, has argued:

> If one refuses the identification between socialism and collective property in the means of production and instead sees a need for different forms of property (private, state, cooperative) as well as a not incidental role for the market in relation to the possible implementation of planning instruments, it becomes hard to define or characterize a "socialist society" as one in which the reigning economic and social systems are defined in terms totally opposed to those found in a capitalist system. (1990, 101)

A leftist counterhegemonic project seeks to reconcile a populist but heterogeneous social basis; democratic political institutions; and a distinct,if not altogether different, accumulation model and strategy.

Expanded democratizations demonstrate the dilemmas inherent in the role of organized labor in future social settlements. As in Portugal, trade unions can be easily drawn into the larger ideological and regime- or project-defining components of the process. They face the choice of radical opposition to a weakened capitalist class or a more conciliatory stance meant to help firms survive, keep employment up, and sustain a fragile social coalition. Employers also must determine whether to collaborate or militantly oppose unions. The pattern of democratization also has inplications for the degree to which organized labor is ignored, symbolically courted, meaningfully incorporated, or offered a decisive role in shaping the new regime and social settlement. When intraregime softliners are ascendant or in coalition with hardliners, a conflict model of industrial relations might be fostered to diminish the role of trade unions, which are unnecessary to the consolidation of that coalition's program. By contrast, when extraregime softliners have a more central role in democratization, they might foster a neocorporatist northern-style regime, as the PS and PSD attempted through the UGT labor confederation and the CPCS. Left and right hard-liners (CGTP, CIP) both might agree—as they did in Portugal—that a voluntary corportist arrangement requires the excessive recognition of the legitimacy of reformist unions and capitalists. Neither the Communist unions nor the employers' association proved particularly inclined to accommodate the other as long as capitalist hegemony remained uncertain.

The Portuguese experience suggests that when a dishegemonic transition yields to deradicalization and reconstruction of some degree of bourgeois control during the consolidation, unions are compelled to accept a generally antagonistic role toward the state, defending largely from outside whatever economic positions and political gains might be salvaged, or pursue a more conciliatory posture. The latter tries to ensure some degree of participation in policy-making at the cost of ideological concessions (rejecting a historic class-struggle position and gravitating toward the harmony-of-interest premise) and specific compromises typical of neocorporatist arrangements. Reformist and neocorporatist unions (such as the UGT) under dishegemony face the difficulties of acknowledging the class-based political accomplishments of the transition, while revolutionary ones (such as the CGTP) must confront the reality of reformist rule within an increasingly capitalist system.

These factors aid in outlining the characteristics and trajectories of democratic transitions and consolidations among a variety of countries, especially authoritarian and essentially capitalist ones undergoing change. The forms of democratization I have mentioned underline key differences among countries whose cultural heritage might otherwise predispose observers to assume a basic symmetry in democratization paths. In southern Europe, the democratization differences between Spain and Portugal demonstrate that despite cultural and socioeconomic similarities, the countries are at best fraternal twins. Many of the variables I have cited about Portugal were useful for developing a general conceptualization of the democratization process as a whole.

How does this analysis of democratization—especially expanded democratization—relate to the historic transformation of the former Soviet bloc? As I argue in the next section, the former Soviet bloc is a reverse case of expanded democratization—from real socialism to some form of democratic capitalism. By adapting my previous discussion, I can address important components of the democratization processes underway on Europe's eastern periphery. Ironically, the concept of a counterhegemonic project as a part of expanded democratization may be derived from the leftist experience of Portugal, but in the contemporary world it may be best applied to the dissolution of the debatably leftist Soviet model of political economy.[20]

EXPANDED DEMOCRATIZATION IN THE FORMER SOVIET BLOC

There are some difficulties involved in applying the set of conditions and variables used to analyze democratization in capitalist countries to the former Soviet bloc. Initially, these stem from the degree to which the Soviet model of political economy transformed property relations, making the concept of dominant class theoretically problematic. Because the analysis of Portugal's democratization begins with divisions over accumulation strategy (see table 8.1) and implies that differently situated segments of capital correspond to alternative policy options, the absence of private capital as a key actor requires some conceptual adaptation. Systemic differences between a regulated market economy and a centralized one are especially important when considering the degree of autonomy that sectors and firms have to identify the quantity and sources of inputs and markets. Even a strongly regulatory state rarely stipulates in detail the kinds and quantities of products or services that firms can produce, although its policies may provide incentives and controls that directly or indirectly influence many private decisions.[21] In a market economy, the intrinsic functional interdependence of different-sized firms and sectors cannot be assumed; rather, competitive divisions between small and large firms, capital and labor intensive sectors, state-of-the-art industries and less advanced ones all serve to divide firms and shape the kinds of accumulation strategies they favor. Private actors also retain considerable political discretion to shape state policy to correspond to the interests of firms divided along such lines.

Centrally planned economies reduce or eliminate the role of private actors and assume the functional interdependence of firms and sectors. In theory, accumulation strategies should maximize the interests of the whole system, although in practice splits between industries as well as structural rigidities and inefficiences in the economy are typical.[22] Because the state is the all-encompassing actor rather than merely an outside regulator, economic crises can stimulate debates not only about specific strategies, but also the larger issue of the utility of the statist accumulation model. Thus, strategic debates about the prospects of decentralized decision-making for firm managers, the local determination of contracting firms, products, pricing, and marketing can only go so far without questioning the hegemonic character of socialism as an alternative to the market-based anarchy of capitalist production. Traditional debates that occur within planned economies about the roles of heavy and light industries, military versus civilian production, industrial versus consumer production, quantitative versus qualitative indicators of plan fulfillment are only strategic divisions to the extent that they involve mild reforms of planning structures and processes rather than fundamentally new economic mechanisms.

The current transformation of the Soviet model suggests that the division between intraregime hard- and softliners (which might crudely be juxtaposed as military/heavy industry/quantitativists versus civilian/light industry/qualitativists) was eclipsed by the difficulties of adequately resolving these strategic alternatives without examining the broader set of constraints imposed by the prevailing system of property relations and class system. As a result, the extraregime opposition did not simply favor a different set of reformist options but instead a different overall economic context for making choices among options. In this sense, the extraregime softliners constituted those who were more willing to tolerate traditional state-firm relations and a slower pace of reform, while the hardliners corresponded to radical liberals wishing to transform the political economy rapidly along market lines. These programmatic positions could not neatly correspond to obvious class cleavages because the extraregime opposition was not representing an extant domestic class's interest but only that of a *potential* class.[23] This was a bourgeois revolution without a bourgeoisie, although certainly not without the inspiration provided by the commanding presence of a world capitalist system.[24]

Democratization's transitional phase in the former Soviet bloc generally falls within the conditions associated with dishegemonic and expanded democratizations. Depending upon the specific country, a deep division existed regarding economic policy. Attempts to straddle the line between real socialism and incipient capitalism had occurred in countries such as Hungary, but generally political and economic liberalization had been quite limited when contrasted with the ideal-typical Western European model or even the People's Republic of China.[25] In all cases, democratization was abrupt, bordering on revolutionary in Russia, Poland, and Rumania. The coalitions varied somewhat but often took the form of extraregime soft- and hardliners united against the intraregime hard- and to a lesser extent softliners (Russia, Poland, Czechoslovakia, especially on the Czech side). In some cases, intraregime softliners found themselves in uneasy coalitions with extraregime softliners (Rumania, Bulgaria, Hungary to some degree), the relative dominance of either side changing rapidly with events. Dishegemony prevailed in most cases: in Bulgaria, conflicts between the formerly Communist Bulgarian Socialist party and the Union of Democratic Forces impeded the implementation of plans for economic reform; in Hungary, the speed and character of privatization has been the source of constant political debate and realignment despite the election of a center-right government. In Russia, dishegemony has been exemplified by the continuing power struggle between Russian President Boris Yeltsin (following democratization option 5 or 6) and the Congress of People's Deputies (apparently preferring option 3 or 2).

The 5 October 1993 crackdown on Parliament conducted by military forces loyal to Yeltsin showed the limits of a complementary transition to capitalism and democracy without a hegemonic class. Done in the name of democracy, the result was to ban opposition parties and censor or close antagonistic presses. Initially, Yeltsin stipulated that parliamentary elections, scheduled for 12 December and meant to produce a Parliament more legitimate than the preceding one, would effectively bar a wide range of parties from competing: half of the 450 seats were to be filled from candidate lists put together by each legal party. This decision was subsequently modified after much criticism of its antidemocratic character.

In a revealing statement by Yeltsin's press minister Valdimir Shumeiko, the contradiction between open-ended democracy and the agenda of installing capitalism without a bourgeoisie was related to the state's role in the media: "as press minister, I proceed from the assumption that the state should have its ideology. The principles of democracy and the free market are the same ideology. I think the state should have a powerful state-owned mass media to promote this ideology."[26] The state was to act like the hegemonic class, directly using state media to propagate the ideology that otherwise would have fallen to a capitalist class and its press in civil society.

The Russian situation parallels Portugal's in two important ways. In Portugal, the 1975 elections for the Constituent Assembly clarified the balance of democratically legitimate political forces and clearly showed that the Communists and far left were a minority. This was similar to the results of the referendum held on 25 April 1993 in Russia, which showed that a reformist tendency had survived the short-term association between austerity and a market-accumulation model. An important difference was that the referendum did not have the same impact: its distinct institutional implications reflected a branch-versus-branch conflict rather than a party-versus-party one. The results of the referendum further undermined the legitimacy of the legislative branch and bolstered the potentially authoritarian aspects of an ascendant executive. In Portugal, the legislature was a constraint on the Gonçalves governments, which would have otherwise gone farther away from capitalism if possible. The inability of the Russian political system to generate a stable and meaningful party system early in its transition is a significant distinction. Its main impact has been to place an extraordinary burden on Yeltsin and the executive branch as the carriers of capitalist democracy.[27]

The second event that parallels the Portuguese experience involves the October crackdown on Parliament and the 25 November 1975 suppression of the Portuguese far left. In both Portugal and Russia, those elements most resistant to capitalism were the object of a military operation meant to liquidate their presence in key places in the state. In Portugal, however, the crackdown was an effort to protect and enhance the functioning of Parliament and the government that reflected its balance of represented forces. The Socialist party played a pivotal role in defending parliamentary democracy, finding allies among softliners in the military. In Russia, no party played a clear role as defender of democracy because the crackdown targeted parties and Parliament.

The Russian situation indicates that, as in Portugal, the delineation of a viable, largely capitalist accumulation strategy may depend first upon consolidating the hold of the state away from anticapitalist elements. In this sense, Lenin's clearly undemocratic view that the state must be smashed before redirecting its hegemonic project seems justified, especially to the extent that a very weak capitalist presence in civil society makes it hard to rely on normal hegemonic transformations brought about by threatened bourgeoisies elsewhere. Capitalism was much stronger in Portugal than in Russia; therefore, civil society was better able ultimately to generate reliable, coherent political parties to support a democratic transition to a Europeanist accumulation project. What remains to be seen is whether the Yeltsin-guided transition to capitalism produces a new expansive hegemony compatible with democracy or the fatalism and resignation more typical of a passive revolution in which democracy and capitalism constitute antagonistic directions of change.

Even in Poland, where an anti-Communist workers movement was instrumental in bringing down the old order, a seven-party coalition delayed passage of the government's privatization plan, which would have brought about a people's capitalism composed of twenty mutual funds. The situation highlighted the difficulties of merging into the world capitalist system without an indigenous bourgeoisie: "deputies on the right and left criticized the plan, saying it would take 600 state companies worth $10 billion out of government hands and turn operating control over to private investment managers, many of whom would be foreign" (*Washington Post* 19 March 1993). Between 1990 and 1993, there were five different privatization ministers (*Economist* 13 March 1993, p. 5). The difficulties of agreeing on a hegemonic project that could surmount the left's statism and the right's nationalism was indicative of the general dishegemony found in post-Communist societies experiencing expanded democratization.[28] As in many other Eastern European countries, a severe dishegemony was partly reflected in the presence of numerous political parties, none able to claim a true mandate for its program.[29] The election to power of the former Polish Communists, allied with the Peasant party during the fall 1993 elections, shows that democracy and capitalism are not intrinsic partners, especially when political forces focus upon alternative accumulation strategies with distinct impacts upon different parts of the population and the absence of a widely shared social settlement.

To a greater degree than in Portugal, the legacy of a single-party rule in many countries stifled the opposition's pretransition efforts to organize itself before democratization. With the abrupt collapse of the old regime, the transition was likely to be longer. Typically, elections only eliminated the intraregime hardliners from power and resulted in a highly fragmented Parliament without a stable party configuration. This has made it very difficult to frame hegemonic projects effectively into major electoral choices that can be translated into executive control. Because the transformation of the economy into a capitalist mold was not essentially driven by a class of entrepreneurs but by a relatively autonomous state supported largely by shifting negative majorities united against some aspect of the old system, the executive often remained perilously weak. This replicated one aspect of the Portuguese transition insofar as the left was especially united by anti-fascism; in a similar sense, nationalists, reformers, and radicals were united by anti-communism but remained divided on vital aspects of the new political-economic agenda.

Consolidation phases have hardly appeared in many Eastern European countries; in Portugal, a less divisive situation required two years before consolidation started. More important, despite the great incentive to adopt a Euromodel of political economy (given the importance of European markets and EC membership), dishegemony prevailed to a substantial degree until the 1987 elections, more than thirteen years from the start of the transition. Based on the Portuguese experience, the timing of the democratic consolidation and the end to dishegemony in Eastern Europe and Russia seem far off. It will depend on several variables. The structure of electoral cleavages plays an important role due to the relative structural weakness of the extraregime-led elements who cannot yet depend upon the support of a powerful set of private controllers of the means of production. They must disproportionately depend upon the intrinsic legitimacy of the hegemonic project to gain the compliance of resistant elements throughout society and in the state apparatus.[30]

In countries where agriculture remains important (Rumania, Bulgaria, Poland, and Russia), electoral cleavages are also shaped by the system of landholdings engendered under the old order. In Russia, for example, smallholdings were crushed during Stalin's collectivization, and large cooperatives or state farms were created. The small farmer cannot yet provide a conservative basis of rural support for a capitalist hegemonic project. In Portugal, proletarianized landed estates were strongly predisposed to the Communist side; events in Russia may show the same to be true. By contrast, in Poland the collectivization effort was very limited and has produced a situation similar to the northern part of Portugal, where smallholders generally were pivotal in providing an immovable electoral bloc of support for procapitalist parties, especially when coupled with the antileftist bias of the Catholic church. Naturally, in the same way that leftists took advantage of the political conjuncture during the transition to erect cooperative farms in Portugal, rightist reformers in Eastern Europe, Russia, and during AD and PSD rule in Portugal sought to expand and consolidate a system of private farms.[31] In Portugal, leftist attempts to foster a politically supportive land-tenure system faced enormous political and economic obstacles. They could not rely upon outside support from Western countries and international organizations; domestically, the ruling coalitions also showed little tolerance for providing financial and technical support to institutions and areas dominated by the Portuguese Communist party. Conversely, in Russia and elsewhere, the right could rely upon some financial, technical, and moral support from the West, although domestically it often faced the limited willingness of local officials to cooperate in privatization efforts. As Yeltsin realized, although the Russian Communist party was made illegal, the Russian state had not been transformed; instead, it had been taken over by new masters in Moscow. Yeltsin's desire for a new constitution and his stern warnings to obstructionist officials reflected the split between the power structure in the periphery and the objectives of the forces nominally in power at the center.

In some countries, the electoral support needed to overcome the impasse typical of dishegemony will reflect the larger degree of industrialization and electoral import of nonagricultural strata. In these contexts, the critical role of industrial workers is subject to the same strains found in Portugal. Inherently predisposed to leftist appeals meant to reduce vulnerability to the vicissitudes of the market, industrial workers are also pulled by a desire for stable employment and personal income growth. In Portugal, the inability of the Salazarist model to produce either an adequate social safety net or a compelling and sustainable growth rate inclined many workers to support the opposition. A plurality were attracted to Socialist dishegemony, which seemed to offer both a welfare state and income growth without wholesale adoption of a purely liberal or statist economy. Only a minority favored the more revolutionary course of the Communists and far left.

In post-Communist countries, workers face the same challenges of supporting an accumulation model and strategy that can tie collective class welfare with individualized prosperity. While the appeal of the strongest anti-Communist voices may find favor with parts of the working-class electorate for some time during the transition, hardline liberals advocating radical privatization without the promise of a social safety net will be hard pressed to sustain popular support in face of mounting layoffs and the curtailment of factory-provided social services.

In Russia, the case of Ivan Guirdov, organizer of a miners' strike in 1989 that presaged the collapse of the Soviet Union, provides an excellent illustration of the contradictions of post-Communist expanded democratization for workers. Having requisitioned the director's office of the Vorgashorskaya mine, he proclaimed himself "100% for free markets and privatization" but then stated that he would not allow the mine's coal to be sold through middlemen and would "oppose selling the enterprise to an owner who will then tell the workers what to do" (*Economist* 6 March 93, 56). Although the appeal of market-engendered prosperity held some attraction, the idea of reconstituting capitalist-class domination without a global safety net or specific social compromise in exchange for potential prosperity remained an uncertain bargain, especially in countries such as Russia where economic conditions have been particularly difficult.[32]

Judging by events in Portugal, short-term austerity associated with the party or leadership of a given political tendency tends to undermine support for the overarching hegemonic project. If austerity yields mainly declining incomes and rising unemployment under opposition rule, expansion of the ruling coalition to include intraregime softliners may be inevitable. In addition, key actors may determine that polarization might better clarify the political situation despite the risks associated with such a strategy.[33] In the former Soviet bloc, the limited credibility of the left as representatives of the working class makes factors impeding leftist hegemony reinforce rightist popularity among workers in spite of relatively long periods of economic distress and dishhegemony associated with democratization.

The dishegemonic character of post-Communist societies also applies to social settlements. In Portugal, Communist-influenced unions fought efforts to incorporate within a capitalist but neocorporatist framework of industrial relations for over a decade. This was fueled by the anti-fascist feelings directed at the ruling circles and the sense that popular counterhegemony might lead to another, more proletarian alternative. In the former Soviet bloc, Communist unions were associated with the ruling circles much like the corporatist unions in Salazar's regime. The critical difference between the two transitions lay in the fact that popular counterhegemony had a proworker hue in Portugal and a procapitalist one in the former Soviet bloc. This means that workers' movements favorable to popular counterhegemony in post-Communist cases found themselves in the politically and socially awkward position of supporting the replacement of one form of domination (real socialism) for another, presumably more benevolent one (real capitalism). Having gained autonomy from party and state control, workers organizations must come to terms with the historic dimension of the labor movement either to find the best possible working arrangement with capital or to reinvent socialism as something distinct from welfare-state neocapitalism nurtured by social democracy, or real socialism advocated by intraregime hardliners.

The Portuguese service sector was extremely heterogeneous. Including a vast number of occupations that varied greatly with regard to status, income, managerial prerogative, and links to capital, it also exhibited considerable political fluidity. Some parts actually supported the Communists, but the bulk of its members were split between the Socialists and Social Democrats. The political collapse of the Socialists, the rise of the PRD, and finally the PSD's majority in 1987 were shaped partly by the electoral fluidity of the service sector.

The class ambiguity of this sector presents a special challenge during expanded democratizations. Depending on a country's level and form of socioeconomic development, the service sector might be composed of menial and mental labor, low and high status, materialist and postmaterialist values. Like the working class, it faces significant organizational hurdles to its representation, with the distinction that its solidarity as a class is even more precarious due to its internal heterogeneity. Secondary cleavages based on nationalist ethnic, or religious rivalry often inspire service-sector support for hegemonic projects directed at reinforcing nonclass identification and blaming economic problems on nonclass groups, the decline of empire, the presence of foreigners, and foreign ideologies. This is apparent in the former East Germany and among nationalists in Russia and elsewhere. Nevertheless, because many of the former Communist states severely neglected the development of a modern service sector, the transition to democratic capitalism can be expected to produce much employment growth. This might tie the sector to the process of political-economic change and induce it electorally to sustain the liberal elements in spite of short-term policy failures.

My examination of the social character of expanded democratization has shown that just as the transition to socialism was limited by the obligation under parliamentary democracy to electorally represent anti-Socialist strata, the transition from socialism will be affected by the electoral predispositions of the strata and cleavages produced under the old regime. Much as Lipset and Rokkan (1967) suggest, each social revolution produces two cleavage dimensions: between the old and the new order; and, over time, among the members of the new order. Cleavages stemming from the old order reflect the identities, class dynamics, and institutional conflicts that were associated with or temporarily quieted during the predemocratic period. In the former Soviet bloc, this has involved a resurrection of pre-Soviet cleavages involving church and state, center-periphery relations, and ethnic divisions—old cleavages suppressed for many decades by the regime. Additionally, it has started to superimpose the complexity of modern capitalist class and value cleavages against both the pre-Socialist and the Socialist cleavages. The success of a capitalist expanded democratization, to say nothing of a left counterhegemonic drive, is challenged by the likelihood that "declining strata [will] typically exercise a political clout beyond their numerical size or economic importance, due to their entrenched positions in the power structure and their cohesion in the face of external threats" (Dalton 1984, 456). Thus, they will attempt to exploit cleavage patterns to their own advantage.

During periods of acute economic crisis, attempts to implement a different accumulation model and strategy whose theoretical benefits must overcome the ill-effects of contemporary malaise makes reformers and revolutionaries alike vulnerable to counterattacks by the displaced ruling circles. Electoral processes facilitate the association between the broad policy goals of the change agents and short-term reversals or declines. This suggests that transitions either to or from socialism may be facilitated by a relatively autonomous, executive-centered regime whose vulnerability to short-term electoral pressures is minimized. In most cases, the transition away from the old order has not been purely democratic in an institutional sense; often it is stimulated from below by mass movements and from above by the willingness of key institutional actors such as the military or the ruling party to permit change. With the installation of electoral politics and the declining relevance of street politics, the political representation of more enduring cleavages surfaces. The strength of antipathy for the old order and the relatively abstract attraction to building democracy cannot carry the liberal hegemonic project across social cleavages indefinitely. What begins by looking like popular counterhegemony may, as time passes, be transformed completely in former Communist countries. The extraregime softliners, perhaps aligned with the hardliners, may come to realize the attractiveness of slow liberalization with possible democratization or democratization led by intraregime softliners in which they are the new intraregime elements and may favor the passive revolution or two-nations hegemonic projects. Once radicals in the face of real socialism, they may now be tempted to become a traditional right wing pursuing real capitalism.

While expanded democratization can open the path to some form of Western-style regime, postwar settlements, even in the major Western European countries, have been traversed by change. As the next section will argue, countries embarked on the quest for a European model of political economy may be pursuing an evasive target. Major economic restructuring and new political alignments affirm that dynamic change continues to be associated with capitalist development. What Marx remarked about capitalism in the *Communist Manifesto* seems no less true today: "All fixed, fast-frozen relations . . . are swept away, all new formed ones become antiquated before they can ossify. All that is solid melts into air, all that is holy is profaned, and man is at last compelled to face with sober senses, his real conditions of life, and his relations with his kind" (Tucker 1978, 476).

WHICH REAL CAPITALISM? THE TRANSITION FROM ORGANIZED TO DISORGANIZED CAPITALISM AND EXPANDED DEMOCRATIZATION IN THE SEMIPERIPHERY

The problems associated with reconciling capitalism and democracy within a hegemonic project partly reflect the changing nature of capitalism at the time when political change occurs. Not only do regional differences within Europe point to alternative configurations of a capitalist political economy, but a broad historical perspective suggests that the general nature of capitalism has been undergoing substantial change. Societies in both the South and the East have confronted not only the question of whether real socialism was a desirable option—it was not—but what type of real capitalism would be better. In Western Europe, models of democratic capitalism have been fluid and problematic.[34] I suggest that the postwar settlement was more a product of compromises made possible by a temporally distinct and exceptional set of circumstances associated with a specific phase of capitalist development. Recent democratizers' attempts to re-create such a settlement are hampered by the broad changes in capitalism since World War II.[35]

Lash and Urry (1987) have elaborated a thesis about the end of organized capitalism that summarizes several major trends in postwar capitalism. They have argued that, following a period of liberal capitalism that lasted through the first half of the nineteenth century, the next hundred years produced a fundamental change in capitalism. The models of perfect competition and night-watchman state were replaced with organized alternatives. These involved decisive differences both at the top (the regulatory state and an economy typified by concentration and cooperation between finance and industrial capital) and at the bottom (the welfare state, organized class interests, and negotiated social settlements). In turn, the authors argue that organized capitalism has been superseded by disorganized capitalism that applies to both domestic environments within advanced capitalist countries and the general world pattern of capitalist development. Disorganized capitalism transformed the initial postwar settlement and has lessened the likelihood that current democratizing countries will develop or sustain settlements associated with capitalism's organized phase.

While Western European countries experienced a change from organized to disorganized capitalism, countries in Eastern Europe and Iberia typically remained politically and economically overorganized under dictatorships. These countries now must search for a model that does not foster disorganization that produces underorganization, resulting in a collapse of state integrity (Yugoslavia) or third-world–style underdevelopment. Movement toward the perimeter of the core rather than deeper into the perimeter of the periphery or lower to the semiperiphery remains the ostensible goal of these states, which have many characteristics in common despite the variability of their recent histories under Soviet or U.S.-European influence.[36]

Using Arrighi's(1985a) concept of core-semiperiphery-periphery in terms of per-capita GNP, figure 8.1 shows that in 1993 traditional core countries such as Germany and the U.S. had per-capita GNPs close to $20,000. Other European countries (France, Belgium, the Netherlands) were somewhat below that figure, ranging between $15,000 and $18,000 and thus constituting the lower end of the core. Between $10,000 and $15,000 were countries on the core's perimeter (Italy, Great Britain, Spain). The semiperiphery encompassed countries that ranged roughly between $5,000 to $10,000, including Cypress at the high end and Portugal at the low end. With the exception of the former Czechoslovakia, most Eastern European post-Communist countries (Bulgaria, Hungary, Yugoslavia, Poland) actually were outside the semiperiphery and might be counted in the perimeter of the periphery. Albania and Romania, by contrast, were probably within the periphery.

In the long run, these countries at Europe's edge will probably pursue a strategy of incorporation within the European Union (as the EC has become with the passage of the Maastricht Treaty). Despite relative backwardness, weak bourgeoisies, and external dependencies, expanded contact with Europe's core could be a powerful stimulus to modernization and prosperity. Conversely, as Europe confronts its own social and political problems of adjustment to a more competitive world, a less clear alternative of resistance to incorporation might materialize. Papadantonakis (1985, 104), generalizing about Mediterranean countries in a manner that might apply to Eastern Europe as well, has argued, "In resisting peripheralization, these countries will be forced to resist incorporation by the European core. In accepting incorporation as the solution to their semiperipheral problems of underdevelopment, on the other hand, they may be trading these problems for the ones associated with a new, tighter than ever, peripheral status of renewed, (albeit subtler) underdevelopment." Papadantonakis's point seems to be that to resist peripheralization, these countries would have to engender relatively independent development efforts. Incorporation by the core fosters a deeper dependency and unshakable peripheral identification that might run counter to improving outcomes such as GNP per capita. Such speculation about alternatives to incorporation must be balanced by the larger point that under increasingly disorganized capitalism, and after the collapse of both Soviet-led and autarkic Salazar-style efforts to induce development without incorporation, the most likely future will be one of dependent incorporation with possible growth rather than nationalist (capitalist or

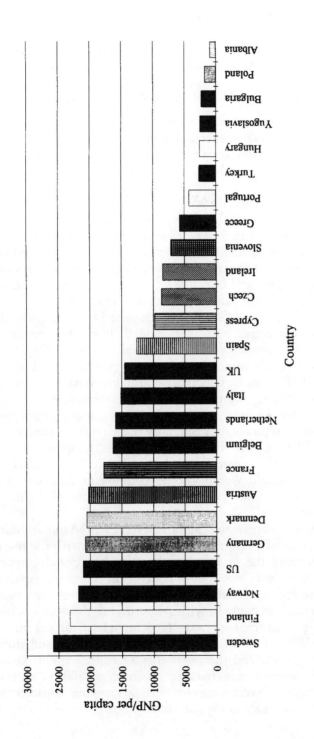

FIGURE.8.1. GNP Per Capita for Selected Countries

poration with possible growth rather than nationalist (capitalist or centrally planned) alternatives that have already foundered.

Organized and Disorganized Capitalism

The transition from liberal capitalism to its organized and disorganized counterparts had several distinguishing points, including (1) changes in the character of markets, firms, and sectors; (2) changes in the relationship between the economy and the state; (3) changes in the scope of state functions in general; (4) changes in the number of participants within politics and the form such participation takes; and (5) ideological and cultural changes.

The first point refers to the growing "concentration and centralization of industrial, banking and commercial capital" and the increasing regulation of markets by the state and cartels in organized capitalism (Lash and Urry 1987, 3). This was reflected in the panoply of links between banks and industry. Industry moved away from consumer and into producers' goods as the importance of the secondary and extractive sectors expanded. Firms became more bureaucratic and impersonally controlled, owners playing a decreased role in management. Industries were concentrated within a few sectors that might be regionally dominant. With the increase in economies of scale, the number of workers employed in each plant rose. In some cases, markets included overseas empires controlled by a colonial power, but generally these political economies were distinguished for the strong spatial (that is, national) association between the state, capital, and the work force. Particularly in the aftermath of World War II, this association made it easier to reach internal settlements given the interdependency of the major economic actors.

By contrast, disorganized capitalism represented the declining relevancy of nationally controlled economic spaces with the rise of global markets and the predominance of multinational corporations. As the state was less able to control its economic environment and new regions offered investment alternatives, dominant classes displayed less concern with perpetuating the social settlements of the organized period. Neocorporatist arrangements became more difficult to sustain in the face of regional and global economic integration and the possibility of capital flight. Lower wages, weaker unions, and reduced business regulation in less-developed countries were coupled with a growing capacity for decentralized coordination of industrial production to erode the industrial base in the older capitalist countries. Increasingly, services became economically preponderant; a service class without the political traditions of the industrial proletariat now defined the new politics in which classic right-left divisions were less salient.

Portugal, like other countries flanking the major European states, tended to pass through relatively weak liberal periods of capitalism and featured excessively organized capitalism in the form of authoritarian corporatism.[37] Lash and Urry have suggested that smaller countries whose industrialization was relatively late and that had strong residues of precapitalist relations tended to feature such overorganization; and indeed this appears to fit the Portuguese case, as well as most Eastern European ones, quite well. Nevertheless, while countries such as Sweden also had a relatively late spurt of industrialization but ultimately embraced the classic northern democratic neocorporatist regime, Portugal, Spain, Greece, and Eastern Europe did not. Instead, to varying degrees they were organized in the sense of linking banks and industry, using empires for markets (at least Portugal and Spain), and regulating the economy through the state. They did not have the same drive for industrialization and expansion of a manufacturing base. Until the establishment of U.S. hegemony in the postwar period, the anarchy in the interstate system reinforced an accumulation strategy based on autarkic and mercantilist principles.

The postwar period featured a dramatically changed international environment in which the Soviet Union and the United States established basic developmental paradigms and engendered global institutional, military, and economic mechanisms to encourage state conformity in their respective spheres of influence. Market-oriented accumulation strategies sponsored by the U.S. gradually eroded the legitimacy of the illiberal and overorganized hegemonic projects that remained in the Western sphere. Some parts of southern Europe engaged in more serious industrialization efforts during the late 1950s and early 1960s but without the democratic social and political settlements found elsewhere.

In the Soviet sphere of influence, a renewed emphasis on industrial production depended on the adoption of even more organized approaches to economic development, but again without the democratic and capitalist accoutrements found in the West. In both southern and Eastern Europe, transformations of the social structures increased pressure from below for the regimes to consider liberalization and disorganization in political and economic domains.

As these countries have faced democratization in recent years, the chances for reproducing the democratic postwar settlement of Western Europe have diminished, even though it may remain as an ideal that brings softliner reformers together. In some ways, these semiperipheral states were possible beneficiaries of disorganized capitalism. Their spatial proximity, cultural affinities, and economic vulnerabilities made them good candidates for precisely the type of investment that was no longer as appealing in the core capitalist countries. In the latter countries, the disorganization of capitalism was a condition for a spurt of capitalist development in the former. But organized capitalism historically depended upon a vibrant national bourgeoisie, even if it often operated in concert with international capital. By contrast, recent democratizers have featured weak (as in Portugal or Greece) or nearly nonexistent (former Soviet bloc) national bourgeoisies; foreign investment and Western aid has been more closely associated with dependent development and less with collaboration between foreign and national capitals acting with a rough degree of equality.

Dishegemony thus appears in the expanded democratizing countries as an expression of a highly fluid period of historic transition. It is a repudiation of the previous accumulation model, which took the worst features of organized capitalism—authoritarian political system, repression of autonomous trade unions, a tendency toward bureaucratic centralization, statist domination of the economy combined with concentration of capital—and failed to bring about an effective and sustainable model of economic development premised upon a broad and democratic social settlement. This provided the impetus for market and liberally oriented economic and political change—in effect, an effort at controlled and deliberate disorganization. Yet especially in the former Soviet bloc, the continued importance of nationalist and economically statist policies is an admission of continued dependency upon the state in the absence of a strong national bourgeoisie that could provide a powerful hegemonic project on its own. Moreover, it also represents a fear of losing national identity and control associated with dependent development.[38] What remains to be seen is whether the gradual replacement of dishegemony by a more clearly capitalist system, such as the one now emerging in Portugal, is an inevitable by-product of unstable dishegemonic political economies. The expanded democratization of the former Soviet bloc raises anew the question of whether there is a development model other than dependent capitalism in an era of disorganized global capitalism.

For countries lining Europe's rim, the decline of organized capitalism in the core has had diffusion effects. Not only are industrial relations in flux, but new social movements based on nonclass issues such as the defense of the environment, resistance to economic development, antipathy to nuclear energy, and struggles for women's and minority rights have further reduced the importance of traditional materialist class cleavages, unraveling the outlines of the postwar settlement. The choice of the developmental model in the semiperiphery gets increasingly complicated as these countries are forced simultaneously to organize (catch up with the postwar settlement) and disorganize (take part in its transformation).

The Portuguese experience highlighted the limitations of a weakly industrialized country's attempt to organize and disorganize simultaneously. While the core European countries had experienced industrial surges between 1890 and 1910, Portugal's industrialization effort during that time was insufficient to create the basis for a largely industrial economy. The labor movement gained strength during the decade after the fall of the monarchy (1910–20), but its small numbers limited its effectiveness. By the time of the 1974 coup, Portugal had attained a level of industrial and social development more characteristic of organized capitalism. But not all the political actors could easily accept a key element of the northern postwar settlement—neocorporatist collective bargaining—given the history of overcentralization and repression linked to Salazar's authoritarian and agrarian corporatism. In addition, given Portugal's need to rely upon its comparative advantage of low wages within the context of disorganized capitalism in the rest of Europe, the resurrection of neocorporatism even after the passage of time has been slow and inconclusive.

Authoritarian corporatist societies, like Communist ones, had emphasized the orchestration of events from above while repressing autonomous pressures from below.[39] Democratization helped cast off the political constraints upon demands from below and the predisposition to structure the economy from above. With the need to foster development through large infusions of foreign capital, the most likely hegemonic project finding general acceptance may be one that continues to decentralize the state and disintervenes in markets while still attempting to introduce a viable social safety net. This social-market approach resembles the postwar experience of the Federal Republic of Germany, which also sought to retain capitalism and overcome the nefarious residues of a totalitarian state while creating a broad basis of legitimacy through an expanded welfare state. That model, with some postmaterialist additions, has been visible among the Socialist and Social Democratic parties in Portugal and the PSOE in Spain. It is less clear whether that model retains its postwar relevancy in a period of dependent development when no national bourgeoisie stands committed to a specific internal settlement with the state and the labor movement.

Events in Portugal postponed the creation of suitable political conditions for such a hegemonic project. The revolutionary upsurge during the transition heightened the saliency of class issues under the coalition of extraregime soft- and hardliners. Unlike organized capitalism under democracy, which allowed reformist, class-based parties to press the dominant classes and the state for a distinct role and welfare function, overorganized corporatism precluded such an outcome. Denied the ability to press such claims and faced with a crisis in accumulation strategy, industrial workers in Portugal sought to make up the time lost through a massive release of proletarian initiatives. This clashed with Portugal's insertion into the global processes of disorganized capitalism and meant that the political resolution would be dishegemonic at first, with the Socialists playing the role of the working-class sympathetic party pledged to a modern welfare vision but also a catchall party appealing to non-class issues. The PSD embodied even more of the traits of the ideal-typical party of disorganized capitalism to the extent that it was more profoundly catchall and less class sympathetic. Expanded democratization placed special obstacles in the way of the formation of a new hegemonic projects that the main parties, explicitly or implicitly, favored.

In some ways, the revolutionary interlude in Portugal hastened the process by which dependent development appeared. The nationalization of industry stripped the indigenous bourgeoisie of its commanding heights within the national economy and established an incipient statized economy that could not be politically or economically sustained. In a world increasingly structured around private multinational capital and free trade, the eventual reprivatization of industry would necessarily open the doors to foreign capital on a large scale. The revolution had not helped produce the Swedish solution: a hegemonic social democracy able to wean a steady stream of concessions based on universalist principles from a national bourgeoisie. Perhaps because the revolution had gone too far by expropriation but was never able to go far enough to reorient the economy completely, it became unlikely that the left could build effective electoral coalitions from below between workers and farmers and from above among organized labor, left parties, and the national bourgeoisie. Instead, the turbulent transition and subsequent dishegemony may have ultimately done too little for either the top or the bottom and thus helped deny Portugal the historic class-oriented but reformist gains associated with organized capitalism.[40]

As in the other cases of expanded democratization, combining structural weakness, political democracy, a viable internal social settlement, and the search for national identity in a postimperial world into a legitimate hegemonic project has proven to be a formidable undertaking.[41] Dishegemony appears as a transition between the past and a future whose outlines can be only partly discerned from the history of postwar settlements in Western Europe.

CONCLUSION

Political democratization and social settlements share a trait once noted by Max Weber: both bring up the question of legitimacy because it is the "generally observable need of any power, or even of any advantage of life, to justify itself" (Roth 1978, 953). Democratizing situations clearly bring into question the legitimacy of the legal order and thereby the specific form that domination assumes: parliamentary, dictatorship, patrimonial, and so on. But domination in its broader significance applies to any advantage of life as well as the legal order. As Weber put it, "in times in which the class situation has become unambiguously and openly visible to everyone as the factor determining every man's individual fate, that very myth of the highly privileged about everyone having deserved his particular lot has often become one of the passionately hated objects of attack" (Roth 1978, 953).

Social settlements refer to the legitimacy that societal arrangements attain in the aftermath of such periods. Less dramatic than the vaticinal end of class society, the transformation of the basic patterns of class interaction is still salient as a research topic and as part of world-historic phenomena. Democratization sharpens the debate over the legitimacy of the old social settlement, whose resolution depends upon understandings that vital actors work out among themselves, taking account of the historical constraints upon their choices.

The Portuguese experience with expanded democratization has shown that, despite serious social contestation, the fusion of political, social, and economic moments need not end in civil war or authoritarianism. Portugal was once viewed as exceptional because among the three southern European dictatorships, only it faced a revolutionary interlude and dishegemony. Yet today in a world that is replete with expanded democratizers in the face of the collapse of Soviet communism, the question may be whether Portugal was simply one of the first countries to seriously confront "times in which the class situation has become unambiguously and openly visible to everyone as the factor determining every man's individual fate" and still emerge with parliamentary democracy and some semblance of a workable social settlement in place.

NOTES

CHAPTER 1

1. Gunther et al. (1986) provides an excellent overview of this dimension of Spain's transition and consolidation phases. McDonough (1986/87) examines the relationship between Spanish party and government legitimacy. Schmitter (1975b) places much attention on the role of the military and the leadership qualities of the Portuguese civilian leaders when accounting for the reasons for the "liberation by *golpe*" in 1974. Aguiar (1983), Bruneau (1984), and Bruneau and Macleod (1986) are examples of works on Portugal that examine parties and the political system in detail. Chilcote (1987) has compiled an outstanding annotated bibliography concerning the Portuguese revolution and its aftermath.

2. I have commented on the limits of the Schmitter et al paradigm of democratization in Nataf (1987).

3. Bruneau's previous work (1984) includes more commentary on socioeconomic changes.

4. Opello's more recent contribution (1991) is generally historical and ties fewer strands from political science literature into the analysis.

5. Nataf and Sammis have commented extensively on Poulantzas' argument (Chilcote 1990). Naturally, the specialist literature on Portugal is vast and composed of a variety of themes as Chilcote's (1987) bibliography can attest. Mailer (1977) and Kayman (1987) are two other examples of efforts to study events in Portugal in a synthetic light.

6. This view has been criticized by Nataf and Sammis in (Chilcote 1990).

7. Giner included more nuances in his review of historical differences among these countries than some have. See his "From Despotism to Parliamentarism: Class Domination and Political Order in the Spanish State" (1980).

8. See, for example, McDonough (1986–87) for such an analysis.

9. Its relevance increases, however, during the consolidation phase as the political economic paradigm gains legitimacy and interests organize chiefly to press demands within its framework.

10. Skocpol (1979) uses a managerially inspired and state-centered approach to highlight the effects of revolutionary change upon the structure of the state, whose centralization is seen as a means for restoring control over society. In cases of expanded democratization, the nature of the social settlement seems more important in shaping the state because it might be subject to decentralization should liberals govern or centralization if the left is electorally successful. In any case, the outcome remains more fluid than expected in a revolution whose political outcome differs from parliamentary democracy.

11. The issue of capitalist development as opposed to Soviet socialist forms has clearly become more controversial as a limiting condition for using class analysis. The contradictions within the Soviet model of political economy have slowly led to a transformation in the structure of power away from the managers and party officials to a nascent bourgeoisie attempting to use divisions and lack of legitimacy within the former group to assert political economic forms better conforming to its own hegemonic pretensions, primarily in the form of market capitalism with overtones of political democracy. This issue is further explored in chapter 8.

12. In addition, some authors emphasize the global context of domestic class conflicts, particularly with regard to the place of a specific social formation within the global division of labor. Poulantzas (1976), for example, divides his book into a discussion of the imperialist world context; the dictatorships, the United States, and Europe; the dominant classes; the popular classes; and the state apparatuses.

13. For instance, Jessop mentions the following circumstance. The City, the economically hegemonic segment in Great Britain, instituted an accumulation strategy that was initially compatible with its financial interests and the interests of industrial capital. Over time, however, the interests of the two diverged, leading to the decline of industrial capital and ultimately the British economy.

14. Przeworski and Wallerstein (1985) argue that democratic capitalism reached a crossroads by the mid-1980s because Keynesian demand management had come under attack from supply-side theorists who once again highlighted the importance of accumulators-producers over consumers. Kesselman (1983) discusses course reversals in France during the early Mitterand years.

15. Note that Hancock (1989) places West Germany more clearly in the neocorporatist camp.

16. The implications of these distinctions for democratization in Eastern Europe will be discussed in chapter 8.

17. The conditions making this possible include the elimination of the landed upper classes from control over state policy and the development of a labor-farmer alliance under social democratic governments, as in Sweden. Harsher economic conditions in the 1980s, combined with the growth in white-collar employment and ecological or antinuclear movements, brought about more conflict over the accumulation strategy.

18. Panitch (1976) has argued that in Great Britain, corporatism was essentially a mechanism for defusing working-class radicalism and co-opting the union movement. Bornstein and Prezeworski present a different perspective: that of a class compromise relatively favorable to the working class but clearly within the framework of a capitalist accumulation model.

19. In Bornstein's analysis, Italy and France clearly fit this characterization while Great Britain does not. This fact reinforces the regional character of the split between northern and southern Europe.

20. See, for example, Peter Hall (1984) for a review of some of these differences.

21. This party was originally called the Popular Democratic party but changed its name by phase 2 to its current name. I refer to PPD/PSD in historical discussions pertaining to events before phase 2.

22. The UGT was formed by the combined efforts of the Socialist and Social Democratic parties (see chapter 6).

Chapter 2

1. Schmitter (1975a, 1979) and Poulantzas (1976) have tended to emphasize the dependent capitalism view; Sousa Santos (1990) has quoted Lopes Cardoso and emphasized the specificity of Portuguese capitalism; the regime itself tended to gravitate to the middle-ground identity.

2. See Cotta (1937, 5–6) for a concise summary of the budgetary changes introduced by Salazar, which, along with increased taxation, led "miraculously" to a budget surplus and inspired faith in Salazar as a financial genius. Wheeler (1978) provides an assessment of circumstances leading to the fall of the Republic. Wairda (1977) reviews constitutional and policy developments under the corporatist regime.

3. Manuel Braga da Cruz (1982) discusses the relationship between Catholic integralism and Salazarist ideology. See Jorge Campinos (1975) for a general overview of the regime's ideology.

4. Cited in Morais and Violante (1986, 36).

5. About 50 percent of the work force in 1930 was involved in agriculture. Historically, the wheat-growing estate owners of the south had sought a measure of protectionism to sustain high prices for their product. The earlier Republican regime had at first continued this strategy; but after failing to stimulate any notable increase in output and seeing the price of bread rise during World War I, it began to import wheat that sold more cheaply than the domestic product. Ultimately, landowners responded by decreasing grain output and fostered a growing trade deficit. Attempts to change the land tenure system in the south had been strongly opposed by the landowners because this entailed the breakup of large estates into smaller family farms worked by landless laborers and northern peasants who now provided cheap labor for the estate owners. The owners came to oppose the Republic partly because of its strategy for agricultural development and partly because of its tolerance for rural trade unions.

6. The tie with the interests of the monopolistic groups was evident even during the 1930s because the percentage of the fertilizer market controlled by CUF went from 48 percent in 1930 to 66 percent in 1937 (País et al. 1978, 338).

7. Sammis (1988, 113) cites sources claiming that in 1937, while textiles made up 47 percent of all exports to the colonies, nearly 90 percent of all textile exports were sent there.

8. Cited in Morais and Violante (1986, 40).

9. Correia de Oliveira, cited in Rafael et al. (1976, 31).

10. Rafael et al. (1976) emphasize that by controlling industries in which large producers had already established substantial market share, the government prevented new entrants from challenging the dominance of the monopolistic groups. While this is partly true, all the industries to which the *condicionamento* applied (both in its more limited original form as well as after its 1937 expansion) were at least numerically dominated by small firms with fewer than twenty-one workers. Moreover, modernizers such as Ferreira Dias argued against the *condicionamento* precisely because it impeded industrial concentration and contributed to weak productive structure. See Moura (1974, 116) for more information on firm size within specific industries and Almeida (1961) and Amaral (1966) for details about the *condicionamento*.

11. Correia de Oliveira, cited in Rafael et al. (1976, 31).

12. It is not obvious that these policies in fact integrated the circuit of capital in the sense of leading to the economic supremacy of industrial capital (Jessop, 1983). Such policies may have slowed growth rates and the development of industry by forestalling increases in productivity and maintaining artifically high prices, although in the context of world depression it may also have prevented the elimination of many industrial firms. Nevertheless, what contributed to balancing the political interests of dominant class segments was not necessarily identical with what might have been ideal economically, especially in the postwar period.

13. The passage of the National Labor Statute (1933) led to the emergence of corporatist, state controlled unions obliged to resolve differences with employers within the corporatist framework.

14. Hegemony may include not only the structural and policy dimensions, but also the ideological and institutional ones. Moreover, instrumental representation within the state points to the direct representation of class segments by regime incumbents. The difference between structural-policy hegemony and institutional-instrumental hegemony is the focus of Sousa Santos in his references to the 1950s.

15. Cunhal's views are contrasted with those of other Portuguese politicians in Nataf (1987b, chap. 4).

16. Derived from Rafael et al. (1976, 13).

17. Kayman (1987) provides a useful overview of the groups.

18. According to Sammis (1988), by 1926 industrial firms held more social capital than commercial ones due to a sharp decline in commerce after World War I. This did not mean that the long-standing debate between commercial and industrial capital over free trade would end. According to Telos (1982, 330–31), the Union of Economic Interests, "intending to congregate all owners' associations [, was] clearly dominated by commercial interests." It constituted an umbrella organization which remained torn by the conflicts between "merchants [who] wanted commercial freedom . . . and industrialists [who] wanted to increase protectionism." Before the world depression, commercial capital could turn to agriculturists such as the wine producers who favored free trade and to a much lesser extent the southern landowners on general grounds including the increased costs which protectionism would add (that is for agricultural machinery and higher labor costs as labor shifted to urban areas with industrial expansion). Thus, Salazar was remarkable mostly for his ability to forge a set of policies that appeased several segments of the dominant class, which had been previously beset by controversy during the First Republic.

19. This section draws heavily on Sammis (1988, 200–201).

20. Rafael et al. (1976) note that the new emphasis on infrastructure was coupled with the creation of state companies such as CML, CP, and CTT. Although this increased the state's role in accumulation, it was not intended to displace private accumulation because these areas of investment required heavy expenditure and possibly low returns. In other words, they were natural monopolies.

21. Armando de Castro (1977) provides a detailed overview of the economic role of the colonies as well as ties between Portuguese and foreign capital. Ramiro da Costa (1977) also reviews economic development in Portugal.

22. The hegemonic combination of corporatism, authoritarianism, and colonialism could not be overcome by the heterogeneous offerings of the opposition, which included Republicans, Socialists, Communists, Monarchists, and others. In any case, the corporatist regime's legitimacy improved as the cold war helped undermine anti-fascist unity among the extraregime elements while anti-Communist sentiments tore apart the Democratic opposition.

23. These changes are mentioned in Rafael et al. (1976, 110–15). See also Manuel Porto (1984, 88–89) for trade figures.

24. Sammis (1988, 221) argues that "overall, Europe received a higher percentage of each industrial export between 1960 and 1970 except for food and drink, and chemicals. The colonial share of textiles, nonmetallic minerals, machinery and transport equipment significantly decreased, with Europe receiving a higher percentage."

25. Sammis (1988) mentions that overlaps between land ownership and ownership of monopolistic groups, among other mechanisms, were essential for increasing the propensity for groups to appease landowners. These ties point out the need to examine carefully the empirical links among family members involved in different segments of capital. These segments are, after all, conceptually defined by our theories; they are not necessarily understood in the same way by the actual owners of the means of production. They, and not simply the conceptual segments, must learn to live with political and economic compromises. Overlapping ownership certainly might ease the way.

26. But it should be noted that the terms of adhesion allowed Portugal to retain many protective tariffs.

27. Fernandes and Alvares (1972, 39), quoted in Sammis (1988, 224).

28. A more detailed analysis of the ideological positions of the Socialist and Communist parties and leaders is found in Nataf (1987, chap. 4).

29. for a longer review of the history of the Democratic opposition, see Raby (1988).

30. The precursor to the current Socialist party, the Associacão Socialista Portuguesa, formed the CEUD in September 1969.

31. A useful summary of the chronology of this period can be found in PCP (1982). Costa (1979) provides an overview of the labor movement.

32. See Dogan (1985) for a discussion of how France avoided a civil war during the May 1968 events.

33. For details about the origins and subsequent actions of the MFA, see Blackburn (1974), Almeida (1977), Maxwell (1975), Fields (1976), Dinis (1977), Porch (1977), Graham (1979), and especially Carrilho (1985), who elaborates extensively upon the sociology of military recruitment, organization, and performance in the most comprehensive treatment of the subject available.

34. See Harsgor (1976, 15–16) for a discussion of this event.

35. Spínola, who in *Portugal and the Future* (1973) had advocated a negotiated conclusion to the colonial wars, was not directly a participant in the planning and execution of the April coup. The Europeanist tendency associated with the industrially oriented groups and foreign capital was represented to some degree by others in the MFA, although it is likely that without the impulse provided by officers close to the extraregime opposition, the coup might never have been attempted. Spínola's ties to the MFA were tenuous from the start: he represented an approach to decolonization and accumulation that contrasted with those closer to the opposition, which favored a more radical break. The coup symbolized the limited tolerance of many officers for another attempt at renovation with continuity. See Carvalho (1977) for his version of the coup and Spínola's role.

36. For details of his thinking during this period, see Osório (1988). Sá Carneiro's views can be found in Carneiro (1972, 1975a, 1975b).

37. See, for example the speeches in Gonçalves (1976).

38. This was soon followed by the establishment of COPCON, a military police that eventually sided with revolutionary hardliners in various popular struggles.

39. It did have an antimonopolist component as revealed in its political, economic, and social program issued in February 1975.

40. For example, Manuel Serra's challenge to the Soares wing of the PS occurred during this period, resulting in Serra's defeat and the formation of the more radical but ultimately inconsequential Frente Socialista Popular (FSP).

41. The agrarian reform law was passed on 29 July 1975. Cutleiro (1971) describes life under the old regime in the Alentejo.

42. This was linked to the formation of the Unitary Revolutionary Front (FUR), which temporarily brought together the PCP with other revolutionary parties. FUR provided support to SUV as a means of undermining the sixth provisional government and the influence of moderates in the Revolutionary Council.

43. A report outlining the events and circumstances leading to the 25 November episode can be found in Veloso and Freitas (1976).

44. João Cilia (1976, 14) discusses the contradictory stands of the PS during this period, although he dismisses the question of parliamentary democracy as a problem of the bourgeois parties, whose role was to "manipulate and divide the unity of the people . . . intending to justify the reconciliation of classes and legitimating exploitation." See also Pereira (1976) for a broader discussion of parties, institutions and socioeconomic transitions.

45. At the PCP's eighth congress in 1976, mention was made of the need for a "policy of subsidies to deficit-laden enterprises to maintain adequate price levels for essential goods and services," all part of a general program to sustain employment by "augmenting internal production of goods with the goal of progressively substituting imports" (PCP 1976, 263).

CHAPTER 3

1. Socialist leader Mário Soares has argued that the Communists rejected a "Common Program of the left" in 1974 because "at that moment it already had a well-defined project for the conquest of power, by force [and] privileged its alliance with the MFA" (Soares 1979a, 14). This statement exemplifies Soares's continuing mistrust of the PCP's commitment to building democracy. See Arroz (1977) for details about the 1976 elections.

2. Some of the Socialist provisions were softened after the periods of constitutional revision in 1981 and especially 1989. Nevertheless, I am emphasizing the Socialist aspects as they emerged from the transition. Article 80 of the constitution dealt with the basic fundamentals of socioeconomic organization and specified that "the socio-economic organization of the Portuguese Republic is based upon the development of socialist relations of production, through the collective appropriation of the principal means of production and land, as well as natural resources, and the exercise of democratic power by the working classes." Article 81, section c mentions the obligation of the state to "eliminate and impede the formation of private monopolies, through nationalization or other forms [of state inter-

vention]" without mentioning public monopolies. Section h mentions the need to realize an agrarian reform; section n, presses forward with Socialist relations of production; and section o stimulates working-class participation in the definition, control, and execution of all significant economic and social measures. Article 82, section 2 grants the possibility of "expropriations of landed estate owners (*latifundários*) and large property-owners and capitalists or stock-owners without giving any indemnization." Of particular notoriety is article 83, which declares that "all nationalizations effectuated after the 25th of April, 1974 are irreversible conquests of the working classes." Other articles with such Socialist or left features are numbers 55 (workers' commissions), 59 (unrestrained right to strike), 60 (prohibition of lockouts), 61 (cooperatives and self-management) as well as a series of articles under part 3 dealing with other aspects of economic organization such as the plan, land reform, the financial system, and the structure of property.

3. The policies of the various governments are discussed in greater detail in chapter 7.

4. Bruneau and Macleod (1986, chap. 2) discuss some of the tensions facing Eanes during this time, particularly the problem of the role of the military.

5. As subsequent chapters reveal, the PSD's stance was not without some merit. A sizable part of the Portuguese working class was still inclined to strong Catholic beliefs, which made the relatively secular left less atractive. The PSD became the Catholic left alternative.

6. Deputies on the right and left tended to view ideologically opposing parties as more extreme, while parties within their own camps were typically classified as less extreme. Gunther et al. (1986) report a similar phenomena in Spain.

7. This has been discussed somewhat in Nancy Bermeo (1986, sec. 3).

8. See Morais and Violante (1986, 368) for a review of the events leading up to the resignation of Balsemão and Eanes's decision to call for new elections.

9. The scores for the PSD and CDS during the AD coalition were calculated based on the share each party obtained of the total right electoral total for 1976: 65 percent for the PSD and 35 percent for the CDS.

10. See Nataf (1987b, 324–42) for a more detailed discussion of Socialist history and ideology.

11. Chilcote (1990) has discussed the relevance of traditional class concepts to the analysis of Portuguese and southern European politics.

CHAPTER 4

1. Clearly the Eurobarometers are vital for comparative public opinion research including several European countries. In Nataf (1992) I use such data for an explicit comparison of public opinion in Spain and Portugal, while my earlier work (1990) compared ecological and survey methods.

2. Unfortunately, there was no direct follow-up question asking, "What party do you feel attached to?"

3. Portuguese respondents rarely admit to having favored a party other than the one they presently voted for. Thus, "party last vote" does not reflect known outcomes from prior elections: in table 4.1, only 4.5 percent admitted voting for the PRD in 1985, about the same number who claim that they would now vote for the party. Naturally, this makes it very hard to trace defectors.

4. In phase 2, the AD governments gained only a small electoral advantage over the left, due largely to the sharply higher totals for the PCP. Communist decline, as yet uncompensated by possible left alternatives such as the newly formed Platform of the Left, has decisively tipped the electoral balance to the right and assured its hegemonic pretensions over the Portuguese political economy.

5. The ten-point scale was reduced to three categories: 1–3 equals left, 4–7 equals center, 8–10 equals right. Therefore, the center naturally appears larger because it entails four points on the scale rather than three.

6. The respondents favoring "order" clustered somewhat around the PSD and CDS in the October 1987 Eurobarometer, although the relationship was still weak.

7. The relation between party tendency and the "change" variable was insignificant in 1985 but *was* significant for every subsequent poll except Eurobarometer 29.

8. This variable was supplied by the Eurobarometer and was only further recoded to remove extraneous entries.

9. This might suggest, for example, that the right tended to be nationalist and traditionalist rather than simply protective of privilege. A larger questionnaire, however, would tap the critical issue of whether a softliner-hardliner distinction was present in public opinion, corresponding to the one discussed in chapter 2 regarding the Portuguese ruling circles.

10. The party-religion and party-"sacrifice for the environment" relationships were statistically significant.

11. Anti-fascism and fear of exclusion from the political process may have animated PCP voters' zeal for libertarian issues because the party's overall stand on liberal democracy was equivocal. Alternatively, party leadership may have underestimated or chosen to ignore the importance of these items to PCP voters.

12. The relationship between "condition of the economy compared to last year" and "party last vote" was statistically significant for both 1985 and 1987.

CHAPTER 5

1. The terms *radical* and *counterhegemonic* emphasize that in the Portuguese case, conflict during the consolidation phase went beyond questions of macroeconomic management to fundamental structural considerations. Dahl (1966) makes a similar distinction between *policy* and *structure*.

2. Much of the literature that initially examined Portuguese politics during the 1970s emphasized the Stalinist nature of the PCP, which implied that it was not truly revolutionary (Mailer 1977) or a dangerous revolutionary party unavailable for coalitions within parliamentary democracy (Livermore 1977). Stoleroff and Patricio (1991) provide an updated analysis of PCP thinking. For some elaboration of the ideological struggles on the left, see also Lomax (1983) and Nataf (1987b chap. 5).

3. To what extent the MFA's program suggested a radical, antimonopolist direction is questionable. The program mentioned goals such as combating inflation, eliminating protectionism, stimulating savings, intensifying public investment (in infrastructure, welfare, and education—not nationalizations), helping agriculture and gradual land tenure reforms, all mostly compatible with the Europeanist accumulation strategy. But it also mentions at one point "a new political economy, placed at the service of the Portuguese People, and in particular the most disfavored strata, having as an immediate preoccupation the struggle against inflation and high living costs, which would necessarily imply an anti-monopolist strategy" (See section B6, article a, in the Programa do Movimento das Forças Armadas Portuguesas, as cited in *Dossier 2a República*, vol. 1 [Lisbon: Editora Afrodite, 1976] 203. Whether this meant nationalizing the monopolistic groups (as some on the left sought) or otherwise breaking them up in combination with the end of the *condicionamento industrial* (as liberals desired) was clearly open to political interpretation.

4. As president, Soares had no difficulty asserting that Portugal should remain "integrated in the European Community and in a system of alliances—NATO" (Soares 1988, 56).

5. Part of the right's animosity was also directed at the MFA, which until the 1982 constitutional revision had a organ that could determine the constitutionality of legislation. Given the MFA's greater tolerance for dishegemony, the right placed a high priority on "civilianizing" government.

6. I am not suggesting that this *was* actually the case—only that the right could influence the electorate by making the argument. Eugénio Rosa (1978), for example, considers phase 1 as a period in which right-wing policies were enacted and places the blame for economic troubles squarely upon those policies. His views on the AD governments are found in Rosa (1982).

7. See Gaspar and Vitorino (1976) for a detailed review of the geography of the 1975 elections to the constituent assembly. Medeiros (1978) provides a good introduction to Portugal's human geography while Batista (1985) reviews changes in the social structure. Figueiredo (1988) has a detailed discussion of the development of regions in Portugal. Nataf (1987b, chaps. 2 and 3) also examines regional electoral phenomena.

8. The following are the six regions including the districts and the number of *concelhos* (smaller census and electoral units) they include:

Region	District	Number of Conselhos
North Coastal	Braga, Porto, Viana de Castelo	40
North Noncoastal	Bragança, Guarda, Vila Real, Viseu	64
Center Coastal	Aveiro, Coimbra, Leiria	52
Center Noncoastal	Castelo Branco, Portalegre, Santarem	47
South Coastal	Faro, Lisboa, Setúbal	43
South Noncoastal	Beja, Evora	28

9. See Silva (1979) for some of the details.

10. This north-south contrast was less obvious with respect to traditional cultural values and behaviors in general, only that the south retained a certain autonomy from church control that was lacking in the north. Some *concelhos* in the south had very low church attendance rates—Setúbal (5.7 percent), Sintra (4.1 percent), and Barreiro (3 percent)—while others in the north had very high ones—(Vila Nova de Familiacão (60.7 percent), Guimares (63 percent), and Viana de Castelo (59.8 percent). These figures are based on church self-reporting as found in Silva (1979). Freitas et al. (1976, 90) give some idea of the land-tenure system: 314,000 farms were under one hectare and covered 125,064 total hectares, while only 27,100 farms were over twenty hectares but covered 3,223,254 total hectares. The vast majority of the large estates were in the south.

11. A combined edition of the Portuguese social science journal *Analise Social* (1985) has several contributions that refer to changes in demography (see Barata 1985, Ferrão 1985).

12. Cabral (1978) discusses Portuguese semi-proletarianization.

13. Coefficient values:

PCP '80 –0.87	PRD '85 –0.46	PS '80 –0.34	CDS '83 0.7	PSD '83 0.9
PCP '83 –0.89	PRD '87 –0.75	PS '83 –0.22	CDS '85 0.72	PSD '85 0.93
PCP '85 –0.88		PS '85 –0.09	CDS '87 0.63	
PCP '87 –0.80		PS '87 –0.34		

14. This is not to imply that the CDS and the PRD were the only parties whose voters defected to the PSD because nearly halving the PCP's total did not result in an equivalent PS rise. Some PS voters probably defected to the PSD, while some PCP voters went to the Socialists.

15. The PRD was decidedly based in urban areas, accounting for the Socialists' relative urban-rural balance in 1985. Given the Communists' strength in the industrial areas, the PS could not expand beyond a certain point barring a dramatic decrease in PCP support.

16. The importance of this social category in a less-developed economy such as Portugal's is due to the impact of the low-skill, labor-intensive, and often tourist-oriented service sector as a major component of the overall economy.

17. Traditional distinctions in the literature about the old and new middle class often obscure the underlying distinctions among service-sector workers. Especially in postindustrial countries, the new middle class is typically composed of white-collar employees and civil servants and "exemplifies the shift of the labor force toward service, government, and technology." It is seen as a social stratum that "neither owns nor produces capital [and is] integrated neither into the unionized working-class milieu nor the old middle-class milieu" (Dalton, et al. 1984, 107). In less-developed economies, the service sector may be large but is composed of relatively low-status roles, with low education requirements and skill levels. While the physical distinctions between the manual working class, factory life, and proletarian culture generally may remain, the relations of production and life chances may be more similar than different.

18. Small changes occur when missing cases are counted: farmers and fishermen were 10 percent; the service sector was slightly under 40 percent; manual workers were 50 percent. This survey underrepresented the primary sector and overrepresented the manual workers.

19. The variable "respondent's occupation" was used. For the purposes of assessing the class nature of party support, other social categories (students, military, housewives, retired, unemployed) were excluded.

20. The turnout levels as shown in Eurobarometer 28 were primary sector, 67 percent; manual workers, 54 percent; white collar/professionals/executives, 62 percent; business owners, 76 percent.

21. See Bermeo (1986) for additional details about the land-reform program.

22. Kousser (1973) has also argued that such results should be interpreted as indicating strong trends rather than specific values. He explains the methodological aspects of ecological regression, as do Langbein and Lichtman (1978). See Dogan and Rokkan (1969) for a fuller discussion of ecological methods.

23. Actually, the occupational category seems to include all those in the primary sector, such as fishermen and possibly miners.

24. The small number of respondents for all subgroupings increases the Eurobarometer's margin of error and implies that analysis based on them should be subject to additional confirmation. This is a good reason to compare survey and ecologically derived calculations because both have their specific limitations.

25. Chi square .004; Cramer's V .18; Eta .18.

26. This was probably due to the large number of manual workers (especially for the PCP) and white-collar workers (especially for the PS) who were in the middle quartiles.

27. Seculars were those who ranked "importance of God" between 1 and 6 on the ten-point scale.

CHAPTER 6

1. According to Vilanova (1978), the PCP jostled with the revolutionary syndicalists over strategy and tactics during the early 1970s. The Communists were certainly not alone in organizing the working class before the dictatorship's fall, which accounts for the later conflicts between the Communists and the far left. Vilanova covers the period 1975–78 from a revolutionary syndicalist position. See also Sá (1981) for another historical perspective on the Portuguese labor movement.

2. Manuel de Lucena (1976, 108–18) discusses these laws in some detail. For Lucena, the initial liberalizing laws were simply one component of Caetano's general policy of modernization, meant in part to integrate the Portuguese working class into industrial capitalism. The Communists argued that the liberalization was simply an attempt to "sow illusions and provoke passivity" within the opposition. For the PCP, the new laws were a

reaction to the growth in labor strength and discontent, particularly heightened by strike activity in the preceding years and months (PCP 1982, 185). The Intersindical has claimed that the Caetano period reflected the growing contradictions within the regime, which sought to broaden its social base, institutionalize enterprise conflicts within established trade-union and employer relations, and assuage international public opinion, especially the International Labor Organization. But "the fascist dictatorship, corroded by profound contradictions, could not give itself the luxury of such a 'liberalization,' since the workers' economic struggle at the level of enterprises and unions rapidly degenerated into a political struggle against the fascist regime and the colonial wars" (CGTP-Intersindical 1974, 7–8).

3. In a prescient survey of possible models of regime evolution, the SEDES group characterization of *um outro socialismo* identifies many of the features that materialized during 1974–76 (see SEDES 1974). For more on the regime that Otelo Saraiva de Carvalho stood for, see *Bases para o Programa de Candidatura* (1976) in which he emphasizes the "need to defend, reinforce and develop all forms of workers' organizations and especially the popular base organizations such as the workers' commissions, neighborhood and residents' commissions." He gives special priority to these decentralized institutions rather than to the more bureaucratized trade unions. In a sad commentary on the history of anarchist schemes for decentralized popular participation, Otelo was held in an investigation of terrorist attacks in Portugal for his possible connection to the underground group Forças Populares-25. As during the First Republic, the inability to sustain anarchist institutional forms may have led to much demoralization and the subsequent resort to more desperate measures. For additional commentary on the residents' movement, see Downs (1989).

4. These were decrees 215-A/75 and 215-B/75.

5. This was reflected particularly in the growing importance of the Comissões de Delagados Sindicais, as opposed to the Commissões de Trabalhadores, in the defense of immediate workers' interests. In addition, the popular assemblies and courts that arose during the Gonçalves period disappeared as the MFA centrist elements consolidated their power. Mailer (1977) provides an overview of some of these patterns during the revolutionary period. Vilanova (1978) also discusses this period in terms of union developments. Although the 1976 constitution (article 56, paragraphs b and c) gave workers' commissions the right to supervise factory management and involve themselves in the reorganization of production, the minority Socialist government passed a law in July 1976 that restricted such involvement to purely economic aspects—a further sign of the decline of decentralized workers' control over the economy.

6. See Vilanova (1978, 23).

7. The polemics surrounding the Carta Aberta, as well as some of the salient documents of the period, have been compiled in Oliveira (1978). As I explain later, decree 215-b/75 was revoked by the Socialist minority government on 1 October 1976.

8. On this issue, the far left tended to side with the Communists; they, too, saw neither ideological nor strategic advantage in the representation of political tendencies. It is ironic that the hostility of the anarcho-syndicalists to the emergent Communist party of the 1920s was based precisely upon the question of the ideological politicization of the unions. See Sousa (1977, passim).

9. This discussion draws heavily on Vilanova (1978, 1–20), who provides the breakdowns of the unions. Cesar Oliveira (1978) also discusses this in his preface to *Tudo Sobre Intersindical e Carta Aberta*.

10. The list in Oliveira's work (1978, 18–19) includes Union of Clerical Workers of Lisbon; Union of Bank Workers of the South; Union of Merchant Marine, Aeronavigation, and Fishing; Union of Retail Workers of Lisbon; Union of Pharmaceutical Industry and Sales; Union of Clerical Workers and Commerce of Aveiro; Union of Engineers of the South; Union of Teachers in Greater Lisbon; Union of Metalworkers of Aveiro; Union of Construction Workers of Leiria; Union of Clerical Workers and Cashiers of Vila Real and Bragança; Union of Bakers of Vila Ral and Bragança; Union of Clerical Workers and Cashiers of Faro; Union of Bakers of Faro; Union of Hotel Workers of Faro; and Union of Clerical Workers of Coimbra.

11. The Communists were partially interested in obtaining some sort of compromise with the Socialists but were unable to offer much due to pressure from the far left as well as a certain inflexibility arising from the party's vested interest in maintaining organizational control over the labor movement. In effect, the PCP could not easily compromise on control over the unions without also undermining its only long-term basis for national power. The March 1975 elections for the Constituent Assembly made it clear that the PCP could not expect to carry much electoral weight in the near future. Like other Communist parties in electoral settings, its main hope for strategic leverage lay in maintaining control over the trade unions. In addition, the Socialist party was at that time strongly supported by anti-Communist and Social Democratic forces of all sorts, both domestic and foreign. In an important sense, the purpose of the Socialist party was not to foster unity with the Communists, but to prevent them from gaining power. In practice, this meant isolating the Communists and revolutionary groups and making them appear outside the mainstream of pluralist political and social life. Thus, both Communists *and* Socialists had important constraints upon their options.

12. According to Vilanova (1978, 19), revolutionary syndicalism was strong throughout the textile industry but also in specific unions outside it.

These included Dental Workers, Security and Cleaning Services, Clothing of Porto and Braga, and Shoemakers of São João de Madeira. These occupations wer either squarely positioned in the service sector without apparent vulnerability (prosthetics) or had low status and high vulnerability (security guards, maintenance personnel).

13. The PS and PPD-PSD relied upon their respective foundations (the Fundação José Fontana and the Fundação Oliveira Martins), which were to provide basic training and skills for future trade-union officials. It has been claimed that foreign financial support was important in funding these foundations and their activities, leading to claims that the new unions were CIA-inspired or linked to the Trilateral Commission of which Socialist Minister of Labor Maldonado Gonelha was a member.

14. Specifically, decree 773/76 repealed decrees 215-A/75, 215-B/75, and 841-B/76. Furthermore, Law 57/77 allowed the manner of obtaining dues to be negotiated between unions and employers but specified that individual workers had to signal their approval of the method "in a declaration to be sent to the employer and union" (as cited in Rosa 1978, 230).

15. Scholars discussing modern corporatism include Lucena (1985), Schmitter (1974), Jessop (1979) Offe (1981), and the classic work of Manoilesco (1934).

16. Interview conducted on 4 April 1982 at the União de Sindicatos de Lisboa.

17. Several journalists covering the Portuguese labor scene have commented that the unions universally overestimate their membership because of the political importance of claiming a large following. But as Kohler (1982, 240) has remarked, when new unions are founded they have to provide the Ministry of Labor with the statutes and an exact list of the membership before they can be legally recognized. This may increase the reliability of the UGT membership claims because most new unions arose under its banner.

17. See especially Castenheira (1981) for details of the union confederations. Castenheira is one of the most astute observers of the union situation, whose many articles in *O Jornal* have contributed to the small number of informed analyses—however journalistic—of the Portuguese labor movement. What is the reason for the greater local activity of far-left members, more than their representation on governing councils would otherwise suggest? One hypothesis is that at the local level, far-left militants might be able to take an active role due to their willingness to confront employers on critical issues and thus risk exposure to possible employer retaliation. This might gain the support of workers in a given plant. At the regional and national levels, however, party identification may increase as the individual candidates are less known to union members, who may vote along party

lines. Union elections rarely have very high turnouts, meaning that ideologically committed members would be likely to have a disproportionate impact.

18. These numbers are almost identical to those listed by Pinto (1973, 15) as belonging to the old corporatist unions. Pinto states that the corporatist unions had a membership of 1,410,840 in 1969. While most of those paying dues were full members (*socios*) more than 560,000 were not (*contribuintes*). This suggests that the CGTP did inherit a large number of passive members resulting from its takeover of the preexisting unions. It also suggests that many members were only concerned with bread-and-butter issues and eschewed the more heated political conflicts between the CGTP and UGT. Thus, if the CGTP performs its collective bargaining functions well, it may retain its vast advantage in membership over the UGT, despite the low electoral appeal of the PCP. The previous structure of Portuguese unions under the dictatorship is covered in Pinto (1973). One rationale for the Socialist law mentioned earlier (on the collection of dues) was to heighten the voluntary aspect of union membership, although the underlying purpose was clearly to weaken the CGTP.

19. Variable 706, which asked whether anyone was a union member, gave a higher figure, 21 percent.

20. Stewart's study of European trade unions provides an overview of the major confederations and union movements in Europe. In France only between 20 to 25 percent of the labor force was organized in the 1970s; in Italy the percentage rose to between 35 and 40 percent (Stewart 1974, 82, 134). See also Roberts (1985) for more recent commentary on European unions.

21. While most unions belong to one of the two confederations, several independent unions of varying political complexion also exist.

22. Pinto (1990, 250) mentions that the "UGT . . . is based on large national or regional unions, with no federations (save three exceptions, each for specific reasons . . .)."

23. The insurance unions, for example, operate in two regional organizations, while the banking unions have three. See Castanheira (1985, 804) for additional details regarding the UGT.

24. Kohler (1982, 241) presents the UGT official figure of eighty three unions in 1979. Castenheira's figures were not strictly derived from the official ones but from a variety of journalistic as well as official government and union sources. His totals were consistently more conservative than Kohler's, who relied upon a narrower range of sources and was generally more distant from the Portuguese labor scene as a whole. Non-Communist–controlled unions were found in a somewhat greater concentration in the center and north as opposed to the south. According to Castenheira,

non-PCP–controlled unions outside of the south included construction workers of the center, agricultural workers of Leiria, agricultural workers of Viseu, shoemakers of Aveiro, domestics (Braga), and motorists of Vila Real. Fishermen of Lisbon, woodworkers of Santarem, and southern butchers were the only non-PCP–oriented southern unions. Among national (that is, not regionally defined) unions, only the merchant marine was outside of PCP influence.

25. All quotations are from the confederation's action program. In addition to ideological commitment, this union orientation was affected by relative weakness at the shop level due to rising levels of unemployment, declining membership, low worker morale, union fragmentation, and employer attacks. By 1985 wages were below the level at the time of the 1974 coup. Real wages shot up during 1974, peaking at the end of 1975. The first Socialist government, facing sharply escalating balance-of-payments deficits, engineered an economic slowdown that took effect during 1977–78. Real wages declined very rapidly during 1977, reaching below the 1973 level in the middle of that year. By the middle of 1979, real wages were 12.8 percent below the mean level for 1973. The relative weakness of the unions was further revealed by the fact that real productivity started a steady upward drive in 1977. By the end of 1978, the gap between productivity and wages favoring workers in 1975–76 was not only reversed but far exceeded it in magnitude. Finally, actual disposable income was further reduced by an increase in taxes of between 2 and 4 percent.

26. The UGT was at one point internally torn by Social Democrats unhappy with the overly politicized orientation of the confederation. See Castanheira (1985, 810) for a discussion of the fate of Tesiresd, whose members were excluded from leadership positions due to their desire to increase the independence of the confederation from the government.

27. The UGT believed that such national bargaining was an integral aspect of its strategy for overall incorporation of the working class within salient policy areas. Thus, such policies were "not only . . . a means of containing inflation, but also . . . a regulator of vast aspects of social and economic life which affect the living conditions of the workers . . . [including] the evolution of prices, salaries, taxes, social security, investment policy, productivity norms, working conditions, and the rights of unions and of workers' commissions in economic life" (UGT 1981,15). To this end, the UGT proposed the fusion of two current institutions, the National Planning Council and the National Income and Prices Council, into a single Economic and Social Committee. The formation of the Permanent Council on Social Concertation in the early 1980s gave institutional shape to this proposal.

28. These items and others were highlighted by CIP president Pedro Ferraz da Costa (1983) in a speech to a general meeting of industrialists. For a review of the nationalized sector, see Martins and Chaves (1979).

29. *Diário de Notícias* (11/25/87). This section relies upon Nataf and Stoleroff (1990); for a review of the logic of competing union confederations, see Stoleroff and Optenhogel (1985). Pimental (1984) reviews the early efforts to institute neo-corporatism.

30. The CGTP's strategy of conducting political strikes had not helped its cause; it lost influence in certain key industrial sectors like ship-building, metalworking, and engineering. In the meantime, the UGT picked up supporters, winning election in workers' commissions in such large enterprises as Lisnave.

CHAPTER 7

1. Martins and Chaves (1979) provide a list of firms either national-ized or with other state participation. They include: banking, insurance, energy, mining, basic industry, light industry, public works, construction, agriculture, fishing, commerce, services, and transports. Her list features nearly a thousand major and minor firms.

2. The series directed by former Minister of Agriculture António Barreto provides a good background and summary of events leading up to the land reform as well as afterward. His own work (Barreto 1987) is particu-larly useful as is Bermeo (1986). For a leftist view critical of the Socialists' policy toward the agrarian reform, see Rosa (1977, 1978).

3. For a longer exposition of the PCP's thinking on political econ-omy and the model of state monopoly capitalism that animated its analy-ses, see Nataf (1987b, chap. 4).

4. As Bruneau and Macleod (1986, 77–97) have emphasized about the PSD during this period, political tendencies and especially personalities collided with regularity.

5. The Nobre da Costa government was vetoed by the Socialists because they felt that it was too directly an affront to their party. Its ideo-logical composition was more acceptable to the PCP, which decided not to vote against the party. By the time of the Mota Pinto government, the Socialists wearily determined that they could not simply oppose every Eanes-appointed government, abstaining in the vote on the Pinto govern-ment's program, which was favored by the PSD and CDS.

6. These goals are elaborated on in Freitas da Amaral's speech to Parliament in Amaral (1982).

7. Silva mentioned that the government had a 6 percent *re*valuation target for the escudo (Silva 1982, 28).

8. The CGTP-Intersindical (1986a) makes several other points regarding the effects of government policies upon income distribution and living standards during this period, arguing that many measures increased income inequality as subsidies were cut, rents were liberalized, income tax rates were insufficiently adjusted for inflation, and so on.

9. The CGTP (1986a, 43) viewed many such measures as part of a "violent offensive against the economic and social transformations realized by the April revolution, against fundamental rights and liberties, with the clear aim of destroying the democratic and constitutional regime." But even it admitted, with regards to the threat of reducing the scope of collective bargaining, that "the defense of workers' rights . . . was in essence guaranteed, despite the offensive against [it]. The employers' attempt to liquidate, in fact, the right of collective bargaining and thereby the elimination of conquests consecrated in collective conventions failed" (CGTP 1986a, 47). This type of inconclusive struggle in which specific skirmishes were laden with hegemonic implications reinforced the overall dishegemonic character of social relations.

10. All references to the 1989 constitution come from *Constituição da República Portuguesa, 2a Revisão, 1989* (Aveiro: Estante, 1989).

11. Catela (1986) reviews the delimitation of sectors issue and summarizes some of the debates involving the major parties, although his discussion is limited to the stands adopted for the 1982 revision rather than the 1989 version.

12. Apparently, disagreements over the treatment of old owners were part of heated discussions between some of those advising President Soares and the Cavaco government, according to one Soares advisor.

13. See Finance Ministry (1987, 32–39) for a fuller discussion of the various measures proposed by the plan for agriculture.

14. Several articles in Silva (1989) review options for the Portuguese economy from the perspective of leading elements in or close to the CGTP.

15. The government report included 132 industries, nearly identical to the number available in the census report. The former did exclude a few industries—notably petroleum refining, which would have changed the totals somewhat. The industries with joint data were sorted by number of firms and then divided in half, forming the basis for each sector. These were each classified into thirds by a coded sum for the measures of industry viability. All the other economic data were derived from INE (1987, 176–84).

16. A Lisbon economic conference held 14–16 May 1986 by the Instituto Superior de Economia yielded a two-volume set of papers that

reviewed a range of relevant topics such as the forms of specialization appropriate given EC integration, the role of social partners, the public sector, the behavior of foreign capital, the effects of development strategies on income inequality, and so on. See Barros (1986). Makler (1983) reviews the fortunes of the industrial bourgeoisie.

17. The top two-thirds of the competitive sector constituted the following percentages of firms, workers, and capital value: 50.3, 56.3, and 47.6. The equivalent numbers for the monopoly sector were 4.3, 11.7, and 17.

CHAPTER 8

1. As Marx once remarked, "history is nothing but the succession of the separate generations, each of which exploits the materials, the capital funds, the productive forces handed to it by all the preceding generations, and thus, on the one hand, continues the traditional activity in completely changed circumstances and, on the other, modifies the old circumstances with completely changed activity." For him, the "more the original isolation of the separate nationalities is destroyed by the developed mode of production and intercourse and the division of labor between various nations naturally brought forth by these, the more history becomes world history" (Tucker 1978, 172). This might be interpreted to mean that as changing circumstances (end of colonies, integration into EC) caught up with the "completely changed activity" (modern productive techniques especially as introduced by foreign capital) in the context of late-twentieth century capitalism, Portugal necessarily lost its specificity and became absorbed into the matrix of ideas and institutions associated with the globally ascendant economic system and dominant class.

2. As cited in *Espresso* (17 July 1993).

3. As Morais (1992, 123) notes, "average wages and compensation [are] still just 24% of German pay packages." Hudson (1989) provides an overview of economic trends through the 1980s.

4. Marx argues in *The Eighteenth Brumaire of Louis Bonaparte* that the living "in creating something entirely new, precisely in such epochs of revolutionary crisis they anxiously conjure up the spirits of the past to their service" (in Tucker 1978, 595). In a general sense this applies to Portugal. Certain avenues consistent with the European framework either conjure up residues of fascism (distaste for corporatism in whatever form) or revolution (antagonisms within the left and the need to deal with nationalized industries), thereby forcing those attempting to institute a new hegemonic project "not [to] make it under circumstances chosen by themselves, but under circumstances directly found, given and transmitted from the past."

5. In a sign that things have come full circle, the Economist (8-6-94) reported that BPA has been subject to "Portugal's first big hostile takeover bid" by the smaller Banco Comercial Português.

6. An article in the weekly *Espresso* (17 July 1993) argues that Soares's recent losses show the effects of the court's changing composition, with leftists becoming less preponderant recently.

7. The backers of independent movements vary by site. In Evora, former PCP members are grouped into the Plataforma de Esquerda, along with members of the MDP and PSR miniparties, and local notables. Discontents among anti-Cavaco Social Democrats as well as Catholics close to the archdiocese concerned with declining living standards may also form a part. In Almodôvar, an ex-Socialist leads the list, along with former supporters and members of the PS, PSD, PCP, and CDS. See *Espresso* (17 July 1993).

8. Richard Snyder (1992, 380) uses the concept of ruler-elite relations to define one of three key relations that shape "alternative transitions from neopatrimonial dictatorships." He differs from my approach by his relative inattention to the presence or absence of structural and policy divisions among segments of the dominant class. Rather than incorporating the more complex concepts of accumulation strategies and hegemonic projects into the analysis of transitions, he simplifies the nature of the relationship into variance "in the extent to which [neopatrimonial dictators] exclude elites from political and economic spoils." He argues that "the degree of exclusion of elites influences the growth of both revolutionary and moderate opposition to the dictator" (1992, 383). In Portugal, the question was not one of exclusion but rather one of excess *inclusion* of dominant-class elements and their representatives, making the resolution of basic policy choices virtually impossible without fundamental institutional change. The concept of dictatorships as neopatrimonial focuses attention primarily on the presence of patronage networks used by the dictator to maintain support. My approach is not necessarily to discount the relevance of such networks but to emphasize instead the role of structural characteristics of the dominant class in shaping the kinds of accumulation strategies that limit rulers' policy alterntives. While Snyder does mention the "relationship of domestic actors to foreign powers," this, too, remains very broadly conceived. Insofar as this entails and underlines the complementary nature of accumulation strategies with predominant patterns of accumulation in the global capitalist system and not simply the instrumental links among visible actors (CIA, World Bank, domestic political parties, or military), I concur that such links help define the scope of plausible political and economic outcomes.

9. Here I agree with Snyder (1992) who insists that the degree of military autonomy from the ruler determines the likelihood that a military-led transition to democracy can occur. Snyder operationalizes the "indepen-

dence of the military" variable by highlighting its control over matériel and officers' career paths, the propensity of discontents to organize, internal cleavages, and the dictator's "capacity to purge elements of the armed forces whose loyalty he questions" (1992, 381). We must also ask, What are the circumstances that allow the military's independence to grow? In Portugal, this was not a fixed relationship but rather a dynamic one in which the colonial wars dramatically altered the military's ability and need to assert itself against the Caetano regime. More fundamentally, it was the inability of that regime to solve the impasse between accumulation models that forced the military to reproduce internally the divisions between intra- and extraregime soft- and hardliners found in the civilian world.

10. The distinction between intra- and extraregime soft- and hardliners is important because it multiplies the number of theoretically possible coalition outcomes and does not simply reduce them to status quo, reform, revolution alternatives, as I shall explain later. Nancy Bermeo (1987) has also highlighted the importance of the pretransition opposition in her admirable comparative review of Spain and Portugal, a point emphasized by Fred Lopez for Spain (in Chilcote 1990).

11. Snyder (1992) places little importance conceptually upon the nature of the popular masses except insofar as they are diffusely related to moderates and revolutionaries. Yet he mentions that in the Philippines, the military did not seize power for itself and block the civilian moderates, and he relies upon the unique "organizational coherence and levels of popular support for the moderate civilian opposition" for an explanation (along with U.S. pressure). In my work, I have drawn the analysis past the short transitional phase and attempted to show the importance of the interaction between institutional actors and social bases in delimiting regime and policy choices throughout the consolidation.

12. Halliday (1992, 25) mentions that the PCP "retains a strong organization, claiming 200,000 members" and that Cunhal "still retains support: the PCP knows that for all his Stalinism—he hailed the August coup in Moscow—his authority commands respect." Perhaps more telling is the following quotation from an unnamed expert about Cunhal (and implicitly the PCP): "He remains true to his principles. He is a great conservative." Without an open debate along the lines mentioned by former Communist Vital Moreira (1990), PCP policy changes (as expressed in the fact that it no longer opposes membership in the EC but only the social or economic costs of integration) will not make the party more palatable to much of its former or potential electorate. For another former insider's view of life in the PCP, see Ventura (1984).

13. I will expand further upon the question of the relationship of democratization and placement in the world system later in this chapter.

14. Dogan (1990, 113) has argued that "comparing always involves extracting a small or large sector from a society" and "the division of the system into segments is the normal course of the comparative approach." Viewing democratization as involving scope over time means that segmentation becomes more difficult as more independent and dependent variables are introduced into the analysis. The decision about where to draw the analytic line is always fluid; even "those who study interest groups always end by reaching a point beyond which the explanation of the differences moves outside the framework of any 'theory of groups'; the contrasts must then be attributed to some element buried in the cultures, social structures, or political systems considered in their entirety" (Dogan 1990, 116).

15. See Lijphart (1971) for these distinctions.

16. This exercise differs from Roniger's discussion of variable forms of democratic transition as well as similar attempts by O'Donnell and Schmitter (1986); Diamond, Lipset, and Linz (1987); and even Stepan (1986) to the degree that this classification scheme explicitly blends the social dimension with the more purely political and formal-legal ones. It does not necessarily reject institutionally based arguments, such as that offered by Dix (1992) in his review of whether political parties are more institutionalized in Latin America and thus offer a better prospect for long-term democratization consolidation. But it insists that any such institutionalization be understood as part of a larger process of developing a viable hegemonic project that includes both institutional forms and a social settlement. See also Diamond (1992) and Diamond and Plattner (1993) for a Hernative perspectives on democratization.

17. For example, a dramatic collapse of the military effort in Africa might have suddenly undermined the hardliners' insistence on maintaining the colonial-protectionist model; sustained Europeanization without the shock of the oil crisis might also have gradually tilted the coalition in favor of the softliners.

18. The Colorado party victory made the issue moot in any case.

19. According to Eric Wright's (1978) analysis, by using Poulantzas's narrow definition of working class to mean those directly involved in productive labor, only 15 percent of the U.S. population would be included. On the other hand, others have focused on the sale of labor power as the key criterion for inclusion in a broadly defined working class. Because the goal is the implementation of a noninsurrectionary strategy of Socialist reform or revolution, this concept provides the basic element: a preponderant numerical majority. What is gained in numbers, however, is lost in programmatic cohesiveness and ambition, as the summary of Przeworski's points shows.

20. As Fernando Claudin (1978) points out, calling that model Socialist implies that socialism, freedom, and democracy are not interdependent; rather, a Socialist base can coexist with a undemocratic political super-

structure. Claudin rejects this position, saying that "the concept of 'undemocratic socialism' is a contradiction in terms" (1978, 63).

21. Carson (1973) explores command and market economies as polar types and reflects upon their strengths and deficiencies as well as the types of mixes that might be found.

22. Alex Nove (1983, 1991) has summarized these strategies in his consideration of feasible socialism.

23. It could be argued that they represented a coalition of international capital in conjunction with elements of the managerial strata, which assumed that their structural microeconomic dominance would make them invaluable liaisons for foreign capital. They appeared to function as a kind of domestic bourgeoisie dependent upon foreign capital for global reorientation of the local economy but with a specific niche preserved in the manufacturing sector.

24. The absence of an indigenous bourgeoisie was also illustrated by the fact that political parties in Eastern Europe have neglected the nomenclatures typically associated with bourgeois parties, such as liberal or conservative. As in Portugal, many countries have relied on an implicit or explicit Christian Democratic, Socialist, Social Democratic party label, although unlike Portugal, explicitly agrarian or nationalist parties have also appeared. In countries such as Czechoslovakia and Bulgaria, parties take diffuse catchall names—Civic Action or Union of Democratic Forces—deemphasizing class interests and broader systemic choices. These circumstances seem germane to a point made by Fehér and Heller about classes: "they are never the fixed, circumscribed, static elements any meaningful structural analysis should operate with. It is rather the dynamic trend, not the blueprint, of the social edifice we can decipher from classes and their conflicts" (1987, 206). Thus, despite the absence of detailed blueprints about the changes in the former Soviet bloc, the class effects seem evident in the dynamic trend toward a market-based economy. It is also important to note that Barrington Moore's (1966) observations about the emergence of democracy (no bourgeoisie, no democracy) are now being critically tested by post-Soviet experiences.

25. Several contributors to Ness (1989) have explored the Hungarian and Chinese cases in detail.

26. *Washington Post* (16 October 1993, p. 14).

27. Moreover, the fact that an elected assembly wrote the constitution in Portugal gave it more legitimacy despite the constraints imposed by the MFA. In Russia, the constitution was placed before the voters much as Salazar did in 1933—as a plebiscite produced by the executive at the margins of an elected legislature.

28. Poland also was first in privatizing a bank, which places "Poland at the forefront of the next step in transforming Eastern Europe's economies—financial reform" (*Washington Post* 7 April 1993). The details of the bank's evolution from "a cash distribution agency of the Ministry of Finance" into a capitalist-style institution reveals other elements that facilitate the dishegemonic transition to democratic capitalism: it required a stabilized currency (which required Western aid); it has meant a reallocation of lending priorities away from state firms to private ones (which now receive 45 percent of the loans); it had to make many uncollateralized loans "granted on the basis of character and the strength of a business plan"; it adopted Western management techniques and had top executives trained in the West; and it took advantage of a $10.6 million investment by the European Bank for Reconstruction and Development for a 28.5 percent share. Moreover, the bank must play a key role in defining the future of major Polish firms, whose bad loans mean either restructuring or foreclosure and liquidation. It operates to determine the delimitation of sectors (both private and public and between manufacturing and services)—a classic case of top-down, finance-capital-led reorganization of capitalism. Yet it is clear that despite its showcase status, Western aid and guidance, and private-sector orientation, it has remained only the first of many such transformations and still gives more than half its loans to state-sector firms.

29. According to the *Economist* (13 March, 1993, p. 5), Poland had nine parties with more than 5 percent of the vote and no party with more than 14 percent. It represented the most extreme case of party fragmentation (twenty nine parties won seats), as Hungary and the Czech republic had six; Romania and Slovakia five; Bulgraia, three; and Albania, only two parties with over 5 percent of the vote.

30. Yeltsin was emboldened by the electoral endorsement of the April 1993 referendum. He then pursued constitutional reforms more actively despite the continued resistance of Parliament.

31. Expanded democratization in Nicaragua parallels others mentioned here. The elections bringing Violeta Chamorro to power on 25 February 1990 resulted in many contradictory policies: the Sandinistas were kept in charge of the military; some firms and farms or cooperatives were reprivatized, but many others were not; organized business groups have been frustrated with the middle course charted by her government, but revolutionary elements have not endorsed the counterrevolutionary reforms.

32. Apparently, conditions in Belarus and Ukraine were even worse; the 1994 elections gave victories to candidates seeking closer ties with Russia. *Time Magazine* (25 July 94) described the Belarus victor as follows: "a dark horse with little experience in domestic or international politics, the former collective-farm boss launched his bid for the presidency of Belarus by pledging that his first official act, if elected, would be to throw the Prime Minister in jail. Then he promised to ban private property, purge the government and squelch free enterprise. Finally in a televised debate, he named

Felix Dzerzhinsky, the ghoulish founder of the Soviet secret police, one of his most admired heroes." This candidate received 80 percent of the vote!

33. This was the strategy of the Portuguese right in the late 1970s when the Democratic Alliance was formed to force a choice between left and right. Naturally, this risked exclusion from power sharing within the regime in the event of a serious electoral reversal.

34. For example, Calleo and Morgenstern (1990) have edited a book entitled *Recasting Europe's Economies* in which national strategies for adapting to the major "changes in economic circumstances forced Western European countries to seek ways to recast their fundamental economic structures and policies" (1990, ix).

35. This is not to say that there is nothing left of a basic Euromodel of political economy. In its dealings with Eastern European countries, the EC reaffirmed at the 1993 Copenhagen summit that four conditions—stable democracy, rule of law, market economy, and acceptable minority rights— must be met before full membership in the EC is possible. These conditions form an irreducible core of the Euromodel.

36. Lange (1985) uses the term *perimeter of the core* to conceptualize Italy's newly arrived status within the core. Arrighi's (1985a) argument that the perimeter concept should reflect "the existence of a no man's land between the core and semiperipheral zone" grants a more specific place for states emphasizing the relative permanence of advanced marginality for some states that border on core status. I extend that concept by arguing that a similar zone may well exist with regard to the periphery, with currently semiperipheral countries slipping either way.

37. See Giner (1986), Chilcote (1990), and Ranki (1985) as well as other contributions in (Arrighi 1985b) for a comparative overview of southern European countries.

38. Naturally, in Russia and Portugal this was coupled to some degree with the collapse of the empires each had established, while elsewhere in the former Soviet bloc renascent nationalism corresponded to the need to solidify a national identity as the Soviet Union disintegrated.

39. This is not to suggest that Communist societies offered no more in the way of social welfare and social mobility than corporatist ones, an empirical point that requires a case-by-case assessment. See, for example, Nagle (1992) for a broad overview of cases.

40. This point should not be overemphasized. The actual capacity of the Portuguese bourgeoisie to accept a modern welfare state, neocorporatist bargaining, and so on was probably never great. Nevertheless, once shorn of the immobility caused by contradictory accumulation strategies and confronted by highly mobilized but reformist workers during democratization,

Portugal may have discovered the *possibility* of a better arrangement than the one that now prevails.

41. Several contributions in Becker et al. (1987), such as Sklar (1987) and Becker (1987a), reflect on the contemporary meaning of postimperialism and touch on its relation to democracy.

BIBLIOGRAPHY

Aguiar, Joaquim. *A ilusao do poder: Analise do sistema partidario português, 1976–1982.* Lisbon: dom quixote, 1983.

Alford, Robert R., and Roger Friedland. *Powers of Theory: Capitalism, the State and Democracy.* Cambridge: Cambridge University Press, 1985.

Almeida, Dinis de. *Origens e evolução do movimento de capitães.* Lisbon: Ed. Sociais, 1977.

Almeida, Pinto de. *A indústria portuguesa e o condicionamento industrial.* Lisbon: Seara Nova, 1961.

Amaral, Diogo Freitas do. *O pais precisa de estabilidade, bom governo, e muito trabalho.* Lisbon: CDS, 1982.

Amaral, Ferreira do. *A industrialização em Portugal.* Lisbon: Anuário Comercial de Portugal, 1966.

Arrighi, Giovanni. "Fascism to Democratic Socialism: Logic and Limits of a Transition." In *Semiperpheral Development,* edited by Giovanni Arrighi. Beverly Hills, Calif.: Sage, 1985a.

————, ed. *Semperiphral Development.* Beverly Hills, Calif.: Sage, 1985.

Arroz, Maria. *As eleiçõs legislativas.* Lisbon: Horizonte, 1977.

Barata, Oscar Soares. "Demografia e evolução social em Portugal." *Analise Social* 21 (1985): 908–94.

Barreto, Antonio. *Anatomia de uma revolução: A reforma agrária em Portugal, 1974–1976.* Lisbon: Europa-America, 1987.

Barros, Carlos P., Jose Manuel E. Henriques, Luis Filipe D. Violante, and Maria Rosa Lopes, eds. *O comportamento dos agentes económicos e a reorientação da politica económica. Vols 1 and 2.* Lisbon: ISE, 1986.

Becker, David G. "Development, Democracy and Dependency in Latin America: A Postimperialist View." In *Postimperialism: International Capitalism and Development in the Late Twentieth Century,* eds.

David G. Becker, Jeff Frieden, Sayre P. Schatz, and Richard Sklar. Boulder, Colo.: Lynne Reinner, 1987.

Becker, David G., Jeff Frieden, Sayre P. Schatz and Richard Sklar. *Postimperialism: International Capitalism and Development in the Late Twentieth Century.* Boulder, Colo.: Lynne Reinner, 1987.

Bermeo, Nancy. *The Revolution within the Revolution.* Princeton: Princeton University Press, 1986.

———. "Democracy and the Lessons of Dictatorship." *Comparative Politics,* 24 (April 1992) 273–92.

———. "Redemocratization and Transition Elections: A Comparison of Spain and Portugal." *Comparative Politics* 19 (1987): 213–31.

Blackburn, Robin. "The Test in Portugal." *New Left Review* (December 1974): 5–46.

Bornstein, Stephen. "States and Unions: From Postwar Settlement to Contemporary Stalemate." In *The State in Capitalist Europe: A Casebook,* by Stephen Bornstein, David Held, and Joel Krieger. Boston: Allen and Unwin, 1984.

Bornstein, Stephen, David Held and Joel Krieger. *The State in Capitalist Europe: A Casebook.* Boston: Allen and Unwin, 1984.

Bruneau, Thomas C. *Politics and Nationhood: Post-Revolutionary Portugal.* New York: Praeger, 1984.

Bruneau, Thomas C. and Alex Macleod. *Politics in Contemporary Portugal.* Boulder, Colo.: Lynne Reinner, 1986.

Budge, Ian, and Vincent Herman. "Coalitions and Government Formation: An Empirically Relevant Theory." *British Journal of Political Science* 8. (October 1979), 459–78.

Cabral, Manuel Villaverde. "Agrarian Structures and Recent Rural Movements." *Journal of Peasant Studies* 5 (1978): 412–45.

Cadilhe, Miguel. *Factos e engredos.* Lisbon: Ed. Asa., 1990.

Caldeira, Reinaldo, and Maria do Ceu Silva. *Constituição política da Republica Portuguesa 1976.* Lisbon: Livraria Bertrand, 1976.

Calleo, David P., and Claudia Morgenstern. *Recasting Europe's Economies.* New York: University Press of America, 1990.

Campinos, Jorge. *Ideologia politica do estado Salazarista.* Lisbon: Portugalia Ed., 1975.

Cardia, Sottomayor. *Socialism sem dogmatismo.* Lisbon: Europa-America, 1979.

Carneiro, Francisco Sá *A liberalização bloqueda*. Lisbon: Morães Ed., 1972.

———. *Poder civil, autoridade democrática e social-democracia*. Lisbon: dom quixote, 1975a.

———. *Por uma social-democracia Portuguesa*. Lisbon: dom quixote, 1975b.

Carrilho, Maria. *Forcas armadas e mudanca politica em Portugal no seculo XX*. Lisbon: Estudos Gerais, 1985.

Carson, Richard L. *Comparative Economic Systems*. New York: Macmillan, 1973.

Carvalho, Otelo Saraiva de. *Bases para o programa de Candidatina*. Political pamphlet, 1976.

Carvalho, Otello Saraiva de. *Alvorada em abril*. Lisbon: Livraria Bertrand, 1977.

Castenheira, José Pedro. "Radiografia do movimento sindical," *O Jornal*, 30 April, 1981, 2–3.

———. "Os sindicatos e a vida politica," *Analise Social*, 21, 87 (1985), 801–18.

Castro, Armando de. *O sistema colonial Português em Africa*. Lisbon: Seara Nova, 1977.

Catela, Miguel. *A delimitação de sectores de propriedadena Constituição e na lei*. Queluz, Portugal, Edições Sílabo, 1986.

CGTP-Intersindical. *Breve história do Intersindical*. Lisbon: CGTP, 1974.

———. *Programa de Acção e caderno reivindicativo*. 2nd ed. Lisbon: Ed. Um de Outubro, 1981.

———. *Do "bloco central" ao governo PSD*. Lisbon: CGTP, 1986a.

———. *Programa da CGTP-IN, Programa de accao, plataforma reivindicativa*. Lisbon: Ed. Um de Outubro, 1986b.

Chilcote, Ronald. *The Portuguese Revolution of 25 April 1974: Annotated Bibliography on the Antecedents and Aftermath*. Coimbra: Centro de Documentação 25 de Abril, 1987.

———. "Introduction." in *Transitions from Dictatorship to Democracy: Compartaive Studies of Spain, Portugal and Greece*, ed. Ronald Chilcote, Stylianos Hadjiyannis, Fred A. Lopez III, Daniel Nataf, and Elizabeth Sammis. New York: Crane Russak, 1990.

Chilcote, Ronald, Stylianos Hadjiyannis, Fred A. Lopez III, Daniel Nataf, and Elizabeth Sammis. *Transitions from Dictatorship to Democracy:*

Comparative Studies of Spain, Portugal and Greece. New York: Crane Russak, 1990.

Cilia, João. *O partido socialista e o processo revolucionário.* Lisbon: Livraria Internacional, 1976.

Claudin, Fernando. *Eurocommunism and Socialism.* London: New Left Review, 1978.

Colliard, Jean-Claude. *Les regime parlementaires contemporains.* Paris: Presses de la Fondation Nationale des Sciences Politiques, 1980.

Costa, Ramiro da. *O desenvolvimento do capitalismo em Portugal.* Lisbon: Assiro and Alvim, 1977.

————. *Elementos para a história do movimento operário em Portugal.* Lisbon: Assirio and Alvim, 1979.

Cotta, Freppel. *Economic Planning in Corporative Portugal.* London: King and Son, 1937.

Cruz, Manuel Braga da. "Notas para uma caracterização do Salazarismo." In *A formação de Portugal contemporaneo: 1900–1980,* ed. A. Sales Nunes, Lisbon: Fundação Calouste Gulbenkian, 1982.

Cunhal, Álvaro. *A revolução portugesa.* Lisbon: dom quixote, 1975.

Cutleiro, Jose A. *Portuguese Rural Society.* Oxford: Clarendon Press, 1971.

Dahl, Robert, ed. *Political Oppositions in Western Democracies.* New Haven: Yale University Press, 1966.

Dalton, Russell J., Scott C. Flanagan and Paul Allen Beck. "Political Forces and Partisan Change." In *Electoral Change in Advanced Industrial Democracies,* ed. Princeton: Princeton University Press, 1984.

Diamond, Larry, ed. *The Democratic Revolution: Struggles for Freedom and Pluralism in the Developing World.* Lanham, Md.: Freedom House, 1992.

Diamond, Larry, and Marc F. Plattner. *The Global Resurgence of Democracy.* Baltimore: Johns Hopkins University Press, 1993.

Diario de Notícias, 25 November, 1987.

Dinis, Almeida de. *Origens e evolução do movimento de capitães.* Lisbon: Edições Sociais, 1977.

Dix, Robert H. "Democratization and the Institutionalization of Latin American Political Parties." *Comparative Political Studies* 24 (January 1992): 499–511.

Dogan, Mattei. *How France Avoided a Civil War.* Beverly Hills, Calif.: Sage, 1985.

Dogan, Mattei, and Stein Rokkan, eds. *Quantitative Ecological Analysis in the Social Sciences.* Cambridge: M.I.T. Press, 1969.

Double, Mary Beth. "Portugal: High Growth Rates Creates U.S. Business Opportunities." *Business America* (6 April 1992): 14.

Dossier 2a República, vol. 1. Lisbon. Edition Afrodite, 1976.

Downs, Charles. *Revolution at the Grassroots: Community Organizations in the Portuguese Revolution.* Albany: SUNY Press, 1989.

Economist. "Portuguese banks: Not yet Norway." *Economist,* 6 March 1993, 56. *Economist,* 13 March 1993. 5. (14 November 1992).

Editorial. *Economia EC* 19 (February–March 1979): 3–4.

Espresso, 17 July, 1993.

Fehér, Ferenc, and Agnes Heller. *Eastern Left, Western Left.* Atlantic Highlands, N.J.: Humanities Press, 1987.

Fields, Rona. *The Portuguese Revolution and the Armed Forces.* New York: Praeger, 1976.

Ferrão, Joao. "Recomposição social e estruturas regionais de classes (1970–81)." *Análise Social* 21 (1985): 565–604.

Figueiredo, Ernesto V. S. *Portugal: Que regiões.* Braga: Instituto Nacional de Investigação Cientifica, 1988.

Finance Ministry. *Program for Structural Correction of the External Deficit and Unemployment.* Lisbon: Imprensa Nacional-Case da Moeda, 1987.

Foweraker, Joe. Corporatist Strategies and the Transition to Democracy in Spain. *Comparative Politics* (October 1987): 57–72.

Freitas, Eduardo de, J. Ferreira de Almedia, and M. Villaverde Cabral. *Modalidades de penetração do capitalismo na agricultura: Estruturas agrárias em Portugal continental, 1950–1970.* Lisbon: Presença, 1976.

Gaspar, Jorge, and Nuno Vitorino. *As eleições de 25 de Abril: Geografia e imagem dos partidos.* Lisbon: Horizonte, 1976.

Giner, Salvador. "From Despotism to Parliamentarism: Class Domination and Political Order in the Spanish State." In *The State in Western Europe,* Richard Scase, ed. New York: St. Martins Press, 1980.

————. "Political Economy, Legitimation and the State in Southern Europe." In *Transitions from Authoritarian Rule: Southern Europe*, eds. Guillermo O'Donnell, Philippe Schmitter, and Lawrence Whitehead. Baltimore: Johns Hopkins University Press, 1986.

Graham, Lawrence. "The Military in Politics: The Politicization of the Portuguese Armed Forces." In *Contemporary Portugal: The Revolution and Its Antecedents*, eds. Lawrence Graham and Harry Makler. Austin: University of Texas Press, 1979.

Gunther, Richard, ed. *Politics, Society, and Democracy: The Case of Spain.* Boulder, Colo.: Westview Press, 1993.

Gunther, Richard, Giacomo Sani, and Goldie Shabad. *Spain After Franco: The Making of a Competitive Party System.* Los Angeles: University of California Press, 1986.

Gonçalves, Vasco. *Discursos.* Lisbon: Edição Popular, 1976.

Hall, Peter. "Patterns of Economic Policy: An Organizational Approach." in *The State in Capitalist Europe: A Casebook*, ed. Stephen Bornstein, David Held, and Joel Krieger. London: Allen and Unwin, 1984.

————. "Policy Paradigms, Social Learning and the State: The Case of Economic Policymaking in Britain." *Comparative Politics* 25 (April 1993): 275–96.

Halliday, Fred. "Atlantic Connection." *New Statesman and Society* (22 May 1992): 25–26.

Hancock, M. Donald. *West Germany: The Politics of Democratic Corporatism.* Chatham, New Jersey: Chatham House Publishers, 1989.

Harsgor, Michael. *Portugal in Revolution.* Beverly Hills, Calif.: Sage, 1976.

Hudson, Mark. *Portugal to 1993.* London: Economist Intelligence Unit, 1989.

Hunt, Alan. "The Identification of the Working Class." in *Class and Class Structure*, ed. Alan Hunt. London: Lawrence and Wishart, 1977.

Industria em revista. "Ultrapassar a contradição." (June 1983): 5.

————. "A 'tricheira' da Constituição." (May 1988): 5.

————. "João Cravinho e as nacionalizações." (June 1988): 5.

Instituto Nacional de Estatística (INE). *Anuário estatistico 1987.* Lisbon: INE, 1987.

————. Unpublished data for *concelho*-level demographics, 1970, 1980.

Jessop, Bob. "Accumulation, State and Hegemonic Projects." *Kapitalistate* 10/11 (1983): 89–112.

———. "Corporatism, Parliamentarism and Social Democracy." in *Trends in Corporatist Intermediation*, eds. Philippe Schmitter and Gerhard Lembruch. Beverly Hills, Calif.: Sage, 1979.

Vitoriano Jose. *O PCP e a luta sindical.* Lisbon: Ediçoes Avante, 1976.

Karl, Terry Lynn, and Philippe C. Schmitter. "Modes of Transition in Latin America, Southern and Eastern Europe." *International Social Science Journal* 128 (1991): 269–84.

Kayman, Martin A. *Revolution and Counterrevolution in Portugal.* Wolfeboro, NH: Merlin Press, 1987.

Kesselman, Mark. "France: Socialism without the Workers." *Kapitalistate* 10/11 (1983): 11–43.

Kesselman, Mark, Joel Krieger, Christopher Allen, Joan Debardeleben, Stephen Hellman and Jonas Pontusson. *European Politics in Transition.* Lexington, Mass: D.C. Heath, 1987.

Kohler, Beate. *Political Forces in Spain, Greece and Portugal.* London: Butterworth Scientific, 1982.

Kousser, Martin. "Ecological Regression and the Analysis of Past Politics." *Journal of Interdisciplinary History* 4 (1973): 232–62.

Langbein, Laura, and Allan J. Lichtman. *Ecological Inference.* Beverly Hills, Calif.: Sage, 1978.

Lange, Peter. "Semiperphery and Core in the European Context: Reflections on the Postwar Italian Experience." In *Semiperipheral Development*, ed. Giovanni Arrighi. Beverly Hills, Calif.: Sage, 1985.

Lash, Scott, and John Urry. *The End of Organized Capitalism.* Madison: University of Wisconsin Press, 1987.

Lijphart, Arendt. "Comparative Politics and the Comparative Method." *American Political Science Review* 65 (September 1971).

Lima, Albano. *Movimento sindical e unidade no processo revolucionário português.* Lisbon: Ed. Avante, 1975.

Linz, Juan J. "Totalitarian and Authoritarian Regimes," In *Handbook of Political Science: Macropolitical Theory.* eds. Fred Greenstein and Nelson Polsby. Reading, Mass.: Addison Wesley, 171–256.

Lipset, Seymour Martin, and Stein Rokkan. "Cleavage Structures, Party Systems and Voter Alignments." In *Party Systems and Voter Alignments*, eds. S. M. Lipset and Stein Rokkan. New York: Free Press, 1967.

Livermore, H. V. *A New History of Portugal.* Rev. ed. Cambridge: Cambridge University Press, 1977.

Logan, John. "Democracy from Above: Limits to Change in Southern Europe." In *Semiperipheral Development*, ed. Giovanni Arrighi. Beverly Hills, Calif.: Sage, 1985.

Lomax, Bill. "Ideology and Illusion in the Portuguese Revolution: The Role of the Left." In *In Search of Modern Portugal*, eds. Lawrence S. Graham and Douglas Wheeler. Madison: University of Wisconsin Press, 1983.

Lucena, Manuel de. *A evolução do sistema corporativo português*. Vols. 1 and 2. Lisbon: p&r 1976.

———. "Neocorporativismo?—Conceito, interesses e aplicaçãoao caso português." *Análise Social* (1985): 819–65.

Mailer, Phil. *Portugal: The Impossible Revolution*. New York: Free Life, 1977.

Makler, Harry. "The Portuguese Industrial Elite and Its Corporative Relations: A Study of Compartmentalization in an authoritarian Regime." In *Contemporary Portugal: The Revolution and Its Antecedents*, eds. Lawrence Graham and Harry Makler. Austin: University of Texas Press, 1979.

———. "The Survival and Revival of the Industrial Bourgeoisie." In *In Search of Modern Portugal*, eds. Lawrence Graham and Douglas Wheeler. Madison: University of Wisconsin Press, 1983.

Manoilesco, Mihail. *Le siecel du corporatisme*. Paris: Alcan, 1934.

Maravall, José Maria. *The Transition to Democracy in Spain*. London: Croom Helm, 1982.

Maravall, Jose Maria, and Julian Santamaria. "Political Change in Spain and the Prospects for Democracy." In *Transitions from Authoritarian Rule: Southern Europe*, eds. Guillermo O'Donnell, Philippe Schmitter, and Lawrence Whitehead. Baltimore: Johns Hopkins University Press, 1986.

Martins, Maria Belmira, and Rosa Chaves. *O grupo estado*. Lisbon: Ed. Jornal Expresso, 1979.

Maxwell, Kenneth. "Portugal under Pressure." *New York Review of Books* 22 (29 May 1975): 20–30.

———. "Regime Overthrow and the Prospects for Democratic Transition in Portugal." In *Transitions from Authoritarian Rule: Southern Europe*, eds. Guillermo O'Donnell, Philippe Schmitter and Lawrence Whitehead. Baltimore: Johns Hopkins University Press, 1986.

McDonough, Peter. "Government and Party Legitimacy in Post-Franco Spain." *APSR*, 1986–87.

Medeiros, Carlos Alberto. *Portugal: Esboco breve de geografia humana.* Lisbon: Prelo, 1978.

Miranda, Jorge. *Nos dez anos da constituição.* Lisbon: Imprensa Nacional-Casa da Moeda, 1986.

Moore, Barrington, Jr. *Social Origins of Dictatorship and Democracy Lord and Peasent in the Making of the Modern World.* Boston: Beacon Press, 1966.

Morais, João, and Luis Violante. *Contribuição para uma cronologia dos factos económicos e sociais: Portugal 1926–1985.* Lisbon: Livros Horizonte, 1986.

Morais, Richard. "Saudade." *Forbes* (25 May 1992): 264–65.

Moreira, Vital. *Relexões sobre o PCP.* Lisbon: Editorial Inquerito, 1990.

Moura, Francisco Pereira de. *Por onde vai a economia portuguesa?* Lisbon: Seara Nova, 1974.

Nagle, John. *Introduction to Comparative Politics.* New York: Nelson-Hall, 1992.

Napolitano, Giorgio. "O socialismo do futuro." *O Socialismo do Futuro* 1 (May 1990): 101–4.

Nataf, Daniel. "Portuguese Democratization: Successful Exceptionalism." Paper presented for panel, "Transitions to Democracy." 1987 *Conference of Southern Political Science Association,* Charlotte, N.C., 6–8 November 1987a.

———. "Social Cleavages and Regime Formation in Contemporary Portugal." Ph.D. diss., UCLA, 1987b.

———. "A Comparison of Ecological and Survey Methods Using Recent Legislative Elections in Portugal." Paper presented at the World Congress of Sociology, Madrid, 9–13 July 1990.

———. "Ideology and Party Systems in Spain and Portugal." Paper presented at the Conference of European Studies, Omaha, 15–17 October 1992.

Nataf, Daniel, and Elizabeth Sammis. "Classes, Hegemony and Portuguese Democratization." In *Transitions from Dictatorship to Democracy: Comparative Studies of Spain, Portugal and Greece,* eds. Ronald Chilcote, Stylianos Jadjiyannis, Fred A. Lopez II, Daniel Natar and Elizabeth Sammis. New York: Crane Russak, 1990.

Ness, Peter van. *Market Reforms in Socialist Socities: Comparing China and Hungary.* Boulder, Colo.: Lynne Rienner, 1989.

Nove, Alec. *Feasible Socialism.* Boston: Allen and Unwin, 1983.

———. *The Economics of Feasible Socialism Revisited.* 2d ed. London: HarperCollins Academic, 1991.

O'Donnell, Guillermo, and Philippe Schmitter. *Transitions from Authoritarian Rule: Tentative Conclusions about Uncertain Democracies.* Baltimore: Johns Hopkins University Press, 1986.

Offe, Claus. "Attribution of Public Status to Interest Groups." In *Organizing Interests in Western Europe,* ed. Suzanne Berger. Cambridge: Cambridge University Press, 1981.

O Jornal, 12 June, 1985, 22.

Oliveira, Cesar. *Tudo sobre Intersindical e Carta Aberta.* Lisbon: Ed. Aqui, 1978.

Oliveira, Correira de. as quoted in João Morais and Luis Violante. *Contribuicao para uma Cronologia dos factos economicos e sociais: Portugal 1926–1985.* Lisbon: Livros Horizonte, 1986.

Opello, Walter, Jr. *Portugal's Political Development.* Boulder, Colo.: Westview Press, 1985.

———. *Portugal: From Monarchy to Pluralist Democracy.* Boulder, Colo.: Westview Press, 1991.

Osório, Helena Sanches. In *Sá rosto, uma Sá Fé: Conversas com Adelino de Palma Carlos.* Amadore, Purtin, Edições Referendo, 1988.

País, José Machado de, Aida Maria Valadas de Lima. "Elementos para a história do fascismo nos campos: A 'campanha do trigo' (1928–1938)—Aspectos politicas-institucionais e ideológicos. *Análise Social* 14 (1978): 321–89.

Panitch, Leo. *Social Democracy and Industrial Militancy: The Labour Party, the Trade Unions and Incomes Policy, 1945–1974.* Cambridge: Cambridge University Press, 1976.

Papadantonakis, Kostis. "Incorporation Is Peripheralization: Contradictions of Southern Europe's Economic Development.' In *Semiperipheral Development: The Politics of Southern Europe in the Twentieth Century,* ed. Giovanni Arrighi. Beverly Hills, Calif.: Sage, 1985.

Pereira, Joao Martins. *O Socialismo, A transição e o caso português.* Lisbon: Livraria Bertrand, 1976.

Pimental, J. M. Rocha. "Concertação social e política de rendimentos em Portugal: Experiência recente e perspectivas para a década de 80." In *Economic and Social Partnership and Incomes Policy*, ed. Cavaco Silva. Lisbon: Univ. Católica Portuguesa, 1984.

Pinto, Mário Carlos Moura. *As estruturas sindicais portuguesa*. Lisbon: GIS, 1973.

————. "Trade Union Action and Industrial Relations in Portugal." In *European Industrial Relations: The Challenge of Flexibility*. Guido Baglioni and Colin Crouch, eds. London: Sage, 1990.

Porch, Douglas. *The Portuguese Armed Forces and the Revolution*. Stanford: Stanford University Press, 1977.

Porto, M. "Portugal: Twenty Years of Change." In *Southern Europe Transformed*, ed. Alan Williams. San Francisco: Harper and Row, 1984.

Portuguese Communist Party (PCP). *VII congresso (extraordinario) do PCP*. Lisbon: Edicoes Avante!, 1974.

————. *VIII congresso do PCP*. Lisbon: Edicoes Avante!, 1976.

————. *60 Anos de luta ao serviço do povo e da patria: 1921–1981*. Lisbon: Edicoes Avante!, 1982.

Poulantzas, Nicos. *Political Power and Social Classes*. London: New Left Books, 1978.

————. *Crises of the Dictatorships: Portugal, Spain, Greece*. London: New Left Books, 1976.

————. *Classes in Contemporary Capitalism*. London: Verso, 1978.

PPD. *Programa do PPD*. Lisbon: PPD, 1974.

Przeworski, Adam. *Capitalism and Social Democracy*. Cambridge Cambridge University Press, 1985.

————. "Some Problems in the Study of the Transition to Democracy." In *Transitions from Authoritarian Rule: Comparative Perspectives*, Baltimore: Johns Hopkins University Press, 1986.

Przeworski, Adam, and Michael Wallerstein. "Democratic Capitalism at the Crossroads." In *Political Economy in Western Democracies*, eds Norman Vig and Steven E. Schier. New York: Holmes and Meier, 1985.

PS. *The Program of the Portuguese Socialist Party*. Lisbon: PS, 1974.

————. *Política económica de transição*. Lisbon: PS. 1975.

————. *Para um Porgugal moderno e solidário*. Lisbon: PS, 1987.

PSD. *Critica ao governo PS.* Lisbon: PSD, 1978.

Raby, David L. *Fascism and Resistance in Portugal: Communists, Liberals, and Military Dissidents in the Opposition to Salazar, 1941–1974.* Manchester, England: Manchester University Press, 1988.

Rafael, Francisco, Jorge Preto, Maria A. Casanova, Maria José Bento, Rui Carvalho, Rui Leonardo Silva and Sílvio Barata. *Portugal: Capitalismo e o estado novo.* Lisbon: Affrontamento, 1976.

Ranki, Gyory. "Problems of Southern European Economic Development (1918–1938)." In *Semiperipheral Development,* ed. Giovanni Arrighi. Beverly Hills, Calif.: Sage, 1985.

Roberts, B.C. ed. *Industrial Relations in Europe: The Imperative of Change.* Dover, New Hampshire: C. Helm, 1985.

Rolo, Jose Manuel. *Capitalismo, technologia e dependência em Portugal.* Lisbon Editorial Presenca, 1977.

Roth, Guenter and Claus Wittich. *Max Weber: Economy and Society.* Berkeley, Calif.: University of California Press, 1976.

Roniger, Luis. "Democratic Transitions and Consolidation in Contemporary Southern Europe and Latin America." *International Journal of Comparative Sociology* 30 (1989): 217–30.

Rosa, Eugénio. *A reforma agrária em perigo.* Lisbon: Ed. Caminho, 1977.

———. *O fracasso da política de direita.* Lisbon: Seara Nova, 1978.

———. *O fracasso dos governos de direita em Portugal.* Lisbon: Um de Outubro, 1982.

Sá, Victor de. *História de Movimento Operário.* Lisbon: 1 Outobro, 1981.

Sammis, Elizabeth P. "The Limits of State Adaptability." Ph.D. diss., UCLA, 1988.

Santos, Boaventura Sousa. *O estado e a sociedade em Portugal (1974–1988).* Porto: Ed. Afrontamento, 1990.

Schmitter, Philippe. "Still the Century of Corporatism." In *The New Corporatism,* ed. Pike de Stritch. South Bend, Ind.: Notre Dame University Press, 1974.

———. *Corporatism and Public Policy in Authoritarian Portugal.* Beverly Hills, Calif.: Sage, 1975a.

———. "Liberation by Golpe: Retrospective Thoughts on the Demise of Authoritarian Rule in Portugal." *Armed Forces and Society* 2 (1975b): 5–33.

————. "The 'Regime d'Exception' That became the rule: Forty-eight Years of Authoritarian Domination in Portugal." In *Contemporary Portugal: The Revolution and its Antecedents*, eds. Lawrence Graham and Harry Makler. Austin: University of Texas Press, 1979.

————. "An Introduction to Southern European Transitions from Authoritarian Rule: Italy, Greece. "In *Transitions from Authoritarian Rule: Southern Europe*, eds. Guillermo O'Donnell, Philippe Schmitter and Lawrence Whitehead. Baltimore: Johns Hopkins University Press, 1986.

Schwartzman, Kathleen C. *The Social Orgins of Democratic Collapse: The First Portuguese Republic in the Global Economy*. Lawrence: University of Kansas Press, 1989.

Secretaria Technico dos Assuntos para o Processo Eleitoral (STAPE). Electoral Results for Legislative Elections (1976, 1979, 1980, 1983, 1985, 1987, 1991).

SEDES. *Portugal novo: Movimentos e partidos politicos*. Lisbon: SEDES, 1974.

Silva, Anibal A. Cavaco. *A política economica do governo de Sá Carneiro*. Lisbon: dom quixote, 1982.

————, ed. *Economic and Social Partnership and Incomes Policy*. Lisbon: Universidade Católica Portuguesa, 1984.

Silva, Augusto de. "Practica religiosa dos católicos portugueses." *Economia e Sociologia* 25–26 (1979): 61–91.

Silva, Manuel Carvalho da, ed. *Emprego, modernização, desenvolvimento*. Lisbon: CGTP, 1989.

Sklar, Richard. "Postimperialism: A Class Analysis of Multinational Corporate Expansion." In *Postimperialism: International Capitalism and Development in the Late Twentieth Century*, eds. David G. Becker, Jeff Frieden, Sayle P. Schatz, and Richard Sklar. Boulder, Colo.: Lynne Rienner, 1987.

Skocpol, Theda. *States and Social Revolutions*. Cambridge: Cambridge University Press, 1979.

Soares, Mário. *Portugal amordaçado*. Lisbon: Arcadia, 1974.

————. *Confiar no PS, Apostar em Portugal*. Lisbon: PS, 1979a.

————. *PS: Fronteira da liberdade*. Lisbon: Ed. Portugal Socialista, 1979b.

————. *A arvore e a floresta*. Lisbon: p&r, 1984.

————. *Intervenções 2*. Lisbon: Imprensa-Casa da Moeda, 1988.

Sousa, Manuel de. *História de sindicalismo em Portugal.* Porto: Affronta-mento, 1977.

Spinola, António Ribeiro. "Portugal and the Future." n.p., 1973.

Stepan, Alfred. "Paths towards Redemocratization: Theoretical and Com-parative Considerations." In *Transitions from Authoritarian Rule,* eds. Guillermo O'Donnell, Philippe Schmitter, and Lawrence White-head. Baltimore: Johns Hopkins University Press, 1986.

Stewart, Margaret. *Trade Unions in Europe.* Epping: Gower Press, 1974.

Stoleroff, Alan, and Uwe Optenhogel. "The Logics of Politically Competing Trade Union Confederations in Portugal: 1974–1984." In *Conflict and Change in Portugal, 1974–1984,* eds. Eduardo de Sousa Ferreira and Walter C. Opello Jr. Lisbon: Teorema, 1985.

Sloleroff, Alan, and Maria Teresa Patrício. *"Changes in the Portuguese Communist Party Strategy and Program."* Unpublished manuscript, 1991.

Snyder, Richard. "Explaining Transitions from Neopatrimonial Dictator-ships." *Comparative Politics* 24 (July 1992): 379–99.

Telos, António José. *As associações patronais e o fim da República.* Lisbon: A Regsa do Jogo, 1982.

Time, 25 July, 1994.

Tucker, Robert. *The Marx-Engels Reader.* New York: Norton, 1978.

UGT. *Programa de acção, política reivindicativa.* Lisbon: UGT, 1981.

———. *Contracto social para a modernização.* Lisbon: UGT, 1987.

Veloso, Maria, and Angela Carrascalão de Freitas. *Relatório do 25 de novembro de 1975.* Lisbon: Ed. Abril, 1976.

Ventura, Carlos. *O socialismo que eu vivi.* Lisbon: O Jornal, 1984.

Vilanova, João. *Sindicalismo em Portugal: 1977/1978.* Lisbon: Assiro and Alvim, 1978.

Vitoriano, José. "Experências tres anos de lutas sindicais." In *O PCP e a luta sindical,* no editor, Lisbon: Edições Avantel, 1975.

Washington Post, 19 March, 1993.

Wheeler, Douglas. *Republican Portugal: A Political History: 1910–1926.* Madison: University of Wisconsin Press, 1978.

Wiarda, Howard. *Corporatism and Development: The Portuguese Experi-ence.* Amherst: University of Massachusetts Press, 1977.

———. *Transitions to Democracy in Spain and Portugal.* Washington: AEI, 1988.

Wilson, Frank Lee. *European Politics Today: The Democratic Experience.* Englewood Cliffs, N.J.: Prentice-Hall, 1991.

Wright, Eric. *Class, Crisis and the State.* London. New Left Books, 1978.

INDEX